Lecture Notes in Computer Science 8345

Commenced Publication in 1973
Founding and Former Series Editors:
Gerhard Goos, Juris Hartmanis, and Jan van Leeuwen

For further volumes:
http://www.springer.com/series/7409

Achim Ebert · Gerrit C. van der Veer
Gitta Domik · Nahum D. Gershon
Inga Scheler (Eds.)

Building Bridges: HCI, Visualization, and Non-formal Modeling

IFIP WG 13.7 Workshops
on Human–Computer Interaction and Visualization:
7th HCIV@ECCE 2011
Rostock, Germany, August 23, 2011, and
8th HCIV@INTERACT 2011
Lisbon, Portugal, September 5, 2011
Revised Selected Papers

 Springer

Editors

Achim Ebert
Inga Scheler
University of Kaiserslautern
Kaiserslautern
Germany

Gerrit C. van der Veer
Open University The Netherlands
Heerlen
The Netherlands

Gitta Domik
University of Paderborn
Paderborn
Germany

Nahum D. Gershon
The MITRE Corporation
McLean, VA
USA

ISSN 0302-9743
ISSN 1611-3349 (electronic)
ISBN 978-3-642-54893-2
ISBN 978-3-642-54894-9 (eBook)
DOI 10.1007/978-3-642-54894-9
Springer Heidelberg New York Dordrecht London

Library of Congress Control Number: 2014936290

LNCS Sublibrary: SL3 – Information Systems and Applications, incl. Internet/Web and HCI

Printed on acid-free paper

Springer is part of Springer Science+Business Media (http://www.springer.com)

Building Bridges – From Non-formal Modeling to HCI and Visualization

In 2011, two HCIV workshops took place at renowned conferences. HCIV is a new major program in Human–Computer Interaction and Visualization. The aim of this initiative is to establish a study and research program that will combine the knowledge of both the science and the practice in the fields of human–computer interaction and visualization. From 2009, HCIV [1] is an official working group of the IFIP Technical Committee on Human–Computer Interaction (TC13). The first workshop at ECCE 2011 [2] focused on "Non-formal Modeling for Interaction Design." The second one was held at INTERACT 2011 [3] with the main topic "Building Bridges—HCI and Visualization." Proposals for both workshops were successfully submitted to the two conferences. After acceptance, the workshops were advertised on academic email lists and on a special website. The submissions to our workshops were made in the form of extended abstracts and carefully reviewed by the organizers. During the workshops the authors presented their work in short talks followed by intense discussions. Furthermore, two very inspiring keynote talks were given by Mary Czerwinski (Microsoft Research, Redmond, USA) and Bob Spence (Imperial College London, UK). In a final discussion, all participants agreed that the topics definitely deserve a visible platform for presenting the single ideas and contributions to the research communities involved in this field. The idea to publish two books based on the outcomes was born. However, after the two fruitful workshops took place, we – the organizers – found that both workshops, despite their contrasting research topics, were very similar in their results and take-away messages. Thus, it seems that (non-formal) modeling, HCI, and visualization are more tightly connected than the literature and conferences imply. Clearly missing are the bridges connecting these important research fields. We hope that this book will help build some of these bridges, allowing us to explore new horizons.

Non-formal Modeling

If modeling is included in the requirements analysis phase of a systematic interaction design method, it mostly focuses on some kind of formalism, e.g., task modeling and requirements specification. However, when designing in collaboration with nonexpert stakeholders this will not work. On the other hand, it is exactly this creative collaboration between stakeholders and designers in a very early design phase which allows us to explore and consider new solutions before these need to be prototyped or implemented.

Non-formal modeling tools and techniques for early collaboration with stakeholders [like sketching, (paper) prototyping, and storytelling] are relatively cheap and, on the other hand, uniquely stimulating techniques for identifying both the boundaries and the opportunities of the design space for interactive systems.

Using visuals, however, is not without pitfalls. Designers who communicate with stakeholders should be aware of how humans perceive and understand. The human visual system, the "mind's eye," relies in large part on the eye and on the processing and the interpretation of the information processed by the brain. Visual design utilizes both. Additional care must be taken to present and highlight important information. Thus, at least a basic knowledge of perceptual and cognitive issues is needed to avoid a poor usage of different features in visual design.

One of the main issues is drawing a user's attention to where it is needed. Here, the so-called preattentive processing, the step that occurs before the attention of the user is concentrated on the visual image, plays an important role. Preattentive processing is performed automatically on the entire visual field detecting basic features of objects in the display. It is done quickly, effortlessly, and in parallel and can therefore greatly improve the intuitiveness of representations. It is a strong instrument for enabling a fast and natural way of acquiring information.

One of the key elements of preattentive processing is the theory of visual or retinal variables, which can be compared effortlessly [4]. Bertin identified eight visual variables: form, orientation, color, texture, value, size, and position (position counted twice). In addition, he divides the characteristics of perception of visual variables into four groups: associative, selective, ordered, and quantitative perception. The knowledge of visual variables and their perception criteria is essential for an intuitive, user-centered interaction design.

All the above-described techniques have in fact been elaborated, and sources as well as resources are available. Teaching design students how to locate and apply them in a creative way strengthens their ability to develop user-centered solutions from the start.

A key problem of visual design in public services and applications is the lack of time and money. The lack of time means stakeholders cannot invest enough time to develop a formal model to define the design process because they are stuck in their principal tasks. The lack of money leads to short-term design processes without having enough time for evaluation. On the other hand, stakeholders mostly cannot really outline their needs because they are often non-professional users, and thus are not able to clearly define their requirements. In fact the design is done based on rare information about requirements followed by the implementation of a rough model as end result. The non-professional users need intuitive, self-explaining systems. If we do not meet this interest, users will not accept a system. Therefore, an important and crucial step is to identify their special needs by involving the users in design decisions. This results in the need of non-formal modeling processes to achieve reasonable results.

Therefore, we need a way to reach an optimized model in interactive design based on the specified needs of the stakeholders. One possible solution might be a more or less "online" evaluation. Once the implementation of different methods has started, the stakeholders have to be involved in the design process by evaluating the current results. This means the implementation has to be based on perceptual and cognitive issues following the steps of the well-known evaluation cycle [5] in a very condensed way. This kind of evaluation tailored for the stakeholders leads to a faster correction of possible faults within the development phase. Implementing a new design method with an immediate evaluation and response by the stakeholders themselves yields an "online" evaluation to reach the users' desires. While evaluating one method, the next method can be implemented. This leads to a user-specified and convenient visual design.

This way is less time consuming because in the beginning some coarse requirements are sufficient to get started. During the design process, it always takes a few minutes to define the next steps because the users get a visual impression of their ideas. Another advantage is to get a visual result of what might be the final result in an early project stage.

Visualization and HCI

Whenever discussing the relationship between HCI and visualization in general or when presenting research results in these areas, questions arise about the differences between these research fields. Are not both fields just the same? And if not, where is the common ground? Can we combine the separate viewpoints and paradigms in a unified and complementary approach, or are we forced to choose one or the other? How can we give the general public (the developers and users of visualization and HCI and the engineers implementing our designs) a precise and practical enough idea about what is happening in these fields and what is not? What are the consequences of the answers on the previous questions: how and what should we teach? What will be the future? This dilemma is a topic of frequent discussion around the water cooler, lecture halls, as well as in the boardroom.

One of the major issues is that it is not easy to precisely define the terms visualization and HCI and there are many interpretations of these two fields that appear to be distinct.

ACM SIGCHI tries to give people a working definition for HCI: "Human–computer interaction is a discipline concerned with the design, evaluation and implementation of interactive computing systems for human use and with the study of major phenomena surrounding them" [6]. However, at the same time the applicability of this definition is significantly limited by adding that it "at least permits us to get down to the practical work of deciding what is to be taught."

Similar imprecise descriptions can be found for visualization. One possibility is the classic definition given by ACM SIGGRAPH: "visualization is [...] the formation of mental visual images, the act or process of interpreting in visual terms or of putting into visual form" [7], although the visualization subcommittee of the SIGGRAPH Education Committee in 1997 provided an alternative: "A computer generated image or collection of images, possibly ordered, using a computer representation of data as its primary source and a human as its primary target" [8]. Foley [9], in 1994, states: "A useful definition of visualization might be the binding (or mapping) of data to a representation that can be perceived. The types of binding could be visual, auditory, tactile, etc. or a combination of these." Kosara [10] tries to better conceptualize the term visualization by defining some criteria forming a minimal set of requirements for any visualization: "Visualization is based on (non-visual) data, produces an image, and results in a readable and recognizable output." Finally, some definitions approach the concept from the point of view of computing: "Visualization is a method of computing. It transforms the symbolic into the geometric, enabling researchers to observe their simulations and computations. Visualization offers a method for seeing the unseen. It enriches the process of scientific discovery and fosters profound and unexpected insights. In many fields it is already revolutionizing the way scientists do science" [11].

As mentioned, questioning similarities, differences, and correlations of HCI and visualization forms an important part of our daily work life. In order to better (or at all) answer these questions, questions like the ones listed below need to be discussed and – if possible – answered:

- What is HCI? What is visualization? What is a working description that is practical for highlighting the special features of each of the fields as well as supporting mutual understanding between them?
- Are there other disciplines involved in this struggle (e.g., visual analytics)?
- How can we take advantage of the two fields and how can we find ways for people with different inclinations to collaborate and take advantage of the strengths of each other?
- What are the similarities of the disciplines? What are the major differences?
- Do we need to really split the domains? Or do we need to join them and provide a joint curriculum for studying and practicing them?
- Can we give definitions that are better applicable in real situations?

Does one need to further research ways of making people take advantage of both disciplines in designing interactive visual systems? In that case, what are the research agenda(s) and what are the top 10 research challenges?

In the current volume, we provide some visions from scholars in these fields, working at – or across – the borders between these fields. Their work may point to possible directions to answer our questions, and will help in the understanding and developing of a holistic cross-discipline.

February 2014

Achim Ebert
Gerrit C. van der Veer
Gitta Domik
Nahum Gershon
Inga Scheler

References

1. HCI & Visualization (HCIV, IFIP WG 13.7). http://www.hciv.de
2. Dittmar, A., Forbrig, P. (eds.): ECCE 2011 - European Conference on Cognitive Ergonomics. In: Proceedings of the 29th Annual Conference of the European Association of Cognitive Ergonomics. ACM (2011)
3. Campos, P., Graham, N., Jorge, J., Nunes, N., Palanque, P., Winckler, M. (eds.): INTERACT 2011, Part I. LNCS, vol. 6946. Springer, Heidelberg (2011)
4. Bertin, J.: Sémiologie Graphique. Les diagrammes, les réseaux, les cartes. Mouton/Gauthier-Villars (1967)
5. Kerren, A., Ebert, A., Meyer, J.: Human-Centered Visualization Environments. Springer, Heidelberg (2007)
6. Hewett, T., Baecker, R, Card, S., Carey, T, Gasen, J., Mantei, M., Perlman, G., Strong, G., Verplank, W.: ACM SIGCHI Curricula for Human-Computer Interaction; Chapter 2: Human-Computer Interaction. Last updated in 2009
7. ACM SIGGRAPH: Definitions and Rationale for Visualization. Last updated in 1999
8. Domik G.: Computer-generated Visualization 1. Introduction to Visualization (2008). www.cs.uni-paderborn.de/fileadmin/Informatik/AG-Domik/VisCurriculum/pdf/introduction.pdf. Accessed 14 March 2011
9. Foley, J., Ribarsky, B.: Next-generation data visualization tools. In: Rosenblum, L., Earnshaw, R.A., Encarnacao, J., Hagen, H., Kaufman, A., Klimenko, S., Nielson, G., Post, F., Thalmann, D. (eds.) Scientific Visualization, Advances and Challenges. Academic Press, New York (1994)
10. Kosara, R.: Visualization criticism – the missing link between information visualization and art. In: Proceedings of the 11th International Conference Information Visualization (2007)
11. McCormick, B.H., DeFanti, T.A., Brown, M.D.: Visualization in Scientific Computing. Comput. Graph. **21**(6), 3 (1987)

Workshop Organization

Achim Ebert[1,2]
University of Kaiserslautern
Gottlieb-Daimler-Straße, 67663 Kaiserslautern
Germany
ebert@cs.uni-kl.de

Gerrit C. van der Veer[1,2]
Open University The Netherlands
Valkenburgerweg 177, 6419 AT Heerlen
The Netherlands
gerrit@acm.org

Gitta Domik[2]
University of Paderborn
Fürstenallee 11, 33102 Paderborn
Germany
domik@uni-paderborn.de

Nahum Gershon[2]
The MITRE Corp.
7515 Colshire Drive, McLean, VA 22102-7508
USA
gershon@mitre.org

Inga Scheler[1]
University of Kaiserslautern
Gottlieb-Daimler-Straße, 67663 Kaiserslautern
Germany
scheler@rhrk.uni-kl.de

[1] Organizer of the 7th HCIV workshop on "Non-formal Modelling for Interaction Design" held at the 29th ECCE conference, 2011.
[2] Organizer of the 8th HCIV workshop on "Building Bridges – HCI and Visualization" held at the 13th INTERACT conference, 2011.

Contents

Building Bridges:
HCI and Visualization
(INTERACT 2011)

Teaching Information Visualization via Creative Design

Bob Spence[✉]

Department of Electrical and Electronic Engineering, Imperial College London,
London SW7 2AZ, UK
r.spence@imperial.ac.uk

Abstract. The importance of Information Visualization is reflected in
the many courses on that subject taught worldwide. The number of those
courses, however, is not of prime importance: what is of real concern is
how they are presented, and to *whom*.

1 Students

It is my view that education in information visualization is required primarily by
two groups of people: those who will become interaction designers and those who
will, at some time in their careers, either commission systems with a significant
element of visualization or be responsible for evaluating such systems. I happen
to teach both types of student: post-Master professional designers at the Technical University of Eindhoven in the Netherlands and first year undergraduates
in Information Systems Engineering at Imperial College London. The material
that follows represents a personal view, one that will hopefully trigger debate.

2 Theory or Practice

It is my strong belief that the best way to become educated in Information
Visualization (and human-computer interaction in general) is to *do it*. For that
reason my condition for presenting those courses is that there be no examination
paper, favouring as it does those with photographic memories: rather I wish to
encourage creativity and design ability. So I ask my students to undertake design
exercises (mostly individually and once as a group) and one design critique.

3 Teaching Environment

The *environment* of my teaching of Information Visualization is of great importance to me. I strive for – and largely achieve – a 'studio' environment, first to
approximate that of a real design house and, second, to avoid the traditional
'me and them' attitude: I certainly learn from the course as well as teach it.
For example, in keeping with a studio environment I ensure that students paste

A. Ebert et al. (Eds.): HCIV Workshops 2011, LNCS 8345, pp. 3–7, 2014.
DOI: 10.1007/978-3-642-54894-9_1, © IFIP International Federation for Information Processing 2014

their early designs on a wall, provide a one minute explanation and then for two minutes respond to questions from anyone who cares to ask them. In that way they receive instant and valuable feedback. Although perhaps unexpected, sketching on large sheets of paper with thick pens is encouraged to capture design ideas in the early exploration and design stages (Greenberg et al. [3]): the use of laptops at this stage is frowned upon and virtually forbidden.

4   Content

My emphasis on *design* is not at odds with a concern with theory, though it is theory *to support design* rather than for its own sake that is my concern. However, difficult decisions must be made about the *content* of a course on Information Visualization: what theory is relevant and the appropriate mix of theory and design. One decision I found easy to make – was the need for clear definitions.

4.1   Definitions

A student would surely be surprised, and disappointed in their teacher, if that teacher cannot provide precise definitions for important concepts. My first concern is to provide definitions where possible, even if they may be contentious. For example, the definition of information visualization I have always used is not shared by most leaders in the field. I refer to two respected dictionaries for the following definition:

visualization (v): the formation of a mental model of something,

with the implication that visualization is a cognitive activity undertaken by a human being and has nothing fundamentally to do with computers. I am pleased that recent publications are recognising the importance of this definition, instead of taking the attitude that the letters v-i-s-u-a-l in the word visualization implies that data can only be encoded graphically. My attitude may seem pedantic, but if we forget what the user is trying to achieve we tread a dangerous path. A visualization is not what we see on a display – it is in the mind.

4.2   Examples

In view of the paucity of relevant theory, Information Visualization is largely taught by a critical review of illustrative examples and the discussion of concepts. For example, a student undertaking their first design of a representation (the marks out of ten in 8 subjects taken by 5 students) may be informed by Bertin's [1] work and the concepts of object and attribute visibility [6], but will find that there is no 'algorithm' guaranteed to lead to the 'best' design (there simply isn't one) and that a design's effectiveness depends upon the ultimate user(s) of the representation.

4.3   The Human User

Information Visualization as a discipline acquired a very bad name in its early years by the preponderance of displays that took no account whatsoever of the human user: they were often primarily exercises in programming. I therefore lay considerable stress on the characteristics of the human user, initially by providing actual – and to my students surprising - examples of phenomena such as Change Blindness, Attention Blindness and Preattentive Processing, but these topics are introduced in context rather than being taught within a separate set of lectures. Similarly, I emphasise the importance of considering the human user by ensuring that the first stage of an interaction design (the final group project) is a careful consideration of who the user is and what their goal and *modus operandi* are. Some students are not aware of the need for this first step and immediately propose, in detail, their 'final' and often impoverished design.

4.4   Restrictions

Occasionally the result of a student project identifies an omission in the teaching of Information Visualization. For example, in response to an exercise asking for a proposal for a new kind of family tree – a task conventionally interpreted as requiring a visual display – one group of my students proposed a family tree made of wood: yes, wood. That tree was visually attractive, stood on a table and had embedded communication facilities such that a family member in one part of the world could easily maintain social contact with another member located many miles away, perhaps with a simple touch and the utterance Hi Gran! Examples such as these are a reminder that a (perhaps unconscious) emphasis on computers needs to be guarded against.

4.5   Interaction

At an introductory level I try to present information visualization in a structured manner, using the generally accepted though simple model of Fig. 1 to identify the essentials of the subject. I have little problem with the topic of representation, by combining a selection of techniques with concepts such as those due to Bertin [1] and to Teoh and Ma [6]. Equally, many examples can illustrate the topic of presentation in both space (e.g., the distortion concept) and time (e.g., Rapid Serial Visual Presentation) and a combination of the two. It is with the topic of Interaction that a structure seems a little elusive, notwithstanding its immense importance to information visualization. The search for a science of interaction advocated by Thomas and Cook [7] appears to be exceedingly challenging, but interaction in the restricted context of information visualization should surely be achievable and taught at first year level. Consideration of the features of interaction in this context strongly suggests the relevance of Norman's Stages of Action [5], a concept I introduce very early in my courses. After all, we have a clear **goal** (the enhancement of a mental model of data); we have '**changes** in the world' (changes in D, R and P – see Fig. 1); we have the

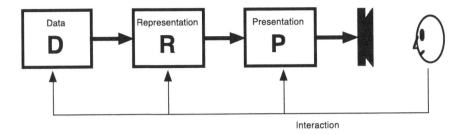

Fig. 1. Model of a system supporting information visualization

ever present requirement to formulate an **action plan** before interaction takes place (and relevant concepts such as sensitivity and affordance); and we have a multitude of devices permitting **execution** – the 'action' of 'interaction'. And the discussion provided by Yi et al. [8] may well be related to another component of Norman's Cycle, the formulation of an **intention**. Consideration of the **perception** and **interpretation** following whatever change occurs in the world (often a visual display) can lead to improvements in the interface being designed. The relevance of Norman's Cycle would appear to extend from conventional navigation in discrete information spaces to the extremely rapid cycle of execution–perception–interpretation–execution involved in the rapid dynamic exploration of complex relationships (see, for example, Neufeld et al. [4]).

5   Visual Analytics

In the context of information visualization the principal value of the newly defined 'discipline' of Visual Analytics can be summarised in a simple statement: Information Visualization exists in context. Acknowledgement of this obvious fact must exist in any course, but not overwhelm it. Simple examples can often suffice to underline this message: the more complex example provided by Colgan et al. [2] is only one of many that can be drawn from many publications extending over the last two or three decades

6   Conclusions

My personal conclusion is that the topic of information visualization is best taught via creative design in a realistic application context.

References

1. Bertin, J.: (1981) Graphics and graphic information Processing, Berlin, Walter de Gruyter: a translation of La Graphique et le Traitment Graphique de l'Information. Flammarion, Paris (1977)

2. Colgan, L., Spence, R., Rankin, P.R.: The cockpit metaphor. Behav. Inf. Technol. **14**(4), 251–263 (1995)
3. Greenberg, S., Carpendale, S., Marquardt, N., Buxton, B.: Sketching User Experiences. Morgan Kaufmann, Amsterdam (2012)
4. Neufeld, E., Kristtorn, S., Guan, Q., Sanscartier, M., Ware, C.: Exploring causal influences. In: Erbacher, R.F., Roberts, J.C., Grohn, M.T., Borner, K. (eds.) Visualization and Data Analysis, vol. 5669, pp. 52–62. SPIE, San Jose (2005)
5. Norman, D.A.: The Design of Everyday Things. Doubleday, New York (1988)
6. Teoh, S.-T., Ma, K.-L.: 'Hifocon': Object and dimensional coherence and correlation in multidimensional visualization. In: Bebis, G., Boyle, R., Koracin, D., Parvin, B. (eds.) ISVC 2005. LNCS, vol. 3804, pp. 235–242. Springer, Heidelberg (2005)
7. Thomas, J., Cook, K.A.: Illuminating the path. IEEE Computer Society, Los Alamitos (2005)
8. Yi, J.S., Kang, Y.A., Stasko, J.T., Jacko, J.A.: Toward a deeper understanding of the role of interaction in information visualization. IEEE Trans. Vis. Comput. Graph. **13**(6), 1224–1231 (2007)

Learning HCI and InfoVis in the Open

Erik Duval[✉], Gonzalo Parra, Jose Luis Santos, Sam Agten, Sven Charleer,
and Joris Klerkx

Dept. of Computer Science, KU Leuven-University of Leuven, Leuven, Belgium
erik.duval@cs.kuleuven.be
http://erikduval.wordpress.com

Abstract. In this paper, we report on our experiences with novel learning strategies for HCI and Information Visualisation, in the context of a computer science master curriculum. What sets our experiences somewhat apart is the focus on openness. This includes the use of Open Educational Resources (OER), as well as open communication between the students, the professor and the general public, through web2.0 tools like blogs, wikis, Facebook and Twitter.

1 Introduction

The work reported here is part of a strong trend towards more open forms of learning. In this context, 'open' can mean many things, including

- open standards that realise interoperability between the different components of a learning infrastructure at the technical level [4];
- open source implementations of such components that enable developers to inspect and modify the source code [11];
- open content that can be shared, repurposed and reused freely - often called 'open educational resources' or OER [5];
- open learning where also the learning activities are more openly shared [7].

We focus on open collaborative learning activities, because we believe that providing students with authentic and realistic learning environments is key to fighting the feeling of alienation and the lack of motivation that characterises so much of formal learning. Providing students with open environments where they work on realistic problems in a dialogue with the wider world is key to addressing this fundamental problem.

Moreover, we position our work in the context of 21st century competencies (information literacy, creativity & innovation, collaboration, problem solving, communication and responsible citizenship), rather than drill-and-practice repetitive fact memorisation or very closed problem solving as is more typical in many university courses. These competencies comprise both skills [6] and dispositions to learn [2]. Basically, the idea is that we should teach students to solve problems we don't know using technologies we don't know, especially in

A. Ebert et al. (Eds.): HCIV Workshops 2011, LNCS 8345, pp. 8–16, 2014.
DOI: 10.1007/978-3-642-54894-9_2, © IFIP International Federation for Information Processing 2014

technology oriented domains like computer science where the domain continues to evolve at increasing speed under the influence of Moore's law [9].

A currently very active instantiation of the open learning idea are MOOC's or 'Massively Open Online Courses' that enable anyone to take courses anywhere [1]. As often well-known prestigious universities organised themselves in networks of providers of such MOOC's and their offerings attract regularly many tens of thousands of learners, the concept of MOOC's has received substantial media coverage [10]. Our course is similar but it is not massive by any meaning of the word: we typically have about 30 students. Our course is open though, but in a different way than MOOC's. Whereas the openness in the latter mainly relates to the low barrier for people to register, we focus more on making students work together and communicate with each other and the team in an open way, through public blogs and Twitter. Our courses are typically only partly "on-line": we do use blogs and wikis and Twitter to communicate, but we also do face-to-face studio sessions throughout the semester.

2   The Courses

In concrete terms, we present here how we have been teaching courses on Human-Computer Interaction (HCI) and, more recently, Information Visualisation (Info-Vis) to computer science engineering students at the University of Leuven in Belgium. Typically, these courses are taken by twenty-five to thirty-five master students in engineering, most of them specialising in computer science. They are optional courses for students with a strong technological focus and background. The HCI course is their first course that focuses on user oriented aspects rather than on technical programming skills.

As such, the main goal of the courses is to make the students change their perspective on how software is evaluated - not from a technical point of view, but focused on how it impacts the user experience. Indeed, evaluation is the main topic of the course: we start with the evaluation of an existing software product (over the years, we have evaluated Mendeley, Google Plus, Pinterest, and others). After this first activity, we start cycles of iterative development, going from brainstorming sessions over user scenario development and paper prototyping to more and more functional digital prototypes and, finally a release 'in the wild', i.e. to the general public. Throughout these activities, we continuously evaluate intermediate versions and the students are expected to document the outcomes of their evaluations and how these outcomes dictate their iterative development cycles.

3   Set-up

The open nature of the course is reflected in the choice of tools that we rely on for organising the learning effort:

- Rather than an institutional Learning Management System (LMS) like Blackboard or Moodle, we use a wiki as the main 'landing page' of the course

Page Discussion   Read Edit View history ▾   [Go] [Search]

Chi 2013

Groepen   [edit]

Navigation

Main page
Community portal
Current events
Recent changes
Random page
Help

Toolbox

What links here
Related changes
Special pages
Printable version
Permanent link

- Team LPG: Peter Bosmans, Laurens Sion, Gert Vanwijn [1] ⧉
- Team TGV: Vincent Goovaerts, Gill Vandenbroeck, Thomas De Vos [2] ⧉
- CHInterest: Maaike Mercelis, Sebastiaan Rousseeuw, Pieter-Jan Verbruggen [3] ⧉
- IGCHI : Kevin Delval, Joris Schelfaut, Wouter Moermans [4] ⧉
- CHI Movez: Michael Gobbers, Nik Torfs, Sander Voeten [5] ⧉
- JeTS-CHI: Jeroen Coninck, Tom Van den Broeck, Simon Chuptys [6] ⧉
- HatCHI: Benjamin Wittevrongel, Willem Mattelaer, Dimitri Vargemidis [7] ⧉
- ChiConCarne: Tom De Buyser, Tom Piot, Alex Witteveen [8] ⧉
- Team S-CHI: Stijn De Haes, An Pirlot, Thomas De Moor [9] ⧉

Future of HCI   [edit]

- Future of HCI videos

Course info   [edit]

- course blog ⧉
- full activity stream ⧉
- badge dashboard ⧉
- badge overview ⧉
- big table ⧉
- username spreadsheet 🔒
- sus scores 🔒
- Comment keywords

This page was last modified on 23 April 2013, at 22:55.

This page has been accessed 1,649 times.

Privacy policy   About HCI Wiki   Disclaimers

Fig. 1. The course wiki

(see Fig. 1). This is important, as an LMS environment is typically set up and under the control of the central institutional services. We replace this environment with a tool that is under complete control of the students: initially, the wiki page only contains a title and empty placeholder text. The clear message, although implicit, is that students are expected to take responsibility for their own learning [3].

– Students typically work in groups of three and communicate with the other groups and teaching staff through public blogs. They are explicitly asked to not only read the blogs of the other groups, but also to comment on the posts of other groups. The intent is to create a community of practice, where learning takes place in an open spirit of collaboration and communication [12].

– Whereas the blogs are intended for more substantial posts and comments on these posts, we rely on Twitter hashtags for more ephemeral messages that create a 'pulse of the course' and support continuous awareness of ongoing activities in the course (see Fig. 2).

Table 1. Statistics on the 2013 HCI course

Number of students	26
Number of blog posts	50
Number of blog comments by students	207
Number of blog comments by staff	57
Number of blog comments by outsiders	12

Fig. 2. The course blog comments and Twitter stream

The result is that the on-line communication happens in a 'class without walls': external people can follow and post to the Twitter stream, subscribe to

Hi Erik,

Victor here, one of the founders of Mendeley. We certainly appreciate your students' comments, I think it's very good feedback! You've managed to highlight three of the main issues we are working on right now (of course, as we are still in beta, many UI elements are still in flux).

Regarding the relationship between the desktop app and the website:

Indeed this should be communicated more clearly. The desktop app is like an "iTunes for research papers", i.e. you can manage, read, and annotate your PDFs locally. The website, on the other hand, is more like a "Last.fm for research": It "scrobbles" your library to the cloud, so you can sync it across multiple devices and access it in a browser. It also generates a catalogue of research (more on that later), Last.fm-like stats about the most popular papers, and it gives recommendations for related research (these are currently only available on article pages, e.g. http://www.mendeley.com/research/evaluation-of-murine-norovirus-as-a-surrogate-for-human-norovirus-and-hepatitis-a-virus-in-heat-inactivation-studies/). We're currently working on an improved "newsfeed" system which will display more of your desktop-app-based research activity on the website and let you and others comment on research papers you've added to your library; likewise, we'll be pulling these newsfeeds, statistics and related research recommendations into the desktop interface right next to your research paper library. This should make the flow of information between desktop and web more visible.

Regarding the registration process:

This was just changed on Friday – there is now a registration form on pretty much any page on the website. However, there has always been a login box at the top right on every page – sorry if that isn't obvious enough.

Regarding the search:

You're right – there isn't any way to search the catalogue of research papers on the website. This is not for a lack of wanting, but because we first had to build a scalable back-end to deduplicate millions of documents on the fly (every day, more than 100,000 papers get uploaded to Mendeley) which could then be indexed. We'll soon be releasing a new interface for searching and browsing research papers, public collections of papers, and researchers.

Hope this was useful,
thanks again,

Victor

edit

reply

Fig. 3. An inspiring reaction from an 'outsider'

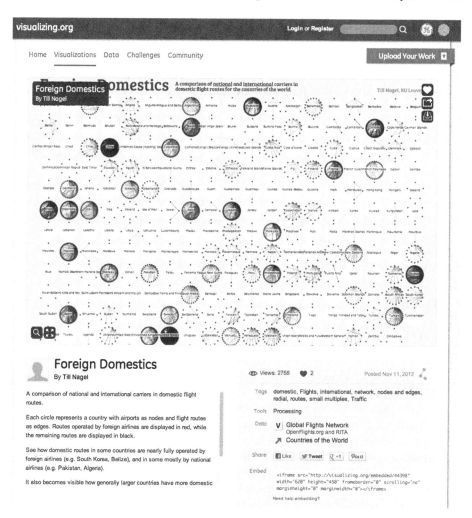

Fig. 4. A winning hackaton entry by Till Nagel

the blog posts, and leave comments on the student blogs. Although this kind of external input is a small percentage of the overall activity (see also Table 1), it contributes significantly to the authentic nature of the course activities: in the words of the students, 'real people' (i.e. not the teaching staff or peer students) take an interest in what they post! One recent example is a reaction from a representative of a software tool, who commented on one of the student blogs to help them with problems they experienced with the tool.

A more inspiring example is that of Fig. 3: in reaction to evaluations that the students blogged about a bibliographic reference manager (mendeley, http://mendeley.com), one of the founders of the company commented on these evaluations. For the students, it is quite motivating to discover that their comments are not only read by the course staff and that these comments may actually serve another purpose than passing an exam or getting a degree.

Another variation on the same theme of openness is participation in 'hackatons', i.e. intensive events where teams design and develop software over a period of a few hours to a few days. In the Information Visualisation course, we participated in the '2012 Visualizing Global Marathon' (http://visualizing. org/marathon2012/), an event from Friday evening until Sunday midnight, with locations across the world. Students were given three data sets at the start and could participate in video conferences with experts on visualisation. A Twitter hashtag organised Twitter messages. After the event, a jury evaluated the results. Actually, some of the teaching staff also participated in the hackaton and one of them, Till Nagel, was awarded a prize for his work (see Fig. 4). Again, this creates an open atmosphere in which students work not only under supervision of the teaching staff on a project that they hand in, but rather work *with* staff in a global community of students, staff and experts, in an intensive setting where friendly competition motivates but doesn't prevent collaboration!

4   Issues

Such an open approach is not without its own issues. We list some of the more important ones below:

– The number and diversity of interactions (Twitter, blog posts and comments, wiki edits, ...) can be a bit overwhelming. This can be problematic for students and staff alike. However, we believe that coping with this kind of 'information overload' (or rather 'filter failure' when this becomes a problem [13]) is an important 21st century meta-skill in itself and that it is actually useful that students acquire this skill as well. Moreover, we also research the use of learning analytics dashboard applications [14,15] that enable staff and students to be aware of, reflect on, make sense of and act on what is going on.
– There are obvious concerns around privacy and 'trusted environments' when learning takes place in this open way: students are sometimes concerned that potential future employers will be able to find out about the mistakes they made in class. On the other hand, our perceptions of what is appropriate to share and what should be private are shifting as technology develops [8]. More importantly, we believe that it is also valuable that students learn to act in public and engage with an external audience, the more so as this is a way to realise a more authentic learning context, as we have argued above.
– There is, of course, a certain overhead involved in the social interactions among students, and between students and the general public. Although we have already mentioned that we believe that mastering social interaction is a useful skill in its own right, there is still a question whether the added effort actually results in more learning - i.e. less time required overall, or better learning outcomes. In fact, grading for these courses is based on the project outcome: in that sense, students are not rewarded directly for social interaction and collaboration. On the other hand, by making use of the opportunities

for interaction, students can receive more feedback about progress on their projects as they proceed, which should result in increased motivation and a higher quality outcome, and thus a higher grade. However, carefully evaluating the impact of the open approach on the learning outcome remains tricky as it is difficult to isolate the effect of our approach from all the other variables that affect student results.

– It is unclear how well this approach would scale from our current group of around 30 students to hundreds or the many thousands of students in MOOC's. On the one hand, as mentioned above, students already now report feeling a bit overwhelmed. Scaling up the courses risks making this problem much more serious. On the other hand, it would be possible to make students interact intensively with just a small subset of a large group. And to channel the contributions from outsiders, so that they would still reach all of the students, unless the participation from outsiders also increases with the student numbers, and we can also partition their contributions to subsets of students. Yet, how to scale up without turning the experience into a set of isolated mini-courses for each subset of students remains unclear.

5   Conclusion

In this paper, we have presented our work on teaching Human-Computer Interaction and Information Visualisation in an open way. Our work is part of a broader evolution towards more open software, content and learning in general. Our basic premise is that a more open approach prepares students better for a 21st century professional career and life in general and that the more authentic context for learning improves motivation and thus increases the likelihood of positive learning outcomes. Although this approach can at times be challenging for students and staff alike, we believe that this openness is essential for deeper authentic learning.

References

1. de Waard, I., Abajian, S., Gallagher, M.S., Hogue, R., Keskin, N., Koutropoulos, A., Rodriguez, O.C.: Using mlearning and moocs to understand chaos, emergence, and complexity in education. Int. Rev. Res. Open Distance Learn. **12**(7), 94–115 (2011)
2. Crick, R.D.: Assessment in schools - dispositions. In: McGaw, B., Peterson, P., Baker, E. (eds.) The International Encyclopedia of Education. Elsevier, Amsterdam (2009)
3. Dron, J.:. Social software and the emergence of control. In: Sixth International Conference on Advanced Learning Technologies, pp. 904–908 (2006)
4. Duval, E., Verbert, K.: On the role of technical standards for learning technologies. IEEE Trans. Learn. Technol. **1**(4), 229–234 (2008)
5. Duval, E., Wiley, D.: Guest editorial: open educational resources. IEEE Trans. Learn. Technol. **3**(2), 83–84 (2010)

6. Griffin, P.: Assessment and Teaching of 21st Century Skills. Springer, New York (2012)
7. Iiyoshi, T., Kumar, M.S.V. (eds.): Opening Up Education. MIT Press, Cambridge (2008)
8. Jarvis, J.: Public Parts: How Sharing in the Digital Age Improves the Way We Work and Live. Simon and Schuster, New York (2011)
9. Kurzweil, R.: The Singularity Is Near: When Humans Transcend Biology. Penguin books, New York (2005)
10. Pappano, L.: The year of the mooc. The New York Times, 4 (2012)
11. Raymond, E.: The cathedral and the bazaar. Knowl. Technol. Policy **12**(3), 23–49 (1999)
12. Rheingold, H.: The Virtual Community: Homesteading on the Electronic Frontier. MIT Press, Cambridge (2000)
13. Shirky, C.: Here Comes Everybody: The Power of Organizing Without Organizations. Penguin Press, New York (2008)
14. Suthers, D., Verbert, K., Duval, E., Ochoa, X. (eds.): LAK '13: Proceedings of the Third International Conference on Learning Analytics and Knowledge. ACM, New York (2013)
15. Verbert, K., Duval, E., Klerkx, J., Govaerts, S., Santos, J. L.: Learning analytics dashboard applications. American Behavioral Scientist, 10p. (2013, in press)

How to Investigate Interaction with Information Visualisation: An Overview of Methodologies

Margit Pohl[(⊠)] and Florian Scholz

Vienna University of Technology, Institute for Design and Assessment of Technology,
Vienna, Austria
`margit@igw.tuwien.ac.at`

Abstract. Advanced information visualisation systems offer many different forms of interaction. Nevertheless, we do not know how useful these interactions are. Researchers have suggested to develop a science of interaction. In this paper we discuss which research methods might be appropriate to study interaction with information visualisation systems. We suggest that thinking aloud, log files and eye tracking are promising candidates. These methods enable researchers to study interaction in more detail than other methods. All these methods have strengths and weaknesses. A combination of two or three of these methods might help to overcome the weaknesses.

Keywords: Thinking aloud · Eyetracking · Log files · Interaction patterns · Triangulation

1 Introduction

Advanced IT systems enable users to interact with them in multiple ways. Users of interactive information visualisation systems, for example, can filter data, show data in more or less detail or represent the data in different visual forms (e.g. as scatterplots or as a graph etc). Such interactions have to be designed appropriately to be useful. User-centered design can help to develop interactive features with a high usability.

The investigation of various forms of interaction has become more important in HCI in recent years [1]. Mirel [2], for example, argues that human problem-solving and open-ended inquiry consist of different high-level activities (e.g. wayfinding, sensemaking, ...). It is necessary to identify interaction patterns, that is "recurring sets of actions and strategies that have a successful record in resolving particular types of problems" [2, p. 35]. The strategies the users adopt to solve problems or find relevant information consist of a certain number of such interaction patterns. Such investigations are necessary for HCI in general, but they are especially relevant in information visualisation and visual analytics. In these areas, systems are developed which are supposed to support human reasoning processes and open-ended exploration specifically. Therefore, Pike et al. [3] argue that a science of interaction is necessary. They assume that interaction

A. Ebert et al. (Eds.): HCIV Workshops 2011, LNCS 8345, pp. 17–29, 2014.
DOI: 10.1007/978-3-642-54894-9_3, ⓒ IFIP International Federation for Information Processing 2014

and cognition are closely coupled and that InfoVis should be designed as dialogic systems where both users and computers pose questions and answers. To design such dialogic systems it is necessary to investigate interaction processes in detail.

The following chapter discusses possible methods of analysis which are especially appropriate for this kind of investigation. In this context, researchers need methods able to represent the various activities which the users engage in while they work with information visualisations. Therefore, methods like interviews or questionnaires are not really appropriate because they cannot give a detailed overview of sequences of activities. In contrast to that, there are other methods like thinking aloud, eye tracking or log files which provide a fairly comprehensive overview of these activities. Categorisation of activities or utterances is necessary to be able to analyse the results of these methods. Based on these categorisations are mathematical approaches like transition matrices (see e.g. Ratwani et al. [4]) and Markov models. In this chapter, we will first describe these methods (eye tracking, log files, thinking aloud). We will discuss their advantages and disadvantages for the analysis of sequences of interactions with information visualisations. We will briefly discuss whether it is beneficial to combine two or more of these methods. Finally, we will present a few examples of the application of these methods in information visualisation and visual analytics. The discussion of the application examples is not exhaustive and can only give a brief idea of how these methods are applied in this area.

2   Eye Tracking

Eye tracking has been used quite extensively in human-computer interaction and usability research (see e.g. [5]). Goldberg and Wichansky [6] summarize usability recommendations based on eye tracking research. These recommendations concern screen elements such as icons, menus, navigation etc. There is also some relevant research on cognitive load [6].

A fundamental assumption of eye tracking research is the so-called eye-mind hypothesis [6,7] which posits that the gaze direction is an indication of what the user is currently thinking about. There is empirical research indicating that this is not always the case. Duchowski [8] argues that peripheral vision also plays an important role in perception. Subjects often remember objects only seen in peripheral vision [9]. Another difficulty in this context is, that it is sometimes challenging to infer what users really are thinking from gaze directions and scanpaths. If a user looks at an object on the screen for an extended period of time, this might indicate that the object is interesting or, on the other hand, that its functionality is not clear.

Eye tracking has several advantages [7]. Eye tracking provides a large amount of objective data about users' attention processes. Such processes sometimes are very fast and unconscious and, therefore, difficult to investigate. It is fairly unobtrusive (in contrast to, e.g., thinking aloud). Eye trackers also usually come with software which provides researchers with interesting visualisations (e.g. heat maps).

Table 1. Advantages and disadvantages of eye tracking.

Eye tracking	
	General advantages
	Large amount of data about users' attention processes
	Fairly unobtrusive
	Eye trackers already provide simple statistics and visualisations
	General disadvantages
	Technical problems
	Labour-intensive data extraction
	Difficulties in data interpretation
	Advantages for the analysis of interaction with InfoVis
	Reflects attention to visual stimuli
	Yields very detailed information about users' scanning strategies
	Challenges for the analysis of interaction with InfoVis
	Generalisations of results from scanpaths difficult because of individual differences
	Definition of AOIs
	Investigation of exploratory tasks
	Difficulty of the analysis of dynamic data

There are also disadvantages. Jacob and Karn [5] summarize disadvantages of eye tracking as follows: technical problems, labour-intensive data extraction, and difficulties in data interpretation (Table 1).

In addition, it should be pointed out that there are usually considerable individual differences concerning the users' scanpaths [10]. This makes generalisation of results of eye tracking studies difficult. A possible solution for this problem is to use small and well defined tasks with clear solutions to get comparable results. Such tasks are usually not very realistic. Results for explorative, open-ended tasks usually differ considerably.

Eye tracking is especially appropriate for investigating interaction with information visualisation tools because it reflects attention to visual stimuli. It can provide detailed information about the users' scanning strategies [11]. Eye tracking can show sequences of the users' activities. The interaction processes of the users with the InfoVis (information visualisation) tool can be analysed in great detail.

There are some specific challenges concerning the usage of eye tracking in information visualisation. Defining areas of interest (AOIs) or regions of interest (ROI) is especially important for visualisations (we will use the terms interchangeably). AOIs should be related to the research question [9]. Unluckily, it is not possible to provide rules for the definition of AOIs. Another problem is the fact that exploratory tasks are especially important in information visualisation and visual analytics. As mentioned above, it is difficult to investigate such tasks with eye tracking methods. In addition, it is still challenging to analyse dynamic data with eye tracking methodologies [7]. Such data are highly relevant for information visualisation and visual analytics. To conclude, eye tracking seems to have great potential for the analysis of interactions with information visualisations and visual analytics, but it is not yet entirely clear how to use this potential.

3   Log Files

Log files are a very well-known methodology of research in Human-Computer Interaction [12]. They were originally used for the analysis of so-called WIMP interfaces (window, icon, menu, pointer), but nowadays their main application area is the assessment of the usability of websites [13].

Log files which can serve as data source for cognitive research are often developed by the researchers themselves. An example for this is described in Sect. 6.3 [14].

The addition of log files to software to analyse the users' behaviour is called instrumenting [15]. The goal of most usability studies using log files, in contrast to that, is to find usability errors and improve the interface. To reach this goal, log files produced automatically by servers or by off-the-shelf software is usually appropriate.

Ivory and Hearst [16] give an overview of various complex systems for the analysis of log files. They distinguish between automated capturing of usage data and the automated analysis of these data. Log file analysis in a narrow sense is the analysis of log file data based on metrics or a mathematical model. The system AMME developed by Rauterberg et al. [17] e.g. uses Markov models and Petri nets to investigate the users' problem-solving processes.

Information visualisation systems often offer interaction possibilities going beyond navigation. Users are supported in zooming and panning, filtering the data, choosing different ways of representing data on the screen or other interaction activities (for an overview of categorisations of interactions see e.g. Gotz and Zhou [18], Yi et al. [19]). Logging all these activities can enable researchers to get some insights about the users' cognitive processes. It is, for example, interesting to know that users sometimes concentrate on details of the visualisation and sometimes on overall aspects and prediction of the behaviour of the whole system [20]. In addition, log files also provide information about the sequence of activities. This enables researchers to investigate whether there are patterns in the users' behaviour. In this context, it is essential to decide which data to capture and how to aggregate these data [15]. It is possible to collect data on a keystroke level, but in many cases such data is not very informative. Higher-level data might be more interesting. To decide which data to collect, a clear hypothesis about the cognitive processes involved in the interaction with the information visualisation system is often necessary. These data often have to be aggregated (e.g., when the same goal can be reached by several methods — menus or keyboard shortcuts) and categorised to be useful for an analysis of cognitive processes. Such an analysis process of log files is seldom described or discussed in the literature (Table 2).

Table 2. Advantages and disadvantages of log files.

Log files
General advantages
Less time consuming than other methodologies
Reflects actual behaviour of the users
Not intrusive, does not influence the users' behaviour
General disadvantages
Difficult to interpret the data (lack of context)
Advantages for the analysis of interaction with InfoVis
Provides detailed information about sequences of interaction
Especially appropriate for the analysis of interactive and explorative InfoVis tools
Challenges for the analysis of interaction with InfoVis
Identification of the appropriate level of granularity of interactions
Identification of the appropriate system of categorisation for the activities

Using log files has several advantages. Compared to other methodologies in Human-Computer Interaction, as e.g. thinking aloud or observation of user actions, log file analysis is less time-consuming, although the amount of work involved in the analysis process should not be underestimated. Log file analysis reflects the actual behaviour of the users, not their attitudes toward a certain piece of software (as in questionnaires or interviews). In addition, log file analysis is not intrusive. Users usually do not notice that their actions are being logged. The method, therefore, does not change their behaviour (in contrast to thinking aloud which influences the users' interaction with the system). One serious disadvantage of log files is that it is often difficult to interpret the users' actions without any knowledge of the context in which this interaction happened. When a user repeats an interaction sequence again and again, this might be an indication of a usability problem or an indication of the user's attempt to gain a more thorough mental model of the information represented on the screen. Log files, are, therefore, often used in conjunction with other methods (thinking aloud, observation,...).

4   Thinking Aloud

Thinking aloud is a methodology which was developed by Ericsson and Simon [21]. The original goal was the investigation of cognitive processes, especially in the context of problem solving activities. It is difficult to analyse such processes exclusively on the basis of observation of visible behaviour because only the results of such activities can be perceived, not the process itself. Ericsson and Simon looked for a methodology to get more information about the processes which happen during problem solving and the strategies problem solvers adopt to reach their goals. This model is based on several assumptions. The theoretical context of thinking aloud is the information processing model of cognition (see e.g. [22]), a theoretical approach in psychology which uses computer based models as metaphors for the explanation of human cognition. Related to this is the assumption that thinking is a serial process which takes place in the working memory and the assumption that thinking aloud provides a complete overview of the cognitive processes. These assumptions are controversial (for a description of these discussions see e.g. [23]).

Boren and Ramey [24] give a comprehensive overview of problems which might arise when thinking aloud is applied in usability research. They point out that cognitive psychology is quite different to usability research, and some of the problems encountered when thinking aloud is used in usability research is due to that fact. In usability research, researchers often encounter system crashes or bugs in using the system which is being investigated. The consequence of such problems is that thinking aloud is interrupted. It is not clear whether an investigation where many such crashes and bugs happen really gives an accurate impression of the users' thought processes. In addition, difficulties in using novel and unstable prototypes often necessitates that researchers talk to subjects to explain relevant issues of using the system. Such behaviour is not acceptable in the context of the original methodology. Boren and Ramey [24] suggest another theoretical framework — speech communication — to allow researchers to conduct more consistent and well defined investigations in usability. The theoretical framework they propose accommodates the current practice in usability research much better than the original theoretical positions formulated by Ericsson and Simon [21]. In addition, we would like to point out that there is another problem with thinking aloud which was already mentioned by Ericsson and Simon [21]. They point out that verbalisation is difficult when problems are presented in a physical form (e.g. the problem of the towers of Hanoi has to be solved by manipulating the disks physically). Subjects concentrate on the manipulation of the objects and are less able to verbalise their thought processes. Using a computer program to solve problems might be a similar situation. Users interact with an artifact and concentrate on mouse movements and navigation, and less on their thought processes.

Nevertheless, thinking aloud has significant advantages compared to methods like eye tracking and log file analysis. It gives insights into the thought processes, goals and motivation of the users of information visualisations. It also provides context to activities of the users and helps researchers to understand what strategies users adopt. Thinking aloud also provides a good impression of sequences of actions, although the granularity of these actions is usually more coarse than the one of log files and eye tracking.

Thinking aloud also has some disadvantages. As mentioned above, the application of thinking aloud in usability research, and more generally to investigate interactions with computer programs poses some problems. In addition, thinking aloud is disruptive and unnatural. Ericsson and Simon [21] argue that thinking

Table 3. Advantages and disadvantages of thinking aloud.

Thinking aloud	
	General advantages
	Direct investigation of cognitive processes during problem-solving behaviour
	Information about thought processes, goals and motivation of the users
	General disadvantages
	Difficult to use in the context of HCI [23]
	Disruptive and unnatural
	Advantages for the analysis of interaction with InfoVis
	Provides detailed information about sequences of interaction
	Provides more direct information about strategies and reasoning processes of users of InfoVis tools
	Provides context for the interpretation of data
	Challenges for the analysis of interaction with InfoVis
	Adaptation of the model of Boren and Ramey [24] for the analysis of interaction with InfoVis tools

aloud only makes the problem solving process longer. Otherwise, the procedure of problem solving is unchanged. There is some reason to assume that this is sometimes not the case [12]. We would also argue that thinking aloud is not a natural behaviour, although people adapt to it fairly quickly. Despite all these difficulties, we think that results gained from the application of thinking aloud can yield valuable insights about the nature of the interaction processes of users of information visualisations (Table 3).

5   Mixing Methodologies

The methodologies described above all have strengths and weaknesses. It has often been suggested that a combination of these methodologies might yield more valid results. Lazar et al. [15], e.g., argue that log files are difficult to interpret and seldom provide contextual information about users and their cognitive processes. They suggest to combine log file analysis with video recordings (analysis of videos of users' interaction processes with software) or direct observation to get more information about the problem at hand. Gilhooly and Green [25], on the other hand, suggest the combination of thinking aloud and log files. Log files enable the researchers to get more detailed and fine grained information about the users' activities. Sometimes, such data can clarify what users meant with their utterances. Thinking aloud can also be combined with eye tracking [7] to be able to interpret the results of eye tracking studies. Subjects are often motivated to talk while they work with the system. A problem occuring in this context is that their eye movements are affected by thinking aloud, and eye movement recordings do not provide a realistic representation of what people are attending to any more. Webb and Renshaw suggest that retrospective methods should be applied in this case (e.g. discussing gaze plots with the users after the experiment). Holmqvist et al. [9] argue that the accuracy of eye tracking data especially suffers in the case of a remote eye tracking system because such systems cannot compensate the effects of fast head movements which usually accompany verbal behaviour. In the case of head-mounted systems, the problem is less serious.

Such combinations of methodologies enable researchers to get more detailed and accurate data than when only one single methodology is used. Such an approach is called triangulation (see e.g. [15]). This also increases the reliability and validity of the results. In their book on mixing methods, Creswell and Plano Clark [26] give an overview of how different research methodologies can be combined. Usually, quantitative and qualitative approaches are mixed.

One example for mixing methods is the study conducted by Jakobsen and Hornbaek [27]. They combined grounded theory, thinking aloud, activity logging, probes and interviews. They argue that the methods in combination "provide stronger evidence of participants' adoption and use" of a specific software. Activity logging, e.g., does not provide any information about the subjects' intents and the context of their work. Thinking aloud, therefore, complements the data from activity logging.

6   Applications in Information Visualization

To illustrate how these methods could be used we will now give some examples of how they were already applied in the field of information visualisation and Visual Analytics.

6.1   Eye Tracking

Goldberg and Helfman [11], compared three different graph types using eye tracking. They defined Regions-of-Interest (Areas-of-Interest) for the sub-elements of the graphs concerned. They measured the time until their participants' fixations first met the ROIs in which the information necessary for the given task was encoded. They also looked at sequences of fixations, observing, for example, that "The second viewed bar graph was generally scanned left to right (except the first AOI), but the first viewed bar graph was not regularly scanned in a particular direction" [11, p. 77].

A similar approach is used by Siirtola et al. [28] where ROIs are defined for elements of a parallel coordinate visualisation, divided in ROIs deemed necessary and relevant to a given task and those which are not. From the eye tracking data they derive the number of fixations that happened before a fixation in certain ROIs, as well as the total number of fixations and the total time spent in it, comparing these for ROI- and task-type, and relating their results to the interactions offered by the visualisation [28].

Another interesting way to use eye tracking is described in Convertino et al. [29] who investigate multiple-view visualisations in different configurations. They use the data to derive a measure of how often their participants moved their focus between views, and relate these values to other measurements taken [29].

Huang et al. [30] on the other hand, consciously avoided using eye tracking data for quantitative analysis, after observing that "currently available measures" are "difficult to relate [...] to specific graph elements such as nodes, links or paths" and decided to employ "Eye movement videos", that is, a video of the screen content overlaid with a marker for the gaze direction during the experiment [30, p. 3:3]. By analysing these they developed new theories concerning human behaviour reading these graphs and then tested the theory by designing and implementing experiments employing classical time-and-error measurements [30].

6.2   Thinking Aloud

As with eye tracking there are different kind data and results one can get with thinking aloud. In evaluating information visualisation systems the concept of insight often is used, though definitions (for a discussion see, for example, Chang et al. [31]) as well as categorization approaches vary, depending among other things on the goals and questions of the study concerned.

Bautista and Carenini [32], for example, use this approach as part of a qualitative and quantitative triangulation (see Sect. 5) in an effort to demonstrate usefulness and improve an information visualisation tool for preferential choice.

HCI often uses time to complete tasks and number of errors as variables of analysis. For explorative tasks in InfoVis other variables are also interesting, e.g. the insights gained during interaction processes. Saraiya et al. [33] conducted a study comparing this kind of evaluation to the more classical method of measuring time and error in the information visualisation domain. They compared three information visualisation techniques of the same dataset and the two methods between subjects. Concerning the insights they use the number of insights (total and in categories, developed in cooperation with domain specialists) and the time spent in the open ended exploration scenario in an analysis of variance. They also note that even though they did not prompt their participants for it they additionally got feedback concerning the usability and visualisations in the insight condition, which might be another interesting factor to consider in the context of methodology choice [33].

Thinking aloud data is usually collected in sessions spanning hours at most, but it can also be a part of a longer term field study, as with Jakobsen and Hornbaek [27], who studied real-life workplace adoption of a source code visualisation tool spanning multiple weeks employing thinking aloud and logging methods, among others. Comparing and contrasting the thinking aloud results with the other methods, they mention that thinking aloud "showed use of the interface across a range of tasks, including some surprising ad-hoc uses" [27, p. 1586].

6.3 Log Files

Log files can clarify many open questions about the interaction processes of users with information visualisations. Bautista and Carenini [32], for example, mention that their log files revealed to them the reason why a certain task showed no significant difference in time-to-complete, even though this task required a functionality that was hidden in one condition and quite prominent in the other. According to them the log files showed that their participants traded the time gained by quicker access to the function for time spent using it [32].

A study conducted at our institute [34] is an example for a more in-depth report of a statistical analysis of log files created during a study of an information visualisation tool (Gravi++).

Building on this, a later study [14] explored the issue of emerging patterns of interactions. Beside the log file data the authors also analysed log files generated by another information visualisation application (VisuExplore) for comparison. While the specific interactions afforded by different tools usually also differ, the authors were able to use a variant of the general categorisation scheme proposed by Yi et al. [19] to group the logged events into higher-level activities, to see if the same general patterns could be found in both tools. To that end they qualitatively identified recurring patterns and also computed transition probabilities between categories [14]. Based on the theory of Distributed Cognition, the authors interpret these patterns as indicators of cognitive activities.

In the study by Convertino et al. [29] already mentioned as an example for eye tracking investigations the authors also statistically analysed their log file data, using the number of different interactions as dependent measure and finding some significant effects for condition and task type, and also relating them to completion time measurements [29].

One advantage of using log files is that the data can be potentially collected over a longer period of time and that the method is relatively non-intrusive, therefore viable for medium or long term field studies, as Jakobsen and Hornbaek [27] demonstrated in the study already mentioned above concerning the in-the-field adoption of a fisheye source code visualisation. Visualising and quantitatively analysing the logs, they could observe the real life adoption of the visualisation component over time and in the context of the surrounding workflow [27].

7 Conclusion

In this paper, we describe three methods for the analysis of interactions with information visualisations. All these methods have advantages and disadvantages. A possibility to overcome the disadvantages would be to combine some of these methods. A careful study of the users' interaction processes with information visualisations could provide more information about cognitive processes accompanying interaction with information visualisation.

We think that in the future it is necessary to discuss methodological problems regarding the investigation of interactions with information visualisations in more detail. Important research has been done to clarify research methods for the evaluation of information visualisations in general [35]. The investigation of interaction sequences is, however, a very specific problem requiring more detailed research.

Acknowledgments. This work is conducted in the context of the CVAST - Centre of Visual Analytics Science and Technology project. It is funded by the Austrian Federal Ministry of Economy, Family and Youth in the exceptional Laura Bassi Centres of Excellence initiative.

References

1. Preece, J., Rogers, Y., Sharp, H.: Interaction Design. Wiley, New York (2002)
2. Mirel, B.: Interaction Design for Complex Problem Solving. Elsevier/Morgan Kauffman, Amsterdam, Boston (2004)
3. Pike, W.A., Stasko, J., Chang, R., O'Connell, T.A.: The science of interaction. Inf. Vis. **8**(4), 263–74 (2009)
4. Ratwani, R.M., Trafton, J.G., Boehm-Davis, D.A.: Thinking graphically: connecting vision and cognition during graph comprehension. J. Exp. Psychol. Appl. **14**(1), 36–49 (2008)
5. Jacob, R.J.K., Karn, K.S.: Eye tracking in human-computer interaction and usability research: ready to deliver the promises. In: Hyona, J., Radach, R., Deubel, H. (eds.) The Mind's Eye - Cognitive and Applied Aspects of Eye Movement Research, pp. 573–03. Elsevier, Amsterdam (2003)
6. Goldberg, J.H., Wichansky, A.: Eye tracking in usability evaluation: a practitioner's guide. In: Hyona, J., Radach, R., Deubel, H. (eds.) The Mind's Eye - Cognitive and Applied Aspects of Eye Movement Research, pp. 493–516. Elsevier, Amsterdam (2003)
7. Webb, N., Renshaw, T.: Eyetracking in HCI. In: Cairns, P., Cox, A.L. (eds.) Research Methods for Human-Computer Interaction, pp. 35–69. Cambridge University Press, Cambridge (2008)
8. Duchowski, A.: Eye Tracking Methodology - Theory and Practice, 2nd edn. Springer, London (2007)
9. Holmqvist, K., Nystrom, M., Andersson, R., Dewhurst, R., Jarodzka, H., van de Weijer, J.: Eye Tracking - A Comprehensive Guide to Methods and Measures. Oxford University Press, Oxford (2011)
10. Nielsen, J., Pernice, K.: Eyetracking Web Usability. New Riders Press, Berkeley (2010)
11. Goldberg, J.H., Helfman, J.I.: Comparing information graphics: a critical look at eye tracking. In: Proceedings of the 3rd BELIV'10 Workshop: BEyond Time and Errors: Novel EvaLuation Methods for Information Visualization, BELIV '10, pp. 71–78. ACM, New York (2010)
12. Preece, J., Rogers, Y., Sharp, H., Benyon, D., Holland, S., Carey, T.: Human-Computer Interaction. Addison Wesley, Reading (1994)
13. Kuniavsky, M.: Observing the User Experience - A Practitioner's Guide to User Research. Morgan Kaufmann, San Francisco (2003)
14. Pohl, M., Wiltner, S., Miksch, S., Aigner, W., Rind, A.: Analysing interactivity in information visualisation. KI - Künstliche Intelligenz **26**, 151–9 (2012)
15. Lazar, J., Feng, J.H., Hochheiser, H.: Research Methods in Human-Computer Interaction. Wiley, Chichester (2010)

16. Ivory, M.Y., Hearst, M.A.: The state of the art in automating usability evaluation of user interfaces. ACM Compu. Surv. **33**(4), 470–516 (2001)
17. Rauterberg, M.: A petri net based analysing and modelling tool kit for logfiles in human-computer interaction. In: Proceedings of Cognitive Systems Engineering in Process Control - CSEPC '96 Conference, pp. 268–275 (1996)
18. Gotz, D., Zhou, M.X.: Characterizing users' visual analytic activity for insight provenance. Inf. Vis. **8**(1), 42–55 (2009)
19. Yi, J.S., ah Kang, Y., Stasko, J., Jacko, J.: Toward a deeper understanding of the role of interaction in information visualization. IEEE Trans. Vis. Comput. Graph. **13**(6), 1224–31 (2007)
20. Friel, S.N., Curcio, F.R., Bright, C.W.: Making sense of graphs: critical factors influencing comprehension and instructional implications. J. Res. Math. Educ. **32**(2), 124–58 (2001)
21. Ericsson, K.A., Simon, H.A.: Protocol Analysis - Verbal Reports as Data - Revised Edition. MIT Press, Cambridge (1993)
22. Anderson, J.: Kognitive Psychologie, 3rd edn. Spektrum Akademischer Verlag, Heidelberg (2001)
23. Gilhooly, K., Green, C.: Protocol analysis: theoretical background. Handbook of Qualitative Research Methods for Psychology and the Social Sciences, pp. 43–54. BPS Blackwell, Malden (1996)
24. Boren, T., Ramey, J.: Thinking aloud: reconciling theory and practice. IEEE Trans. Prof. Commun. **43**(3), 261–78 (2000)
25. Gilhooly, K., Green, C.: Protocol analysis: practical implications? In: Richardson, J.T.E. (ed.) Handbook of Qualitative Research Methods for Psychology and the Social Sciences, pp. 55–74. BPS Blackwell, Malden (1996)
26. Creswell, J., Plano Clark, V.: Designing and Conducting Mixed Methods Research. Sage, Los Angeles (2011)
27. Jakobsen, M.R., Hornbaek, K.: Fisheyes in the field: using method triangulation to study the adoption and use of a source code visualization. In: Proceedings of the 27th International Conference on Human Factors in Computing Systems, CHI '09, pp. 1579–1588. ACM, New York (2009)
28. Siirtola, H., Laivo, T., Heimonen, T., Raiha, K.J.: Visual perception of parallel coordinate visualizations. In: 13th International Conference on Information Visualisation, 2009, pp. 3–9, July 2009
29. Convertino, G., Chen, J., Yost, B., Ryu, Y.S., North, C.: Exploring context switching and cognition in dual-view coordinated visualizations. In: Proceedings of International Conference on Coordinated and Multiple Views in Exploratory Visualization, pp .55–62, July 2003
30. Huang, W., Eades, P., Hong, S.H.: Beyond time and error: a cognitive approach to the evaluation of graph drawings. In: Proceedings of the 2008 Conference on BEyond Time and Errors: Novel EvaLuation Methods for Information Visualization, BELIV '08, pp. 3:1–3:8. ACM, New York (2008)
31. Chang, R., Ziemkiewicz, C., Green, T., Ribarsky, W.: Defining insight for visual analytics. IEEE Comput. Graph. Appl. **29**(2), 14–7 (2009)
32. Bautista, J., Carenini, G.: An empirical evaluation of interactive visualizations for preferential choice. In: Proceedings of the Working Conference on Advanced Visual Interfaces, AVI '08, pp. 207–214. ACM, New York (2008)
33. Saraiya, P., North, C., Duca, K.: Comparing benchmark task and insight evaluation methods on timeseries graph visualizations. In: Proceedings of the 3rd BELIV'10 Workshop: BEyond Time and Errors: Novel EvaLuation Methods for Information Visualization, BELIV '10, pp. 55–62. ACM, New York (2010)

34. Pohl, M., Wiltner, S., Miksch, S.: Exploring information visualization: describing different interaction patterns. In: Proceedings of the 3rd BELIV'10 Workshop: BEyond Time and Errors: Novel EvaLuation Methods for Information Visualization, BELIV '10, pp. 16–23. ACM, New York (2010)

35. Carpendale, S.: Evaluating information visualization. In: Kerren, A., Stasko, J.T., Fekete, J.-D., North, C. (eds.) Information Visualization - Human-Centered Issues and Perspectives. Springer, Heidelberg (2008)

A Participatory Perspective on Cross-Cultural Design

Kasper Rodil[(✉)]

Department of Architecture, Design and Media Technology, Aalborg University,
Sofiendalsvej 11, 9200 Aalborg SV, Denmark
kr@create.aau.dk

Abstract. Designers face a number of challenges in terms of how to design interactive systems with indigenous groups. Every layer of development faces obstacles from designing localized interfaces to facilitating prototype evaluations in the wild. This article argues for the importance of continuous user involvement and participatory design. This is highlighted through explaining ongoing research in the creation of a 3D visualization knowledge management system to support preservation of indigenous knowledge (IK) in Africa. Through the sharing of experiences from the field I underpin the importance of acknowledging users' expertise and knowledge about the design context. Through presentation of a selection of these challenges in localizing systems development I wish to raise awareness of an required sensitivity to cultural differences in IT.

Keywords: Indigenous knowledge · Visualization · Interactive system · Participatory design · User-centered design · Field study · Namibia

1 Introduction

Being users and designers in Western countries we design towards a wide array of available technologies. Through institutionalized teaching of design and acquired principles derived from a plethora of empirical user studies and projects developers can usually rely on these guidelines when creating new projects. Since most of our interface design relies on principles firmly rooted within the demographic from which designers and users share similar characteristics. Large parts of this demographic have been part of the development of interfaces and HCI for a relatively long time. E.g. a user can often apply previously acquired IT skills from one OS to the next generation of that OS etc. Besides having established conventions of how to design interfaces, the users and designers also often share similar underlying conceptual structures -while applied design guidelines in turn sustain the conceptual structures of the users/designers.

One might argue that when users and developers have similar 'expectations' for an end-product - the necessity for radical design seems small. By following design trends we also communicate with users in an expected manner, which naturally has a great value for the user who can interact with a familiarly looking

A. Ebert et al. (Eds.): HCIV Workshops 2011, LNCS 8345, pp. 30–46, 2014.
DOI: 10.1007/978-3-642-54894-9_4, © IFIP International Federation for Information Processing 2014

interface. The designs originating from the same contextual background as the users might not seem radical to users from that context, but for users from other nationalities/cultures a proposed system can pose too much friction to be of use. When designing for indigenous groups or users with a different cultural background to the domain of Western principles of design, development immediately faces barriers on fundamental areas of interaction design, interface design and diversity in ontological categorization of objects. As Heukelman (2006) states: "Working with a user interface designed for 1st world users could make inexperienced computer users feel that it was not intended for their use." [1]. The author further states: "Designers often erroneously believe that they know what the users need, especially inexperienced computer users." [1].

Tools in the Western designer's toolbox are established and well assimilated by Western users, but by perceiving the tools as universal/global solutions the possibility of ignoring localization as a cardinal point for understanding the users and the context is plausible. Early in the process of a cross-cultural project the designer must consider if he/she believes that the design components such as UI icons (is the concept of icons even universal?) are globally transferable or not, and whether this distinction is important for the design or not. While Bidwell & Winschiers-Theophilus (2010) support the claim of the importance of localization: "Localizing interaction design in Africa is critical for improving usability and user experience for African populations" [2]. Winschiers-Theophilus (2009) further explains: "Looking at the history of cross-cultural IT design and usability evaluation shows the originally naïve assumption that IT, being value neutral, only needs to be slightly adapted to its new environment" [3].

The objective of this article is not to question Western design traditions, but to highlight their possible inadequacy when introduced to a completely unfamiliar domain. Both the Western and the unfamiliar domain are by comparison full of differences and unique opportunities. Thus when jumping between those domains designers are subjected to re-evaluate their concepts, which in return might create new ideas and knowledge. One of the ambitions for the following pages is to convey a message that bridging the gap between fundamentally different users/co-designers and designers is not a slight adaptation in design thinking. Nor should the designer be a sovereign authority but could engage in participatory design activities to challenge his own concepts, and seek inclusion of other concepts than those originating from his own context.

The ambition for the first part of the chapter is to create 'food-for-thought' for developers and designers wishing to embark into cross-cultural systems design by outlining some differences/challenges in understanding the users in unfamiliar contexts. Following is an introduction to Participatory Design (PD), then motivation and an overview of a project focusing on developing a locally managed indigenous knowledge system for elders in a Herero village in Namibia is described. The chapter ends with some chosen examples (and references to other publications with more detail) about the importance of PD. The intention for the chapter is not to provide a system description but to highlight some challenges in cross-cultural understanding of and inclusion of differences into the design process.

2   A Critical Perspective on Approaches to Understand Users

When developing a system together with people from another culture, there are naturally obvious differences and similarities between those parties. Some of these differences and similarities are meaningful to include in the design solutions, since they represent local values and sometimes represent an uniqueness not readily perceived by external designers. While IT systems in general are Western constructs based on Western epistemologies, a growing need and realization of cultural differences rendering the notion of universal design flawed has led to approaches to understand the 'other'. According to Hofstede's (2006) research on 'culture dimensions' the majority of the designers in the project team described here has contrasting origin (Scandinavia) compared to the Namibian context on several societal structures and personal value beliefs [4]. The Namibian context and Western designer's origin differs according to Hofstede in the following areas [4]:

– Feminity vs. Masculinity:
   "Minimum emotional and social role differentiation between the genders." Vs. "Maximum emotional and social role differentiation between the genders."
– Individualism vs. Collectivism:
   "Speaking one's mind is healthy" and "Personal opinion expected: one person one vote" Vs. "Harmony should always be maintained" and "Opinions and votes predetermined by in-group."
– Power Distance:
   "Older people are neither respected nor feared." Vs. "Older people are both respected and feared."

Hofstede's theory on cultural dimensions represents one perspective on understanding core differences between cultures and its people. The cultural dimensions do not provide guidelines for developing perfect systems nor should they be used as generalizable facts for a plethora of diverse cultures, languages, and religions in Africa. It provides an outline of the differences between co-designers and designers, but not a detailed guideline for understanding the context.

As Irani et al. (2010) explain: "Some have sought to predict and understand these problems of translating HCI knowledge by drawing on taxonomic models of culture where members of cultural groups are characterized by traits and averages." [5].

Kamppuri (2012) further questions the generalizable nature of these models: "In the same way, even though cultural dimensions are based on questions related to a particular area of life, such as work, it is assumed that the differences found between countries are similar in other contexts, too." [6].

Namibia is an example of clear differences in the national population and is inhabited by 13 different tribes who along with other ethnic groups constitute a highly diversified user base - not fit for generalizations. While some of these groups might have similarities with a foreign designer, an adaptation to this group can not rely on intuition alone. As stated by Teasley et al.: "'Professional intuition' is neither a sufficient nor reliable methodological foundation for producing an 'appealing perceptual experience' in interactive computer systems." [7]. Irani et al. explain: "ICT4D designers face challenges transporting both design conventions and processes of HCI across cultures. HCI's visual conventions have proven not to be universal - systems effective in the US may fail utterly in Japan or South Africa." [5].

The elaborate article on basic psychological and perceptual differences in cultures presented by Henrich et al. (2010) describe the assumption that the generalization of WEIRD (Western Educated Industrialized Rich and Democratic) users/subjects cannot be justified on a global scale [8]. The main conclusion is that the WEIRD population is "particularly unusual compared with the rest of the species" and "there are no obvious a priori grounds for claiming that a particular behavioral phenomenon is universal based on sampling from a single subpopulation" [8]. "The sample of contemporary Western undergraduates that so overwhelms our database is not just an extraordinarily restricted sample of humanity; it is frequently a distinct outlier vis-a-vis other global samples. It may represent the worst population on which to base our understanding of Homo sapiens" [8]. Relating to Henrich's research where samples from one population might inform design in another population leads to the questioning of attempts to provide global guidelines in order to localize cross-cultural design.

By using Bennett's terminology, the designer can choose to hold onto "denial of difference" or seek "integration of difference" [9]. I must make clear here that not all cross-cultural projects require similar nuancing or levels of localization. The project described later requires IK preservation in the 'design' of the system and as 'content' in the system, but I believe the consideration makes sense no matter the project scope. Namibia is a post-colonial country thus a mix of religions, tribes and world views. Being freed from apartheid in the 1990's, and now a young democracy (by Western measurements). Does Namibia have a singular culture or does it constitute of various cultures? Developers should ask (probably at least) three fundamental questions.

- What constitutes the origin and empirical foundation for the knowledge leading to decisions in the design phase?
- What level of localization is needed?
- Is there in the design process room for local differences to be manifested?

By perceiving people living within the same national borders as being belonging to the same group and pertaining the same world views there is a great risk of suppressing the perspectives of the minorities. I would always argue for a much more nuanced view on people than by pooling them into overall user groups. Does it make sense to perceive descendants of European colonialists and Hereros to be having similar values and world views? It might be that the experiences we share and knowledges being brought forward in one Herero community is different from the next Herero community etc. Even within the same community I would claim we could find different opinions towards many things. Cultural models are one way of looking at differences, another approach could be by being informed through in situ dialogue and inclusion of personal perspectives. I must underpin that these two could support each other in our aspirations to understand users and the context. Where the perspective from one elder in one Herero village probably is not the perspective of everyone, nor is the generalized values enough for localizing IT design.

3   An Introduction to Participatory Design

This section presents a brief background for PD as a methodology for users involved in the design process of interactive systems.

User-Centered Design (UCD) as a discipline is spanning a plethora of methods and techniques to facilitate input from end-users to help shape or solve a design problem. Through methods such as interactive paper prototyping [10], personas, use cases and visual ethnography etc. the ambition is to make sure the design fits the users and their contexts. UCD houses an array of iterative conceptual models to ensure user involvement and usability of a system. One of the most known models for evolutionary acquisition of user input is the spiral model [11], which conceptually and practically directs when users through iterations are involved. UCD have proven valuable in contexts/domains where design negotiations are founded on shared principles of power relations, gender roles, and cultural norms through shared means of communication. PD is a process-oriented variant of UCD. One of the tenets of PD is an emphasis of the continuous involvement of users through empowering and egalitarian principles. As Sanders et al. (2010) explain: "Participatory Design today is an emerging design practice that involves different non-designers in various co-design activities throughout the design process." [12].

PD is historically rooted in Scandinavian socio-technical developments for workplaces and within trade unions in the 1970's and 1980's to democratically "re-balance the power of workers and management" [13]. The onset was to explore and apply methods to implement interactive systems that would fit workers and their skills. Nygaard and associates were pioneering PD with the NJMF project initiated in Norway in 1970 [14]. Later followed the DEMOS project in Sweden in 1975 [15]. Project DUE, Denmark 1978 [16]. The UTOPIA project started in 1981 as collaboration between The Nordic Graphic Workers' Union and researchers from Denmark and Sweden [17]. One of the points from the project is that design professionals having technological skills should understand the worker context. The worker (or user) often lack the technological understanding, but have knowledge on context and have the skills within that context.

As Dearden & Rizvi based on [13] explain in their elaborate review: "A common theme has been one of 'mutual learning' where technology designers learn about the setting where technology is to be used, and users continuously learn about technology design and designers" [18]. Kensing and Blomberg (1998) explain: "the epistemological stand of PD is that these types of knowledge are developed most effectively through active cooperation between workers (and increasingly other organizational members) and designers within specific design projects." [13]. Other projects related to the Scandinavian PD tradition are reported by Ehn (1993) in [17].

Although PD has a political origin in workplace democracy the methods associated have increasingly been used to bring users and developers closer. As reported by Gregory (2003), PD is also considering discussions of values in design and that conflicts and contradictions are to be seen as resources in design [19].

As Muller states regarding the political background of PD: "Many researchers and practitioners in PD (but not all) are motivated in part by a belief in the value of democracy to civic, educational, and commercial settings - a value that can be seen in the strengthening of dis-empowered groups (including workers), in the improvement of internal processes, and in the combination of diverse knowledge to make better services and products." [20]. The participatory designer should be a facilitator of communication, a gatekeeper responsible for the fusion of differing knowledges and emphasizing polyvocality as a unique opportunity to create 'better products'.

A cardinal point in PD is regarding the decision making and power balances between designers and participants. Users in UCD processes are urged to provide feedback and ideas during their involvement. They represent a voice in the decisions on terms, interaction design, functionality etc. but the design professionals responsible for a given system solely decide if they decide to listen. As Bratteteig and Wagner (2012) explain it: "While in commercial design projects there may be some sharing of power, participatory design (PD) opens up for systematically including users and other stakeholders in the decision processes in design. It is assumed that their knowledges and skills are also valid in the exploration and evaluation of both big and small decisions." [21].

While Scandinavian PD backbone has a political motive to empower users and an ambition to include domain knowledge into the design of systems with objectives of for instance mutual learning, our design approach is of a more conceptual nature. We are not participatory designers from a particular political nerve but from a realization that our attempts to make 'good systems' would be fruitless unless designed together. Our aspirations to empower the local community is to infuse their perspectives and world views, which is essential since an objective is to represent these local view points within the interface and system design.

The ambition for the following pages is to explain some of the reasons for perceiving the co-designers in Namibia as essential partners in producing functional localized design.

4 Overview of a Project in Designing Localized Interactive Systems to Support Preservation of Indigenous Knowledge

4.1 Background

Namibian Herero youths are currently assimilating knowledge from a curriculum influenced by characteristics of a modern society while being contextually de-situated from decades of traditional transfer of IK, cultural values and sustainable living in the rural areas of Namibia. The modus of traditional dissemination in the rural areas has for generations been through informal master-apprenticeship by practical learning and as oral knowledge transfer between youths and knowledgeable elders in the rural areas. Besides the obvious local benefits in acquiring knowledge on husbandry, herbal lore etc. the tacit knowledge transferred through inter-personal interaction with and within the context effectively adds to preserving local culture, customs and traditions.

Wenger (1998) articulates the often tacit and uncodable knowledge situated within a community of practice as a 'repertoire' [22]. Being absent from the rural areas for large parts of the year the youths are unable to exercise this repertoire locally, thus exacerbating the process of local knowledge management. Confronted with a knowledge paradox on what type of knowledge would aid them and the eco-system in the rural areas in their respective future most optimally, the youths are per governmental regulations left without a choice. Being situated in remote schools for large parts of the year, the effect is a disruption of inter-personal knowledge transfer between curators (the elders) and future curators (youths).

In Namibia, a majority of urban migrants return to their villages in the rural areas, regularly on short visits and permanently after many years of living in the cities. They return to an unmanaged and unmaintained knowledge system. UNESCO highlights the importance of preservation of IK: "The UNESCO Convention for the Safeguarding of the Intangible Cultural Heritage highlights the importance of developing tools and measures to preserve and transmit cultural knowledge of indigenous peoples in terms of traditions, practices, expressions, knowledge and skills that are created and shaped by communities in close interaction with their environment" [23].

4.2   Project Overview

In order to preserve and transmit IK between Namibian community groups separated by age and location, our research project aims to develop an IK management system, which villagers (especially elders) can utilize to manage IK unassisted. The IK content comprises of elders having recorded multimedia, primarily video recordings on where to find healing herbs or how to slaughter a goat according to customs etc., but a system for the elders to store these clips in is much needed.

A major concern and design challenge is the fundamental difference between the orientations of African cultures and the orientations of Western cultures governing designers and technology. It is important to investigate under what conditions the corpus of IK can be preserved and mediated and represented for city living youths with a minimal loss of IK content and meaning. Being developers primarily from other value systems and cultural orientations we are aware of the fact that we are not able to decide, select and handle which particular knowledge is important/relevant. Our endeavors into creating an IK system, investigating the clash of cultures in HCI and the use, reshaping and creation of new methodologies in PD have proven fruitful. But as every layer have been investigated new layers keep surfacing making us rethink and re-evaluate our approaches.

Through introductions made by local researchers in Namibia we have since 2009 worked closely with a community of the Herero tribe located in the Kalahari Desert. The tribe has traditionally been pastoralists in the rural areas of Namibia since settling down (17th and 18th century) in the region. Our approaches to help the community preserve their cultural heritage have been approved by village elders, whom traditionally have decision power in the community and custodians of the IK. Until now the research has been directed to investigating and prototyping possible approaches in creating a system for preserving IK, which is co-designed through methods of PD and where all phases in the development are negotiated locally. Figure 1 shows the evaluation of a prototype running on a 10.1 inch Motorola Xoom tablet.

Fig. 1. Dialogue on a prototype.

Initial work in the project has shown the inadequacy of text-based interfaces to facilitate knowledge management for the so called digitally illiterate elders. Based on ethno-graphical field observations and reflections a number of design options, including speech output, picture-based input and tangible prototypes have been explored, as described by Kapuire & Blake [24]. These advances have all expanded our understanding of the domain we are engaged in. Most importantly they have from the beginning of the project gradually involved the elders, thus also added to the building of trust and helped clarifying our intentions. While attitudes towards the Western academic scene and nature of researchers is usually good in the Western world, academics are not always attributed objectivity and honesty when seen from an indigenous perspective. For instance as noted by Braun et al. (2013), indigenous societies are well-accustomed to researchers flying in, grabbing what they need, advancing their careers and then leaving again [25]. The elders have sovereign authority on allowing and supporting our involvement in their village, and in granting us permission to document our trips with video recorders and cameras.

We conduct the design in-situ using several design probes as means for polyvocal dialogue, and consider the village elders as co-designers. Due to the nature of PD and our attachment to the research site's people everything becomes intertwined in activities as research and as not-research. Due to the project's setting and the nature of PD it is not easy (nor always desired) to pick out individuals for a usability test etc. I would argue for that if our system does not function in the community environment with a burning sun and people unfamiliar with IT, we are not producing anything successful besides our own advancement. Thus instead of the dominating researcher wishing to assume control of the experiment, we often let the interaction unfold naturally while observing.

The Hereros are as a majority of indigenous groups valorizing collectivism, then why should the research methods reflect Western use of IT and individualism? After all, measuring number of clicks in the interface or measuring speed of interaction might not be relevant since some cultures do not rush into action before careful consideration. We are accustomed to the thought of IT as being almost value-free, but IT can be a different experience for non-Western users. As noted by Oyugi et al. (2008) designers should "...consider the degree of replication of Western approaches to usability methods.." [26]. A study by Vatrapu & Pérez-Quiñones (2006) show how interview/interviewee relations can affect the analysis and results: "When the usability methods involve human-human interaction, such as is the case with structured-interviews; then the interaction of the cultures of the two participants must be considered." [27].

Where usability can investigate errors or pinpoint weaknesses in the interaction with the prototype, it is usually defined by the visiting researcher. Similarly are interviews usually following the researcher's agenda. While these approaches can be efficient in a design process, they have inborn difficulties challenging the concepts the researcher design with.

Dialogue is as already emphasized important for understanding and investigating the prototypes' suitability. Dialogue as a participatory activity for challenging one's concepts is vital for representing local view points within the interface and system design. Lakoff & Johnson provide a way to look at it [28]:

- Ideas (or meanings) are objects.
- Linguistic expressions are containers.
- Communication is sending.

This practically means that when the designer evaluates i.e. an interface icon he should be cautious not to measure only the success or failure of his idea, but to challenge the concept of an icon, since it might not exist locally. Due to dialogue being a linguistic form, the researcher should be careful not to run his argument as a 'battle', thus he would loose the cooperative aspects of dialogue, which is important to further his understanding of the concept of the icon.

4.3   3D Visualizations as a Design Approach

Since 2010, we have investigated the potential of 3D visualizations as supportive visual meta-data in sense of creating a virtual context for IK content recorded as multimedia content by village elders, and investigating how 3D worlds can mediate the knowledge transfer between youths and elders [29]. The context embodying the videos can holistically provide visual information on individuals, the nature, objects etc. not easily perceived or missing from the video recordings, thus widening and adding to the information stored in the IK videos.

An example of a virtual scenario could be the collection of herbs for a bad stomach. The video recording could display an interview with an elder elaborating on location and how to find the specific herb in the bush. The reconstructed 3D scenario would visually depict the surrounding environment such as time of the day, people involved in the collection etc. Besides adding to the information from the collected videos, the scenarios are a different approach to manage the structuring and assigning of 'visual' meta-data, which must rely on local concepts and is highly culturally dependent (Fig. 2).

Fig. 2. The figure shows the core idea of a virtual world, where 3D objects constitute the 'building blocks' for the recorded IK.

Some of the current points of focus are investigating any cultural difference of shape, color, camera perspectives [30] of the virtual models for the system. These areas are foundational for in the next phases to have tools for the co-designers to create custom scenarios free from our interference. We have introduced drawing as a method to be informed on conceptual and visual representation of objects and argue "...that this helps to democratize the design and that these methods can be used in the broader contexts of bridging the gap of understanding across cultures where technology or language may fall short [31].

Thus hopefully being representations with closer fitting to the co-designers perspective, ambitions and world-views.

We are currently exploring how elders can design these scenarios themselves; as described in [32], but a future system could potentially house a large corpus of in-situ collected video material. Thus the requirement for a repository and a smooth integration of user generated content is needed. A functional idea in the Western world could be a sorting of videos based on textual meta-data in a large database, where users upload their videos and provide tags for later retrieval by others based on those categorizations and keywords. The work of Hughes and Dallwitz (2007) stress the shortcomings of traditional databases when trying to sort IK. They describe that physical objects may be culturally restricted to be either for both genders or purely for one gender to see [33]. Thus the representations as multimedia of real objects directed the authors to create three parallel databases. Currently we have a focus on the possible inter-cultural differences between ontologies and taxonomies as underlying structures for such databases and interface structures (for an example see Rodil et al. (2013)) [34].

With the visualization approach we deliberately bypass any requirements for skills in textual literacy due to previous experiences in the village. From a PD point of view we argue that text interfaces dis-empower our co-designers. In this approach it must be envisioned that the user is visually browsing what could resemble a virtual village and then e.g. decides to see how a traditional goat slaughter is conducted according to customs. While results are promising with this attempt we are much aware that the complexity of the system might not be possible to align with a pure visualization approach.

The specifications for the final system are ambiguous at this point. Thus being in the middle of the process Brereton et al. (2011) describe as: "The challenge for any design project is to build relations and cross-cultural understanding, so as to ensure that local aspirations are articulated effectively into socio-technical design outcomes." [35].

If we already know the end result we would implicitly disregard user input and stray from a participatory process. Our approach is an oscillation between 'going forward' with a prototype. Then if being promising for co-design and accepted by the parties involved we backtrack to research why it has been effective. Naturally the prototypes reflect thoughtful considerations from developer side. But as experienced many times in the field and reported by other researchers good intentions and sound design choices do not necessarily provide successful prototypes when evaluated locally.

5   Participatory Design in Cross-Cultural IT Design

The majority of our design team does not have an ethnic origin in the context were we design artifacts. As stated by Marcus (2006): "It is difficult for designers/analysts to escape being biased culturally. All designed artifacts are cultural objects." [36]. There is arguebly some truth to Marcus' statement, but probably the 'cultural' part comes from the designer. As Suchman (2002) states: "our vision of the world is a vision from somewhere that it is inextricably based in an embodied, and therefore a partial perspective which makes us personally responsible for it." [37].

The difficulties of exporting systems design across cultures have been reported many times and surely we have experienced it ourselves. From the beginning we have come to terms with the cultural differences as problematic for the design of the IK system and have used PD as a way to consider people engaged with technology and how designs could be harmonized with local influence. In our project having a clear objective of preserving and transferring local IK, we can consider the external designers as potential filters or facilitators in this transfer. We accept that the 'cultural objects' being prototyped might interfere with the representation of culture in this transfer. There is a risk of transforming the knowledge when we represent it through a to the context unfamiliar artifact. And if the knowledge is captured by externals, then synthesized and represented by those externals, it would be questionable to claim that no distortion is taking place?// Mutema (2003) explains on the interpretation of IK: "Understanding is made possible through dialogue, conversation and communication between the researcher and the actors. The inter-subjective nature of the research process allows for the researcher's interpretations to be checked, reinterpreted and evaluated by the actors." [38].

In order to ensure that the system is aligned with the local perspective, we have since the beginning actively sought to involve local future users as being co-designers who are critical towards the ideas presented. The critical nature towards ideas put forward is a tenet of PD, but difficult to facilitate. In this case the notion of power relations can aid in explaining it. For instance it is not new to receive critique from students and test participants in the Western world, if the researcher asks for it. In cultures with different values in power distance, it is more complicated, since it might not be polite to critique people perceived to be higher in the hierarchy. Thus we have invested significantly more effort in explaining that we seek critique.

Iivari (2004) describes three levels of user involvement as being either a 'consultative', 'representative' or 'consensus' type [39]. Iivari describes consensus as: "the responsibility of design is assigned to users, who are continually involved in the design process and have power to make decisions" [39]. We perceive the village elders as being consensual co-designers empowered to shape the IK system under their terms and requirements. The other community members in the village are in traditional sense to be considered as users primarily involved in evaluating the usability of prototypes. Empowerment of users into being co-designers is a central theme in PD.

Ertner et al. (2010) explain on the empowerment of users: "In order for the designer to empower the users, user participation requires more than simply uttering wishes and participate sporadically in the process - users need to gain actual power in decision making and direct influence in the entire process in order to be empowered." [40]. Designers in traditional PD are seen as being able to empower users and thus improving the design. In our particular project, I would claim that the elders equally empower us (along with our technological skills) to partake in designing the IK system.

5.1   Mutual Learning

One's skills are essential for any successful design, but that skills should be traded or reflected - not only to empower users/designers in decision making, but because the trained designer and indigenous co-designers possess different strengths that must be shared, critiqued and evaluated in dialogue. The dialogues are important for enriching the 'contextually illiterate' designer with an updated skill set and in bringing awareness of different perspectives important for developing in a cross-cultural domain. And for the co-designer to acquire technological knowledge – thus being in a more balanced position to critique whatever the designer brings forward. Pearson & Robinson (2013) have a good point when they stress that how can people criticize something if they do not know what they want and the technological capabilities being available [41]. Although PD has mutual learning as a guiding principle it can also come with a cost to design systems intended for a marginalized demographic.

During the development the co-designers gradually familiarize themselves with new technologies, which move them closer to the trained developers in terms of IT skills. While this might be important for the dialogue about prototypes, it is in the meantime important that some anchor remain in the end-users' demographic. Recently we have focused on the design export to other sites to ensure that the designs produced with the elders remain successful within the broad community group. Years of familiarization with technology and design might affect the whole project, since the co-designers might be so skilled and proactive in a system's short-comings, that basic concepts are learned, but not transferable to the rest of the co-designers' demographic.

6   Experiences with Prototypes

From several field trips to our pilot community discussing prototypes and their use, we have learned that fundamental areas must be considered before conducting field studies. One of the primaries is the balancing act of appropriate hardware technology behind a software prototype. Findings presented in [32] highlight the radical shift in co-designer involvement and critique when we exchanged laptop and mouse driven software prototypes with tablets and touch input functionality. When presenting the first proof-of-concept of a 3D visualization to the elders, we experienced reluctance in interacting with the laptop and mouse. The co-designers sat in a larger group commenting on what they saw on the screen, but did not actually try to interact with the prototype. As quoted from [32]: "He (the elder) said that on the other prototypes (laptops) they had to use a mouse, which was difficult, this (tablet) is easy cause he just has to use his hand" (in situ translation). The concept proved to create much less friction when technology device and actual system were both more intuitive to the elders. But from a PD perspective the technology was an active gatekeeper for participation. Designers should consider if their technology of choice hinders participation.

We experienced new perspectives on technology devices and HCI, when these different prototypes were in the hands of the elders. This can be illustrated by findings from a field study investigating how common (common in the Western world) touch input gestures such as two-finger rotation, one-finger drag etc. were perceived in the community and how to decide on implementation of gestures for missing functionality in the prototype called the Homestead Creator. We deliberately left the functionality for rotating virtual objects up for discussion with the community for two reasons. (1) How would they actually try to rotate a virtual object without instructions given? (2) If we informed them of a rotation gesture it would be difficult to decode the local intuitiveness of an implemented choice. And if a local gesture was preferred it is the participatory designer's onus to facilitate inclusion in the methods in contrast to only evaluate the designer's choice.

Another important finding in sense of the involvement of co-designers has been presenting them with proof-of-concepts as rather high fidelity software prototypes, which act as center points of dialogue. Our experience is that when the presented prototype fidelity is too far from an actual designer envisioned output -it becomes harder to critique. That lo-fi can be too far from the vision designers have, thus transferring an abstract concept to people with little experience in IT is difficult. When we presented a smaller part (virtual area of the village); but looking close to the vision of the system of the larger envisioned 3D visualization, we immediately received valuable feedback in sense of ways to recreate the 3D so that it matches the local views on i.e. virtual cows, trees etc. So far all of our prototypes have elements which could function in a final system, but the important discipline for us is to be ready to change them or discard them. Sometimes we experience something unexpected and have to take several steps back to investigate i.e. how perception of virtual camera perspectives in a virtual world might be different for the community members than Westerners trained in using maps. And common to all the prototypes we have developed together is that none of them are meant as final products per se. They are meant as abstracting down and articulating approaches which in the future scope could be the digital IK management system. Being are aware that we are creating the proofs-of-concept and a valid question could be articulated regarding who the actual designer is.

That is why we oscillate between various prototypes and methods to inform our (all stakeholders') design.

I believe that there are many technological approaches to the problem, but we have from the beginning decided to defocus on a specific technology and while the co-designers become gradually more aware of the technological possibilities for a system we in the meantime narrow the field of hardware candidates. E.g. in the case of exchanging laptops with tablets we saw a radical shift in ease of use and constraints set by the physical environment, hence we would never in the future settle on using that particular hardware platform for a situated community IK system. One of the lessons we learned from this example is the differing nature of the feedback we received with different combinations of hardware and software prototype fidelity.

7   Conclusion

When relating the arguments carried in the article to the context of PD in Namibia, we can raise some ideological 'pillars' to support cross-cultural system's development. The system's design must be designed in such a way that it infers the world views from the context's inhabitants. It must be validated locally due to psychological, perceptual, societal etc. differences.

It has been evident through many field trips to the community that we as designers and system developers can not solely rely on skills previously acquired when designing for a much different context than our own. It has been clear that it is possible to develop prototypes and design human-computer interaction that is better aligned with the elders' and rest of the community's ways of using; to them, new technology. But that all phases of development rely on a premise of localization through Participatory Design, and being critical towards the transferability of findings and design ideas from contexts that are unaligned with the new design space. But even more importantly that the designer questions the universality of his ideas. After all when designing together with people with other perspectives it is necessary to include their concepts, thus also actively challenging your own concepts.

Acknowledgements. I wish to thank all Erindiroukambe's community members for friendships and for giving me personal experiences I treasure highly. I also wish to thank the members of the project team for their dedication of investigating these important challenges, and especially my supervisors for continuous dedication and feedback.

References

1. Heukelman, D.: Can a user centered approach to designing a user interface for rural communities be successful? In: Proceedings of Conference CHI-SA, January 2006, pp. 51–58 (2006)
2. Bidwell, N.J., Winschiers-Theophilus, H.: Under development: beyond the Benjamins: toward an African interaction design. Interactions **17**(1), 32–35 (2010)
3. Winschiers-Theophilus, H.: The art of cross-cultural design for usability. In: Stephanidis, C. (ed.) Universal Access in HCI, Part I, HCII 2009. LNCS, vol. 5614, pp. 665–671. Springer, Heidelberg (2009)
4. Hofstede, G.: Dimensionalizing cultures: the Hofstede model in context. Online Readings in Psychology and Culture (2006)
5. Irani, L., Vertesi, J., Dourish, P., Philip, K., Grinter, R.E.: Postcolonial computing: a lens on design and development. In: Proceedings of the 28th International Conference on Human Factors in Computing Systems, CHI '10, pp. 1311–1320. ACM, New York (2010)
6. Kamppuri, M.: Because deep down, we are not the same: values in cross-cultural design. Interactions **19**(2), 65–68 (2012)
7. Teasley, B., Leventhal, L., Blumenthal, B., Instone, K., Stone, D.: Cultural diversity in user interface design: are intuitions enough? SIGCHI Bull. **26**, 36–40 (1994)
8. Henrich, J., Heine, S.J., Norenzayan, A.: The weirdest people in the world. Behav. Brain Sci. **33**(2–3), 61–83 (2010)
9. Bennett, M.J.: A developmental approach to training for intercultural sensitivity. Int. J. Intercult. Relat. **10**(2), 179–196 (1986)
10. Buxton, B.: Sketching User Experiences: Getting the Design Right and the Right Design. Morgan Kaufmann Publishers Inc., San Francisco (2007)

11. Boehm, B.W.: A spiral model of software development and enhancement. Computer **21**(5), 61–72 (1988)
12. Sanders, E.B.N., Brandt, E., Binder, T.: A framework for organizing the tools and techniques of participatory design. In: Proceedings of the 11th Biennial Participatory Design Conference, PDC '10, pp. 195–198. ACM, New York (2010)
13. Kensing, F., Blomberg, J.: Participatory design: issues and concerns. Comput. Support. Coop. Work **7**(3–4), 167–185 (1998)
14. Nygaard, K.: The iron and metal project: trade union participation. In Sandberg, A., (ed.): Computers Dividing Man and Work Recent Scandinavian Research on Planning and Computers from a Trade Union Perspective, Number 13. Swedish Center for Working Life, Demos Project Report No. 13, Utbildningsproduktion, Malmø, Sweden, pp. 94–107 (1979)
15. Ehn, P., Sanberg, A.: Management Control and Wage Earner Power (Foretagsstyrning och Lontagarmakt). Prisma, Falkoping (1979)
16. Kyng, M., Mathiassen, L.: Systems development and trade union activities. Computer Science Department, Aarhus University (1979)
17. Ehn, P.: Scandinavian design: on participation and skill. In: Schuler, D., Namioka, A. (eds.) Participatory Design, pp. 41–77. L. Erlbaum Associates Inc., Hillsdale (1993)
18. Dearden, A., Rizvi, H.: Participatory IT design and participatory development: a comparative review. In: Proceedings of the Tenth Anniversary Conference on Participatory Design 2008, PDC '08, Indianapolis, IN, USA, pp. 81–91. Indiana University (2008)
19. Gregory, J.: Scandinavian approaches to participatory design. Int. J. Eng. Educ. **19**(1), 62–74 (2003)
20. Muller, M.J.: The Human-Computer Interaction Handbook, pp. 1051–1068. L. Erlbaum Associates Inc., Hillsdale (2003)
21. Bratteteig, T., Wagner, I.: Disentangling power and decision-making in participatory design. In: Proceedings of the 12th Participatory Design Conference: Research Papers, PDC '12, vol. 1, pp. 41–50. ACM, New York (2012)
22. Wenger, E.: Communities of Practice: Learning, Meaning, and Identity. Cambridge University Press, Cambridge (1998)
23. Unesco: The UNESCO Convention for the Safeguarding of the Intangible Cultural Heritage. http://www.unesco.org/culture/ich/en/convention/. Accessed 12 March 2013
24. Kapuire, G.K., Blake, E.: An Attempt to re-organise digital indigenous knowledge representations to merge local and technological paradigms. In: IKTC 2011, pp. 72–78. http://www.indiknowtech.org (2011). Accessed 12 March 2013
25. Braun, K.L., Browne, C.V., Ka'opua, L.S., Kim, B.J., Mokuau, N.: Research on indigenous elders: from positivistic to decolonizing methodologies. The Gerontologist **54**(1), 117–126 (2014). doi:10.1093/geront/gnt067
26. Oyugi, C., Dunckley, L., Smith, A.: Evaluation methods and cultural differences: studies across three continents. In: Proceedings of the 5th Nordic Conference on Human-Computer Interaction: Building Bridges, NordiCHI '08, pp. 318–325. ACM, New York (2008)
27. Vatrapu, R., Pérez-quiñones, M.A.: Culture and usability evaluation: the effects of culture in structured interviews. J. Usability Stud. **1**, 156–170 (2006)
28. Lakoff, G., Johnson, M.: Metaphors We Live By. University of Chicago Press, Chicago (1980)

29. Rodil, K., Winschiers-Theophilus, H., Bidwell, N.J., Eskildsen, S., Rehm, M., Kapuire, G.K.: A new visualization approach to re-contextualize indigenous knowledge in Rural Africa. In: Campos, P., Graham, N., Jorge, J., Nunes, N., Palanque, P., Winckler, M. (eds.) INTERACT 2011, Part II. LNCS, vol. 6947, pp. 297–314. Springer, Heidelberg (2011)

30. Jensen, K.L., Theophilus, H.W., Rodil, K., Goagoses, N.W., Kapuire, G.K., Kamukuenjandje, R.: Putting it in perspective: designing a 3D visualization to contextualize indigenous knowledge in rural Namibia. In: Proceedings of the Designing Interactive Systems Conference, DIS '12, pp. 196–199. ACM, New York (2012)

31. Winschiers-Goagoses, N., Winschiers-Theophilus, H., Rodil, K., Kapuire, G.K., Jensen, K.: Design democratization with communities: drawing toward locally meaningful design. Int. J. Sociotechnology Knowl. Dev. (IJSKD) 4(4), 32–43 (2012)

32. Rodil, K., Winschiers-Theophilus, H., Jensen, K.L., Rehm, M.: Homestead creator: a tool for indigenous designers. In: Proceedings of the 7th Nordic Conference on Human-Computer Interaction: Making Sense Through Design, NordiCHI '12, pp. 627–630. ACM, New York (2012)

33. Hughes, M., Dallwitz, J.: Ara Irititja: towards culturally appropriate IT best practice in remote indigenous Australia. In: Dyson, L., Hendriks, M., Grant, S. (eds.) Information Technology and Indigenous People, pp. 146–158. Information Science Publishing, Hershey (2007)

34. Rodil, K., Rehm, M., Winschiers-Theophilus, H.: Homestead creator: using card sorting in search for culture-aware categorizations of interface objects. In: Kotzé, P., Marsden, G., Lindgaard, G., Wesson, J., Winckler, M. (eds.) INTERACT 2013, Part I. LNCS, vol. 8117, pp. 437–444. Springer, Heidelberg (2013)

35. Brereton, M., Roe, P., Hong, A.L.: A cross-cultural approach towards designing digital noticeboards with a remote aboriginal community. In: Proceedings of the Indigenous Knowledge Technology Conference 2011, November 2011, pp. 137–139 (2011)

36. Marcus, A.: Cross-cultural user-experience design. In: Barker-Plummer, D., Cox, R., Swoboda, N. (eds.) Diagrams 2006. LNCS (LNAI), vol. 4045, pp. 16–24. Springer, Heidelberg (2006)

37. Suchman, L.: Located accountabilities in technology production. Scandinavian J. Inf. syst. 14(2), 91–105 (2002)

38. Mutema, G.: Phenomenology, hermeneutics and the study of indigenous knowledge systems. Indilinga: African J. Indigenous Knowl. Syst. 2(1), 81–88 (2003)

39. Iivari, N.: Enculturation of user involvement in software development organizations - an interpretive case study in the product development context. In: Proceedings of the Third Nordic Conference on Human-Computer Interaction, NordiCHI '04, pp. 287–296. ACM, New York (2004)

40. Ertner, M., Kragelund, A.M., Malmborg, L.: Five enunciations of empowerment in participatory design. In: Proceedings of the 11th Biennial Participatory Design Conference, PDC '10, pp. 191–194. ACM, New York (2010)

41. Pearson, J., Robinson, S.: Developing our world views. Interactions 20(2), 68–71 (2013)

Recognizing Complexity: Visualization for Skilled Professionals in Complex Work Situations

Arne W. Andersson, Anders Jansson[✉], Bengt Sandblad, and Simon Tschirner

Department of Information Technology, Uppsala University, Uppsala, Sweden
anders.jansson@it.uu.se

Abstract. In our research, we study IT-systems for highly skilled professionals in complex and dynamic work situations. Such situations can be found in e.g. health care, process and traffic control and in administration. The demands on the operators/users are often very high concerning quality performance, efficiency, timeliness, safety, communication and cooperation. Our experience shows that human operators can overview, interpret and in real time use an almost unlimited amount of information, if it is relevant to the situation and visualized according to human capabilities. The solution to the visualization problem is therefore *not* to avoid or hide complexity, but to *cope* with it, to *accept* that the complexity must be there. The challenge is to develop systems for visualization and support, which can be used efficiently in relation to the complexity of the work task. We believe in *recognizing* complexity. First, we describe the scientific foundation of such an approach. Second, we give a detailed example of a complex visualization problem, emphasizing the demanding cognitive operations the operators have to conduct. Finally, we describe the solutions, the visualizations and interactions that make it possible to support the cognitively demanding task, taking care of the complexity without losing the rich amount of information necessary for the operators in different situations, but without adding unnecessary complexity in terms of complicated handling of the user interface and the information systems. Some of these visualizations now run in real systems and have been evaluated, and we end up by suggesting recommendations for successful visualizations in complex work tasks.

Keywords: Complex and dynamic work situations · Design of operator systems · Visualization

1 Introduction

1.1 The Research Field

In our research we focus on the design and use of IT-systems for highly skilled professionals in different types of complex and dynamic work situations. The demands on such experts, e.g. process operators, traffic controllers, health care staff in intensive care units and professionals in more complicated administrative organizations, are

A. Ebert et al. (Eds.): HCIV Workshops 2011, LNCS 8345, pp. 47–66, 2014.
DOI: 10.1007/978-3-642-54894-9_5, © IFIP International Federation for Information Processing 2014

often very high concerning quality, efficiency, timeliness, safety, communication and cooperation. Our experiences show that organizations and the technologies often are not designed to support skilled professionals in their demanding tasks, and that much of the problems are related to which information that is visualized and how. For different reasons the information systems do not comply with the complexity of the work. In Endsley et al. (2003) this is formulated as: "In the face of this torrent of 'information', many of us feel less informed than ever before. This is because there is a huge gap between the tons of data being produced and disseminated, and our ability to find the bits that are needed and process them together with the other bits to arrive at the actual needed information. That is, it seems to be even harder to find out what we really want or need to know".

To our opinion, the solution to the visualization problem is *not* to avoid or hide complexity, but to cope with it. We believe in *recognizing* complexity. The challenge is to design, develop and deploy systems that can be used efficiently despite the complexity of the work tasks. The design of information and control systems, and the user interfaces, must match the complexity, the needs and the capabilities of the human operators.

1.2   Contents of the Paper

This paper starts with a specification of the concept complexity in order to be able to explore and discuss it in a systematic way. This is based on recent theoretical progress in the area of cognitive psychology and human-computer interaction. A second concept of importance in our research is dynamics. Here, we also give a definition, following modern literature on dynamic decision making. An example of a design solution is presented, and with its help we describe why human cognition in general is well adapted to complex and dynamic tasks, but only if the design solutions comply with the general principles identified below. We also present a more detailed example of a complex visualization problem, emphasizing the demanding cognitive operations the operators have to conduct. Here, we describe the design solutions, the visualizations and interactions that make it possible to support the cognitively demanding task, without losing the rich amount of information necessary for the operators in different situations, and without adding unnecessary complexity and usability problems. The paper ends with a discussion about why recognizing complexity and understanding the dynamics are important in relation to the operators' understanding of the work domain and control situation.

1.3   Earlier Studies and Experiences

We base our results and recommendations on a number of earlier research and development projects. Examples are train traffic control, process control in different organisations, train driving, high speed ship operation, health care systems, home care and administrative work in large organisations. Here we have both analysed existing control systems and operator interfaces and participated in design, development, deployment and evaluation of new systems and interfaces. The work has always been very user centred, involving professional operators in all phases of the projects. Our experiences are that traditional models and methods for design of control systems and operator interfaces very often fail in understanding the complexity of the controlled system and the control tasks and do not deliver systems and interfaces that efficiently support skilled operators. We will explain why such pitfalls often are encountered and how they can be overcome. The conclusions and recommendations we present in this paper are on another level than traditional interface design heuristics in human-computer interaction and guidelines that can be found in literature or in corporate guidelines. Our focus is on understanding and accepting the complexity and to design interfaces which support complex tasks and not add unnecessary usability problems.

2 Background

2.1 Separating Complex Tasks from Complicated Systems

Let us start with a working definition of complexity. With complexity we here mean the richness and properties of information that is given by the process that is to be controlled, i.e. the essential part of the operator's work. This is not (only) a question of the amount of information, but much more of the properties such as the number of system states, their interdependencies, nonlinearities, time delays, unpredictable behaviour and disturbances, discrete decision possibilities etc. Our view on complexity is in line with Endsley et al. (2003), i.e. separating system complexity from operational complexity and cognitive complexity (display and task complexity). However, we want to separate complexity from dynamics, which is further discussed below. The richness of information is perceived and handled, often with an astonishing level of expertise, by users and operators in different complex and dynamic work situations. Our own experiences in this way relate to train traffic dispatchers, train drivers, high-speed ferry operators, nurses and doctors at intensive care units, process operators in nuclear power industry and paper mills. In recent literature in cognitive psychology, the knowledge that expert users of this kind have is discussed under the heading of *intuition*. For example, in the recently published and seminal book on human thinking, Kahneman (2011) suggests that there exist two basic conditions for being able to develop expertise and intuitive skills in different kind of work contexts:

1. An environment, or surrounding, that is sufficiently regular in order to be predictable
2. A possibility to learn these regularities through extensive and long-lasting practice

When both these conditions are satisfied, we can expect human operators to develop intuition and expertise based on knowledge and best practice. Such precise judgments have been studied by for example Klein and his associates (Klein 1993; 1998). An experienced car driver can normally, and without high cognitive workload, handle intense rush-hour traffic, manoeuvring the car from one location to another at the other end of the town, and in real time monitoring what is going on inside and outside the car. We monitor and adjust speed and position of the car by controlling gear, brake and throttle, observe the behaviour of thousands of other cars, bicycles, pedestrians, traffic signals etc. We can evaluate and take a large number of decisions, sometimes several per second. During this very dynamic and complex process we can, provided that we really are experienced drivers, be cognitively focused on some problem of another kind, e.g. concerning what we are going to cook for dinner or if the newly employed co-worker really is well integrated in our work team. Skilled intuitions, based on recognition-based decisions, seem to develop when the opportunities to learn are generous (Kahneman and Klein 2009). Moreover, Ericsson et al. (2006) have suggested a range of factors that influence the rate of skill development. Among these, the kind of learning people employ, level of engagement and motivation, and the kind of self-regulation processes people use seem to be important. Here, we find a connection to the model for system development we have used in analysing and designing systems in the different domains mentioned above (Tschirner et al. 2014).

Instead of trying to reduce patterns that are rich of information, we should try to include these patterns into the design of modern information systems. This is in line with Norman (2010), who argues that we must learn to live with complexity, not to reduce it. But how do we do that? One problem here is that there seems to be confusion about the use of the term complexity. Many information systems are regarded as complex because their design has failed to adapt to the actual context. But this is to confuse things. A better term for such maladaptive designs is that they are complicated, and that they make things more complicated than necessary. There are numerous examples of complicated systems, caused by e.g. the organization or the design of the information systems. This can make the work more difficult because the operator must focus on the wrong things, e.g. on how to interpret information or how to navigate in the hierarchy of the information system rather than on solving the problems related to the control tasks. Complicated systems of this kind reduce the operator's possibilities to cope with the fundamental complexity of the controlled process.

The design challenge is to accept and not hide the complexity of the work as such, and at the same time not to add unnecessary complexity in the interface.

When we study different work settings, where skilled professionals shall handle very dynamic and complex situations, we see that it is not always easy to understand requirements and find solutions to how the professionals must be supported and how relevant information should be visualized. One purpose of this paper is to discuss this problem in relation to a case study, and we will describe some important aspects related to how information is visualized and used in these situations and the problems and solutions we have identified.

2.2 The Properties of Dynamic Systems

Dynamic should not be confused with "in movement", i.e. the contradiction to stationary. Dynamic is the contradiction to static and means that the system has certain important characteristics. A dynamic system e.g. develops over time even if it is not interacted with, it will keep on developing even when the interaction is stopped, and a control action at one time will sometimes not have an immediate effect but is only recognizable after some time. In order to understand the current and future behaviour of a dynamic system, it is necessary to know the prehistory of the system and how it has been interacted with. In order to reach a certain desired state in future, it is necessary to know the current state of the system and how to interact with it in a relevant way during some time period. It is necessary to be able to observe the system in enough detail including its history, the goals to be reached must be specified, a model describing the dynamic properties of the system must exist, and there have to be appropriate possibilities to interact with the system. In the case of human control, the model of the system is the operator's mental model. It can easily be understood that much of this requires efficient visualization of information.

In practice, most systems that we are trying to control are dynamic. To manoeuvre a large and heavy ship, to control a nuclear power plant or a paper mill, to plan and control train or air traffic, to monitor the state and give therapy to a patient in an intensive care unit or to handle a complex electronic case in an administrative organisation are examples. In such and many other situations, human operators, marine officers, pilots, process or traffic controllers, physicians, nurses, case handlers etc have the task to monitor, plan and control a complex and dynamic process. For this they require information visualized in an appropriate way. Often this means much, complex and dynamic information. When we study operators' handling of dynamic systems, we base this on a model (Jansson et al. 2014) that explicitly focuses on the models humans develop and the goals they formulate as consequence of the characteristics of the control systems, i.e. the controllability and the observability. Both these properties are important for the ability to develop knowledge on how to approach a system and how to reach desired effects. This model is based on studies on how humans manage dynamic decision tasks (Brehmer 1992). Controllability and observability are always operationalised in some way, i.e., they manifest themselves in some kind of visualization. The visualization is a key factor for the ability of a human operator to handle a dynamic system.

2.3 An Example

In this paper we argue that the control of complex and dynamic systems requires complex and dynamic information. Skilled professional operators and users must be supported with information systems that help them to cope with the difficulties they are facing. However, in practice we often see that the developers, in the design of information systems, often try to avoid, reduce, hide or neglect this. The main reason for this is probably both that the designers are not expert enough to understand the complexity of the situation and the needs of the users, and that the users themselves are not aware of the complexity and cannot express their requirements verbally. Another reason can be that the developers deliberately hide the complexity of reasons such as "it will be too complex for the users to handle" or that "it will be too complicated to develop and maintain". The result of not recognizing the complexity will most often result in very poor support for the users and that their possibilities to cope with the challenges in their work tasks are severely limited.

Our interpretation of this is that, if we reduce or hide the complexity and dynamics that are needed, we cause severe problems for the skilled professionals. They will have problems to work efficiently not because of the complexity of the work, but because the lack of efficient support. In other words, avoiding or hiding complexity will add another type of complexity related to the user interface, and the users will experience an unnecessary cognitive workload. "Too little information will result in cognitive overload". This is a statement that goes in the opposite direction compared to what can be found in the major body of literature on design and visualization today. In Edsley (2003) it is argued that "People can only pay attention to a certain amount of information at once. ... A considerable amount of additional work is required to find what is needed and extra mental processing is required to calculate the information the operator really wants to know. This inevitably leads to higher than necessary workload and error". We have found that people can pay attention to extremely large amounts of information, if relevant and visualized in a way that corresponds with our perceptual and cognitive abilities, e.g. the Gestalt laws.

In the case of train traffic control, see Fig. 1 below, the information on the large screens forms a very complex and dynamic pattern. The skilled traffic controllers can despite this have a very good control of what is going on, without consciously focus on the individual information elements. If something important or unexpected

Fig. 1. The information of a very complex process, here in train traffic control in an urban area, forms a pattern that despite its complexity can be perceived and efficiently interpreted by skilled professional traffic controllers.

happens, they will immediately perceive this and turn their attention to this for further analysis and actions.

Another aspect of this example, which we will discuss more below, is that the complexity shown here is not what they actually need for efficient control. The information visualized here does not reflect the real time dynamics of the train traffic system. To visualize this, other information sets must be a part of the observability for the traffic controllers.

We have found, from several case studies, that skilled professional users in complex work require systems that support them and allow them to use both their advanced professional and their basic human cognitive skills. The users in such work environments also have the normal human cognitive limitations. The design of the system must not come in conflict with these. This makes the design and visualization process very difficult. User-centred design does not mean presenting users with just the information they say they want or need at any given moment (Endsley et al. 2003). To understand the needs of the users and to find an appropriate visualization requires more than traditional user centred models.

3 Human Cognitive Skills and Limitations

Today, there is general agreement within research in cognitive psychology that human cognition is well adapted to a natural ecology. Our cognition is efficient and effective in relation to the tasks we are set to handle in such surroundings. This is especially true for what recently has come to be known as System 1 (Kahneman 2011). This system is believed to produce suggestions for interpretations and actions continuously to System 2. This latter system will only be activated if there are reasons to believe that the normal conditions are no longer valid, and that reflective thinking and problem solving is needed. This latter kind of thinking is constrained, mainly by being forced to bring all information to the working memory, which is known to have very limited capacity. Thus, when we argue that too little information will give cognitive overload, it is because the working memory has to continuously check and scan a new dialogue or a new window with information, without being able to relate the different presentations to each other in a semantically meaningful way. The design solutions are in these cases not adapted to the requirements of System 1, which immediately activates System 2 and prompts for a solution. System 2 reacts to the situation in its own way, which is considerably slower, by allocating a lot of attention to this new task, with the result that other on-going cognitive processes are interfered with and interrupted.

System 1 is associated with low level processing, high parallel capacity and low cognitive constrain, but also with rapid and efficient pattern recognition, and use of Gestalt laws. It has almost an unlimited capacity to overview, perceive and interpret information, also in real-time. On the down side, System 1 comes with a number of consequences in terms of biases (Tversky and Kahneman 1974; Kahneman and Tversky 1996), but as mentioned above, it is believed that operators of the kind we study are able to develop expertise and intuitive skills without exhibiting these biases, since they deal with a sufficiently regular and predictable environment and are using the possibility to learn about these regularities through extensive practice (Kahneman and Klein 2009). However, this is true if, and only if, the visualization of the information is well adapted to the needs of the operators. If not, the support system will be perceived as making things more complicated, often inducing the need to call System 2 into work. System 2 is limited in capacity and very sensitive to different kind of disturbances. When using working memory, it is often System 2 that has to carry out these processes.

4   A Case Study: Train Traffic Control

The train traffic system of Sweden is geographically divided into eight control areas. Train traffic in each area is controlled from a centralized traffic control centre (TCC). At the TCC, information about the traffic process status is presented in track diagrams on large distant panels, see Fig. 1 above, and/or on several computer screens at the workplace, see Fig. 2 below. Operators, the traffic controller here called dispatchers, monitor the train movements and control train routes by automatic or manual remote blocking systems. Track usage is controlled either by automatic functions or by manually specifying and executing interlocking routes for each track section. Today's control systems are often designed to support the operator's possibilities to react on and to solve disturbances and conflicts when they occur. In order to meet increasing future demands, new principles and technical solutions are required for efficient train traffic control. Controllers should be able to follow the dynamic development of the

Fig. 2. The same control centre as in Fig. 3, but here re-designed for visualization using a number of large size screens at each individual workplace.

traffic system over time and rather prevent disturbances than solving them when they already have caused delays.

This project has been a long research cooperation between our department and the Swedish Transport Administration. It started with a deep analysis of the present systems for traffic control and the problems experienced there. Requirements and prototypes of new systems and interfaces were successively developed and evaluated in close cooperation with groups of experienced traffic controllers and managers. After detailed laboratory experiments a full scale test systems was developed, deployed and tested in two different traffic control centres. The evaluations have shown that the new systems, based on the type of recommendations presented in this paper, contributed to radically improved performance. The professional traffic controllers were supported to move from control of the technical infrastructure to control of the traffic flow and to more optimal handling of traffic perturbations and disruptions (Sandblad et al. 2010).

One main objective has been to shift the control paradigm from low-level technical control tasks into higher level traffic re-planning tasks (Kauppi et al. 2006). Re-planning tasks must be supported by efficient user interfaces that allow the train traffic controller to be continuously updated and able to identify and evaluate present and future traffic conflicts so that these can be taken care of in time. The traffic controller must have high situation awareness (Endsley 1996). Improving train traffic control is a very cost effective way to better utilization of existing infrastructure. The traffic controller can be pro-active and prevent conflicts.

When the traditional traffic control work was analysed, several interesting and important findings related to visualization were made. Some of these are the following.

Today's control systems are designed to support the operator's possibilities to react on disturbances and to solve problems and conflicts when they have occurred. A paper-based time-distance graph is used as a tool for planning. Train dispatchers change the traffic plan by drawing new time table lines in the graph. The paper graph is then used by the dispatcher to remember what needs to be done and at which time. Since the new traffic plan is not automatically introduced into the system, there is great risk that the different automatic functions in the system will work against the new plan. Automatic support systems are not predictable enough to the dispatchers, because of their internal complexity. Automates can cause automation surprises by performing control actions that contradict the dispatchers plan. Bainbridge (1983) called this "the irony of automation", that when workload is high, automation is of the least assistance. To avoid automation surprises, train dispatchers are often forced to take full control by inhibiting all automatic functions in the disturbed area and solve the situation manually. Planning is mainly a mental process and the dispatcher must remember the plan without support and give control commands at the appropriate time. This causes a high cognitive workload and disturbs problem solving.

When decision making of the traffic controllers was analysed, we found that the information they base their decisions on was not directly available on the panels and screens. They had to observe what was available and then cognitively generate the information they actually need. This is an extremely complex cognitive task and requires advanced mental models and long experience. One concrete problem is that the exact position and speed of the trains are not visualized, since this information is not available from the signalling system. The only information available is the occupation of a track segment, indicated as red on the panel. By observing the shift from one segment to the next, the controllers "know" the position, speed and identification of each train. If the train suddenly stops, this is not visualized but will after some time be understood by the controllers since the red segment does not shift as expected.

The controllers' understanding of what dynamically happens, past, present and future, is not based on any visualization of dynamic information. Instead the controllers must remember what happened earlier, sometimes by writing things down, measuring time delays using a stop watch and perform control actions without any support that shows predictions of future events.

To summarize, the control of this extremely complex and dynamic system is today not supported by relevant and usable information systems and the visualization, although rather complex, does not show any dynamic or directly decision relevant information.

A project was initiated where researchers and a group of experienced dispatchers worked together, in a very user centred way, to describe and analyse today's systems and problems, to develop a new control strategy and to design prototypes of new, better information systems. A special focus was on aspects related to complexity and understanding of the dynamic properties of the train traffic control system.

The result was a completely new control principle and a completely new visualization of information to the dispatchers (Kauppi et al. 2006). The new control principle means that the dispatchers, i.e. the traffic controllers, will be supported by completely new systems for re-planning, traffic control and visualization. In the new system they are supported to monitor the dynamic movements of all trains in their control area, to identify disturbances and traffic conflicts and efficient tools to solve these conflicts by re-planning directly in the interface. The traffic plan is executed automatically when the planned train movements are approaching present time. An example of the new interface is shown below in Fig. 3. The re-planning tools (Fig. 4) and some details on indication of traffic conflicts (Fig. 5) are also shown below.

The new control system and traffic controller user interface have been fully developed and evaluated in full scale operational traffic control at two control centres in Sweden. Evaluations have shown that the concept and design contribute to improved support to the dispatchers and better planning of train traffic (Sandblad et al. 2007).

The most important differences and improvements achieved, compared to the old control principles and operator interfaces, are:

- The dispatchers, i.e. the traffic controllers, can now focus on identifying the disturbances and conflicts and make appropriate changes in the traffic plan. This is supported by visualizing decision relevant information and supporting re-planning. The execution of control commands is completely automated, something that earlier was a main task and took cognitive capacity from the problem solving activities.

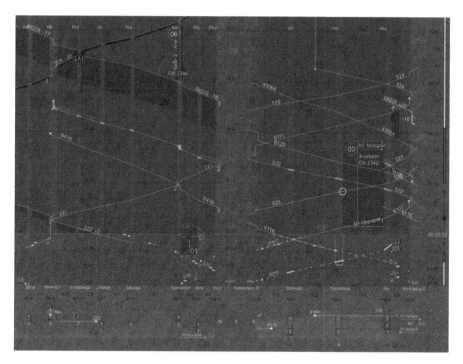

Fig. 3. The new traffic controller user interface. The interface shows the train traffic plan, deviations from the original plan, the planning via a time-distance graph, the present state (train position and speed), the history, planned maintenance work etc. Static information is e.g. the track structure.

- The interface shows history, present time and future plans. In this way the dynamic properties of train movements and signalling system are continuously visualized.
- The interface shows all decision relevant information simultaneously and in real-time, which minimizes unnecessary cognitive workload.
- The effects of re-planning actions are always directly visible, so the dispatchers have a direct feed-back on their actions.
- The traffic plan can be made available to all involved actors in the traffic process, e.g. train drivers and railway companies, which minimizes the need for oral communication.

5   Recommendations

Experiences from several applied research projects that we have been involved in or have detailed knowledge about, together with the more theoretical background described above, allow us to make some more general conclusions and recommendations.

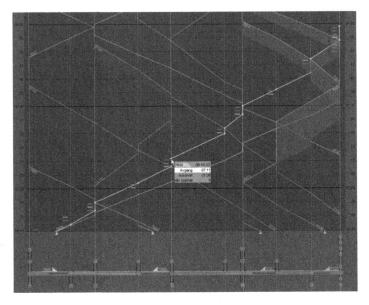

Fig. 4. The re-planning tasks are performed directly in the graph. A train is selected and highlighted. The selected graph line can be manipulated using the mouse scroll wheel. In this way all re-planning tasks can be performed directly in the interface and the resulting plan is directly visible. Examples of re-planning tasks are changing departure and arrival times, track usage, train speed etc.

5.1   Recognizing Complexity in Design of Visualization

If a work situation is complex, and if the process that is controlled is complex and dynamic, then the human operators will depend on complex information to perform their tasks. It is never a good idea to hide the complexity or to try to be "user friendly" by simplifying things in a way that does not support skilled professional users. Skilled professionals rely on complex information to perform their work. Therefore, the design of an operator system must be based on how we can support the operator's work in an efficient way, recognizing complexity and solving the conflict between complexity and good design.

"Cognitive overload" most often comes from visualizing too little or irrelevant information and of using bad coding and design. If well designed, the human operator can overview, interpret and handle very large, almost unlimited, amounts of information. If the information needed for the complex and dynamic tasks is not visualized in an appropriate way, the human operator must develop and use very advanced mental models and the very limited capacity of the short term memory. This will cause "cognitive overload". Already very small amounts of information can be impossible to use if not properly designed. Information overload in a complex and dynamic situation comes from showing too little, not too much!

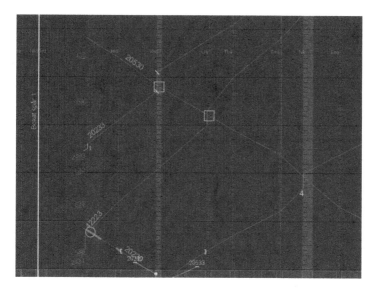

Fig. 5. Example of visualization of different types of conflicts. Conflicts are automatically detected and indicated. Yellow circles here mean a line conflict, e.g. two trains meet on a single track line. A yellow square means station track conflict, i.e. two trains are planned to use the same station track. During re-planning the removal or appearance of a conflict is visualized in real time (Color figure online).

5.2   Recognizing Complexity in the Systems Development Process

The process of analysing the control process and work situation, specifying requirements, designing, developing and deploying the control system and the visualization and interaction in the operator interface must be based on very detailed knowledge about the work performed by the operators. The process must be user centred and actively involve skilled professional users. Traditional process, task analysis and modelling methods can neither capture the complexity of the information the operators need, nor details or requirements concerning visualization and interaction. It is only using iterative user centred methods, prototyping and evaluations that can fulfil the actual demands.

5.3   Recommendations for Visualization

We can, based on the experiences discussed above, give some concrete practical recommendations concerning visualization in complex and dynamic control situations.

Different types of recommendations, guidelines and heuristics for design and visualization of operator interfaces have been presented earlier. In Endsley et al. (2003) a set of recommendations for design of systems and interfaces to support high situation awareness are described. Our recommendations below are to a large extent in compliance with these, but are more concrete and aimed to support the actual visualization.

We must here emphasize that it is never possible to give general recommendations that can be directly applied in the design of a specific system in a specific context. The detailed solution will always "depend on...". But based on the general recommendations, together with necessary knowledge about how to interpret and apply these, the following examples can support the design of usable interfaces for humans in control of complex and dynamic systems.

Below we present some of the most important recommendations.

Show the Whole and the Details Simultaneously. Rationale: If the user/operator has to focus on a specific detail, it is important to show the relation of this detail to the rest of the available information. In many systems the information can either be shown in form of an overview or (and only or) in form of a selected detail. When a specific detail is visualized, the user cannot see the relation of the detail to the whole and cannot see which other details are available and how to find them. In such systems it is easy to get lost and to fail to notice or consider important things that occur in other parts of the system. At least it will add cognitive load that disturb the chain of thoughts.

Example: In an electronic patient record (EPR) system all information about one patient is stored. Very often the EPR contains very large amounts of information related to different medical problems, encounters, episodes and time periods. In an old paper based patient record the physician could hold the whole record in one hand and turn pages with the other. The whole was always visible when a certain page was opened. Today the physicians often report that they lack overview, easily get lost in the record, that they always are afraid to miss important information and that they are slow in reading and spend most of their time searching and navigating. If the whole is always visible, these problems can to a large extent be avoided (see Figs. 6, 7).

Show all Information Needed Simultaneously; Support Continuous Overview of the Whole Process. Rationale: Based on the fact that we humans have an ability to overview, perceive and interpret almost unlimited amounts of information simultaneously and in real-time, if it is properly visualized, we have found that it is often possible to show very large amounts of information simultaneously. This is especially true for skilled professional operators in a complex work environment. When the pattern formed by the information is well known and relevant to the goals of the work, large sets of information can be monitored and analysed with very low cognitive load. This is not surprising since we humans are used to be and act in complex and dynamic environments when we e.g. drive a car in rush hour traffic or walk around in the town on a busy Saturday, meet friends in the crowd and watch for things to buy in the shop windows. If we do not see all information simultaneously, we must start to remember things in our limited working short term memory and use cognitive capacity for navigation etc.

The human operator needs to be continuously aware of what is going on, in order to be prepared to act when needed and to be able to act proactively. Even if the information visualized is very complex, an experienced operator can, if the design supports this, easily scan the images whenever needed and directly without conscious attention identify relevant perturbations or disruptions. If not all relevant details are continuously available, the operator has to actively search for relevant information,

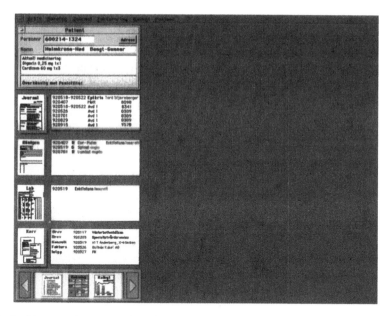

Fig. 6. In this example an overview of the total EPR is visualized. It consists of a patient card with important data that are always visible and four piles of documents together with an index of each pile. The user can choose to open one pile or select a specific document from the index. The menu at the bottom is for navigation to other information "rooms".

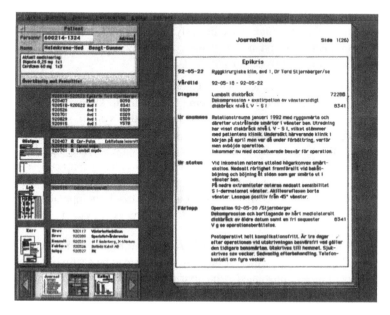

Fig. 7. Here one document is opened for reading. The whole record is still visible and it is easy to identify which pile and document is opened. Reading of consecutive pages is done by turning of the pages. Links between different documents are indicated in the indexes.

something that requires high level attention, makes it easy to miss important things, can lead to safety problems etc.

This also includes the information needed for development of efficient mental models. If the operators continuously can follow the dynamic behaviour of the whole system they will learn to understand the dynamic properties of the system and how they can and should act in different situations.

Example: Figure 8 shows an example of an operator user interface from a process industry. Here the whole process is visible in one single view, together with diagrams showing the dynamic development of different process states. The development of the process can be observed continuously and important changes can be identified and taken care of before they develop into something problematic. The amount of information is not a problem for the operator.

This could be compared to another design, where the operator was supposed to monitor an overview where only some states were observable, together with eventual alarms. When needed, the operator could select a process detail showing one part of the process. In this case there were more than 20 different details available. When one detail was selected, the whole and the other parts are not visible.

In Fig. 3 above, we can see another example. Here the whole train traffic and signalling process, including history and planned future, can be displayed in one single view. When this new traffic controller interface was presented, even experienced controllers were fist afraid that this was too much information to overview and interpret in real-time. Our argument, as being the designers, was mainly that this is actually the information they use today in their decision making and control tasks, but without seeing it. If they do not see the information they must develop extremely complex mental models to handle the situation. When implemented, the controllers rather fast learned to use the interface efficiently and the evaluation indicated that they developed much better understanding of the complexity and dynamics of the traffic process and could improve the control.

Show Dynamic Information. Rationale: Operators of dynamic systems are always interested in the development of the system. They want to know what is going on, what probably will happen, how they can control the system so that a desired behaviour or state is reached etc. If they only see the present state of the system, but are interested in the history, the trend or how fast the state is changing, they have to actively remember or even take notes in order to follow the dynamics. For an experienced process operator the key information are the first and second time derivatives, not (only) the present value. If dynamic data are visualized, the operator can by just scanning over the image get a direct feeling for what is going on.

Example 1: See Fig. 9.

Example 2: In Fig. 8 above, the relevant dynamic information for different process states are visualized. The dynamics of the system states can be easily observed by the experienced operator and unwanted behaviour detected before anything gets critical. This supports high situation awareness and pro-active control. It has shown to be a common main task for process operators to act so that the risks for problematic situations are reduced. To have continuous high situation awareness, and to take care

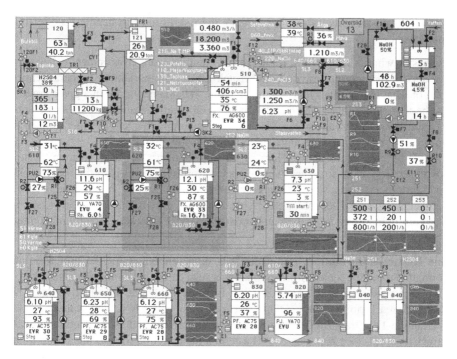

Fig. 8. Example of an operator interface for industrial process control. The visualization contains both static information in the background and dynamic information in the foreground. Information is coded with regard to the importance for the operator. Despite its complexity, for novice users, a skilled operator has no problems to overview and interprets the interface using very low cognitive capacity.

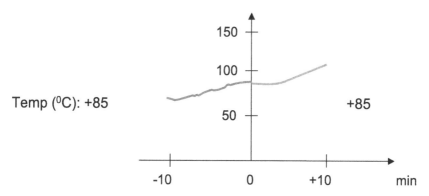

Fig. 9. The temperature can be rather uninformative, while the history and trend are much more relevant for the operator. If the temperature just now is 85 °C, this can have a very different meaning and require different actions, depending on if it is sinking or rising, and how fast.

of perturbations as early as possible, reduce the risk to have to handle chaotic situations later.

Emphasize what is Important. Rationale: In complex work environment, when very large sets of dynamic information are visualized, it is important to support identification of what is important in a certain situation. What is important in a given context must be thoroughly investigated and visualized efficiently. Static structures can be of less importance. Data values (e.g. 85) are more important than entities (e.g. °C). High values can in one context be more important than low ones etc.

Example: See Fig. 8 above. Here very many items are coded in relation to their importance. The static structure that the operator always knows is in the background. Important process parts, states, values etc. are in the foreground. Importance is coded by e.g. contrast, font size, colour etc. Using a medium grey background allows coding using both light (white as background coding) and dark (black as foreground coding) colours.

Time Related Information. Rationale: It is often important for the user to relate information to a time scale. The information as such can only be interpreted in relation to when it was generated and in relation to other data. The information must be visualized in a form that the user/operator easily can relate to a time scale.

Example 1: In train traffic control, the traditional way to present information was by track diagrams (see Fig. 1 above). If a certain track section was occupied by a train, the section was coloured red. But it was not indicated when the section became occupied and when is can be expected to be free again. In Fig. 3 above an alternative visualization is used. All train movements are visualized in form of lines in a time-distance graph. This allows the traffic controller to see the dynamics of the system and relate track occupation to time. The information can be easily interpreted even for large train traffic regions.

Example 2: In the patient record system it can be important for the user, physician or nurse, to be able to relate e.g. laboratory findings, patient encounters, events of medical relevance etc to a time scale. When such presentations are not shown, the users often complain that they "do not see the process and cannot relate different data to each other". This can e.g. be shown by the option to select a view where relevant data are visualized along a lime axis.

Show Effects of Alternative Decisions. Rationale: In the control of complex and dynamic systems the operator often has to evaluate complex situations and decide on what to do and when. Often it is also difficult to predict the possible outcomes, on short and long term, of alternative decisions. One solution can be to allow the operator to try different alternative solution to the present problem and to directly visualize the result of these solutions. This requires that it is possible to separate the decision from the execution, so that the operators are given the possibilities to "play around" before making the final decision.

Example: One example can be seen in Fig. 4. Here the train traffic controller is allowed to try different alternatives for re-planning of the traffic before selecting one. When a certain decision is tried, all consequences such as upcoming conflicts, delays of trains etc. are directly visualized.

Support Development of Mental Models. Rationale: Normally the operator's user interface is designed to support control tasks. We know that an important part of the work of the controller is to continuously further developing their mental model of the controlled system. Even if certain dynamic properties are not directly needed for control, they are essential for development of the mental model.

Example: Show dynamic information continuously. Allow the operator to "play around" and see the effects of manipulations. See Fig. 4 above.

Efficient Coding of Information. Rationale: Visualizing large sets of dynamic data requires efficient coding. Based on theory of perception (properties of the human sight/view/eye system) and cognition, many heuristic rules for efficient coding can be derived. What is a good solution must be evaluated in each specific context.

Example: Different coding mechanisms can be used. Examples are: contrast, use of colours, foreground-background, patterns instead of text, fixed positions, consistency etc.

Visualization of Automatic Systems. Rationale: Automation very often adds complexity to the operator's work. If automatic systems are autonomous, i.e. do not only execute the operators' intention but make decisions according to their own algorithms, it becomes difficult for the human operator to predict what the automatic systems will do, when and why. This will cause "automation surprises" (Bainbridge 1983) and other problems. One common result is the "turn-it-off" syndrome, i.e. the operators turn the automatic system off in order to be in full control.

Example: One solution can be to only use non-autonomous automatic systems, so that they only execute the operator's plans. If autonomous systems are used, it becomes important to visualize what the automatic systems will do, when and why. This can in many cases be extremely difficult.

6   Discussion

We have argued that skilled human operators, in complex and dynamic work situations, must be efficiently supported. This requires that they are provided with systems, interfaces and visualization that help them to cope with the challenges. The solution is not to hide, avoid or neglect the complexity, but to accept it and find appropriate ways to support the skilled professional users. We have found, with support from theories and from a number of case studies, that skilled human operators can handle extremely complex and dynamic situations without cognitive overload. On the contrary, limiting the complexity and showing too little information can often cause cognitive overload since this will cause lack of the information the operators need for understanding and deciding on control actions. Here the visualization is a real challenge. We must efficiently visualize very large, complex and dynamic information patterns. The information presented to the operators/users must be designed to support human and professional skills, without interfering with our inherited limitations or adding unnecessary workload.

Classical heuristics of HCI are too general to guide design of control systems and operator interfaces in very complex and dynamic work situations. The recommendations presented in this paper try to complement traditional design knowledge in this respect.

When we base the design of operator interfaces on the recommendations above, we have found that the operators' work is better supported and that acceptance from the operators is high. They report that they now "have an overview and know what is going on". They can be continuously in-the-loop, have high situation awareness and develop a pro-active behaviour.

References

Bainbridge, L.: Ironies of automation. Automatica **19**(6), 775–779 (1983)

Brehmer, B.: Dynamic decision making: human control of complex systems. Acta Psychol. **81**, 211–241 (1992)

Endsley, M.R.: Automation and situation awareness. In: Parasuraman, R., Mouloua, M. (eds.) Automation and human performance: theory and applications, pp. 163–181. Lawrence Erlbaum, Mahwah (1996)

Endsley, M.R., Bolte, B., Jones, D.G.: Designing for Situation Awareness: An Approach to Human-Centered Design. Taylor & Francis, London (2003)

Ericsson, K.A., Charness, N., Hoffman, R.R., Feltovich, P.J. (eds.): The Cambridge Handbook of Expertise and Expert Performance. Cambridge University Press, New York (2006)

Jansson, A., Tschirner, S., Andersson, A.W., Sandblad, B.: Trading rigor for relevance: GMOC – a conceptual model for cognitive field studies. Unpublished manuscript (2014)

Kahneman, D.: Thinking. Fast and Slow. Allen Lane/Farrar, Straus and Giroux, London/New York (2011)

Kahneman, D., Klein, G.: Conditions for intuitive expertise: a failure to disagree. Am. Psychol. **64**(6), 515–526 (2009)

Kahneman, D., Tversky, A.: On the reality of cognitive illusions. Psychol. Rev. **103**, 582–591 (1996)

Kauppi, A., Wikström, J., Sandblad, B., Andersson, A.W.: Future train traffic control: control by re-planning. Cognition Technol. Work **8**(1), 50–56 (2006). Springer-Verlag London Ltd.

Klein, G.A.: A recognition-primed decision (RPD) model of rapid decision making. In: Klein, G.A., Orasanu, J., Calderwood, R., Zsambok, C.E. (eds.) Decision Making in Action: Models and Methods, pp. 138–147. Ablex, Norwood (1993)

Klein, G.: Sources of Power: How People Make Decisions. MIT Press, Cambridge (1998)

Norman, D.: Living with Complexity. MIT Press, Cambridge (2010)

Sandblad, B., Andersson, A.W., Kauppi, A., Wikström, J.: Implementation of a test system for evaluation of new concepts in rail traffic planning and control. In: Wilson, J., Norris, B., Clarke, T., Mills, A. (eds.) People and Rail Systems. Human Factors at the Heart of the Railways. Ashgate Publ. Comp, Abingdon (2007)

Sandblad, B., Andersson, A.W., Kauppi, A., Isaksson-Lutteman, G.: Development and implementation of new principles and systems for train traffic control in Sweden. In: Ning, B., Brebbia, C.A., Tomii, N. (eds.) Computers in Railways XII, pp. 441–450. WIT-press, Southampton (2010)

Tschirner, S., Jansson, A., Andersson, A.W., Sandblad, B.: GMOC – a conceptual model for analysis and design of human-work interaction. Unpublished manuscript (2014)

Tversky, A., Kahneman, D.: Judgments under uncertainty: Heuristics and biases. Science **185**, 1124–1131 (1974)

Applying CTA to the Design of SA-Oriented Visualizations: Heuristics and Recommendations

Rosa Romero[✉], Sara Tena, David Díez, and Paloma Díaz

DEI Lab - Computer Science Department,
Universidad Carlos III de Madrid, Madrid, Spain
{rmromero,stena,ddiez,pdp}@inf.uc3m.es

Abstract. The effectiveness of visualizations depends on their feasibility to support the goals and tasks of the user in some particular target domain. In order to fulfill this requirement, task analysis has been characterized as a needful activity during the visualization design cycle; however, there is a lack of artefacts that guides the processing of user tasks to design visualizations. This lack of guidelines may hide the identification of such tasks that should be supported by visualization. This fact is especially relevant in operational environments in which ineffective visualization designs may hinder the acquisition of Situation Awareness (SA) and, therefore, lead to the performance of erroneous operational decisions. With the purpose of overcoming this situation, this chapter presents a set of heuristics for addressing the application of Cognitive Task Analysis (CTA) to identify visualization-supported tasks within this type of environments. The definition of such heuristics has relied on the review of the literature about SA-oriented design, visualization, and CTA, and the application of these concepts during the design of control system interfaces. The final aim is to provide a design framework that helps visualization designers to apply task analysis methods to the design of SA-oriented visualizations.

Keywords: Human-centered visualization design · Situation awareness · Goal task analysis · Visualization-supported tasks

1 Introduction

Visualization design is defined as *'the process of designing information to match the processing characteristics of human visual system'* [16]. Aiming at providing effective visualizations, this process consists of a set of transformations, such as data transformations, visual mappings, or view transformations, which can be carried out through two main approaches which are different yet complementary: (1) the *data-oriented* approach: the accomplishment of these transformations is mainly based on data attributed characteristics such as whether an attribute is categorical, numerical, or ordinal; and (2) the *human-centered* approach: these transformations are not only based on data characteristics but also on the user's tasks and the environment. Over the last decade, applying the latter has led to the definition of the concept of

A. Ebert et al. (Eds.): HCIV Workshops 2011, LNCS 8345, pp. 67–79, 2014.
DOI: 10.1007/978-3-642-54894-9_6, © IFIP International Federation for Information Processing 2014

human-centered visualization [9, 16], the general idea of which is that visualization should be adapted to user's needs, skills, and limitations. Based on this ground, and trying to provide some guidance to visualization designers, several authors such as Munzner [11], Wassink et al. [15], or Zhang et al. [16] have proposed models and design frameworks that describe the structure of tasks, users, and functions. Although these models have clear differences among them, they concur in characterizing task analysis as a required process for effective *human-centered visualization* designs. Unfortunately, under the umbrella of task analysis, and the definition of the task performed by the user throughout an activity, there are numerous methods, approaches, and techniques to consider; most of which have not been conceived to fulfil the study of specific domains and systems. Furthermore, since the main challenge in designing visualizations is not only the gathering of the tasks carried out by the user but also the suitable characterization of those tasks, the application of task analysis techniques to the design of visualization is not trivial; applications that have so far mainly relied on the experience of visualization designers. The lack of context-oriented guidelines may cause the highlighting of irrelevant tasks or the collection of inadequate information for a successful visualization design.

The design of unfitting visualization is especially problematic in operational environments in which visualizations support the performance of critical tasks. Operational environments refer to working situations in which an operator controls the functioning of either a critical process or an essential infrastructure. During their activity, operators must be aware of all the incidents, actions, and situations related to the operating situation, monitoring and controlling the state of either the process or the infrastructure. In these environments, the acquisition of Situation Awareness (SA) is a key factor to perform the operation of these critical process and infrastructures [4]. In fact, the analyses of recent problems in a variety of operational environments show the relevance of SA as a major factor in failures propagation [8].

Acquiring SA refers to knowing what is happening around the operation and what that information means at this moment and in the future. SA is therefore a cognitive process directly dependent on the context [6]. Thus, the design of SA-oriented visualizations requires the identification of such context goals that must be achieved by operators as well as the task performed to accomplish such goals and the information required to carry out those tasks. Figure 1 illustrates the detailed scope of SA-oriented visualizations. According to the SA-oriented visualization approach, two different but complementary disciplines guides the design of visualization: Visualization and Human-Computer Interaction (HCI). In this way, Cognitive Engineering methods – such as task analysis or cognitive task analysis- allow designers to identify those tasks that must be carried out by users to achieve specific operational goals. Once these goals, and their corresponding tasks, had been identified, designers could apply different theoretical and methodological visualization foundations to create such information visualizations that assist the achievement of SA. These foundations will be supplemented by a set of SA-oriented design principles related to the design of operational user interfaces. Consequently, at this design approach the key design element will not be the operational information to represent, but the operational goals to achieve by the operators.

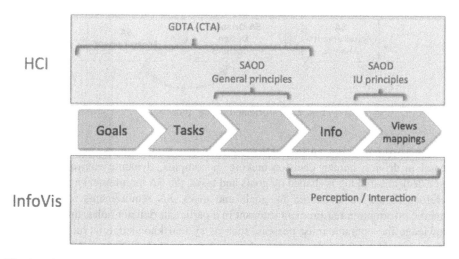

Fig. 1. The scope of SA-oriented visualizations. The design of operational visualization is not guided by the information to represent but to the operational goals to achieve.

This chapter presents a set of heuristics to guide visualization designers during the Goal-Directed Task Analysis (GDTA) of operational environments. GDTA is a CTA method specially oriented to elicit SA requirements within operational environments. The purpose of these heuristics is to reduce the relevance of the visualization designer's experience by systematizing the performance of GDTA within this context. The rest of the chapter is organized as follows. The rationale for defining these heuristics is described in the next section. Section 3 is focused on presenting the theoretical foundations that ground these heuristics. Section 4 establishes these heuristics grouped by three purposes of the task analysis process: the elicitation of visualization-supported tasks, the identification of information requirement to the task at hand, and the characterization of such information requirements. Finally conclusions and recommendations for further work are drawn in the last section.

2   Designing for Achieving Situation Awareness

Nowadays, SA is one of the most relevant concepts of cognitive engineering, one of the foundations for decision-making and performance, and a relevant factor studied in wide-ranging fields. Endsley formally defined SA as *'the perception of the elements in the environment within a volume of time and space, the comprehension of their meaning, and a projection of their status in the near future'* [6]. Much of the operator's efforts in operational environments are devoted to developing SA and keeping it up to date [7]. As a consequence, designing artefacts for supporting this process is a challenging activity, which has been mostly carried out through the SA-oriented design process. This process model, as shown in Fig. 2, is divided into three basic stages: analysis, design, and measurement. According to the scope of this chapter, this section characterizes the first stage, highlighting the deficiencies of the analysis phase from the viewpoint of visualization design.

Fig. 2. SA-oriented design process [4]

The SA-oriented design (SAOD) strategy is based on the idea that SA is fundamental in driving human decision-making in complex, dynamic environments [7]. Since decision-making is shaped by goals and tasks, the SA requirement analysis stage therefore should be addressed by goals and tasks. SA requirements focus on the dynamic information requirement relevant in a particular domain rather than the static knowledge the operator must possess, such as system knowledge or rules, and procedures [6]. These SA requirements are delineated through GDTA. GDTA is a CTA method oriented to seek and document what information operators need to perform their job and how each operator integrates or combines the information to address a particular decision [4]. Conforming to that, this method involves knowledge elicitation sessions with experts aiming at providing an analysis of the information required for each level of SA linked to each goal and task. The steps involved in GDTA are presented below:

1. *Review of the domain*: basic information about the domain of application is crucial for designing systems.
2. *Initial interviews*: the key operators that are playing significant roles should be chosen for applying the GDTA method.
3. *Development of a goal hierarchy*: identification of the major goals and associated tasks should be extracted from the interviews.
4. *Identification of decisions and SA requirements*: experts should be enquired about the tasks that are necessary for accomplishing the main goal. The sub goals would serve to set the direction for clarifying the primary decision needed for each sub-goal and the information needs to accomplish those sub-goals.
5. *Reviewing the goal hierarchy*: additional interviews to experts for reviewing the goal hierarchy are recommended in order to consolidate the information extracted.
6. *Review of the GDTA*: a final review of the final GDTA structure obtained from the application of the method.

Unfortunately, the application of this analysis depicts when it must be carried out, but does not support the how, which must rely on designers' experience. Moreover, since not every SA requirement is relevant from the viewpoint of visualization, designers must be able to distinguish among them for a successful visualization design. An appropriate application of the GDTA method helps designers determine ways to present information to operators in a better way in order to support SA, and consequently, in decision making and performance [6].

3   SA-Oriented Visualizations: Theoretical Foundations

Although the primacy of designer's experience is to carry out GDTA techniques, there exists a basis of knowledge related to both SAOD and visualization design that can be employed by designers to systematize the application of GDTA methods. This basis of knowledge may be considered as a grounded theory for the definition of specific design guidelines.

3.1   Principles for Situation Awareness-Oriented Design

The way in which information is presented to the operator through the interface greatly influences SA [6, 13]. The most applied principles for creating SA-oriented designs are the fifty design principles proposed by Endsley [4, 5]. These principles are based on a model of human cognition involving dynamic switching between *goal-driven* and *data-driven* processing and feature support for limited operator resources. However, they underpin not only SA design interface issues but also how to design automated systems, dealing with complexity or uncertainty. For this reason, the set of principles to consider for designing effective visualizations should be reduced to those focused on the interface design.

- *Goal-oriented information displays.* Goal-oriented information displays should be provided, organized so that the information needed for a particular goal is co-located and directly answers the major decisions associated with the goal.
- *Direct presentation of higher-level SA needs (comprehension and projection), rather than supplying only low-level data that operators must integrate and interpret manually.* As attention and working memory are limited, the degree to which displays provide information that is processed and integrated in terms of comprehension and projection will positively impact SA.
- *Support for global SA.* Providing an overview of the situation across the operator's goals at all times and enabling efficient and timely goal switching and projection.
- *Critical cues related to key features of schemata need to be determined and made salient in the interface design.* In particular those cues that will indicate the presence of prototypical situations will be of prime importance and will facilitate goal switching in critical conditions.
- *Support for parallel processing.* Multi-modal displays should be provided in data rich environments.
- *Use information filtering carefully.* Extraneous information not related to SA needs should be removed (while carefully ensuring that such information is not needed for broader SA needs).

3.2   Visualization Design Principles

A first step in developing effective visualizations is to understand how they enable perception and cognition. The achievement of this purpose encompasses the application of the following set of widely accepted visualization design principles [2, 10, 12, 14].

- *Appropriateness principle.* Visualizations should provide neither more nor less information than that needed for solving the problem.
- *Naturalness principle.* Experiential cognition is most effective when the properties of the visual representation most closely match the information being represented. This principle supports the idea that new visual metaphors are only useful for representing information when they match the user's cognitive model of the information. Purely artificial visual metaphors can actually hinder understanding.
- *Matching principle.* Representations of information are most effective when they match the task to be performed by the user. Effective visual representations should present affordances suggestive of the appropriate action.
- *Principle of congruence.* The structure and content of visualization should correspond to the structure and content of the desired mental representation. In other words, the visual representation should represent the important concepts in the domain of interest.
- *Principle of apprehension.* The structure and content of visualization should be readily and accurately perceived and comprehended.
- *Principle of expressiveness.* The visualization contains all the facts in the data set and only the facts.
- *Principle of effectiveness.* The visualization conveys the information in an effective way.

4   SA-Oriented Visualizations: A Prescriptive Analysis Artefact

GDTA has emerged as an essential approach to study operational environments and address the design of control systems. However, as aforementioned, there is a lack of prescriptive analysis artefacts that systematize the SA requirements analysis for designing SA-oriented visualizations. One solution to this shortcoming will be the collection of heuristics that guides the application of GDTA for designing effective visualization for operational environments. The following subsections explain the rationale of the solution as well as the defined heuristic.

4.1   The Rationale of the Solution

A heuristic refers to a generalizable abstraction based on the design experience. A heuristic provides an educated design rule, a simplification that can be used to address the definition of a fitting solution. In this way, heuristics are less consistent and generalizable than guidelines or principles, but they are a useful mechanism to scope a solution in emerging domains. Moreover, heuristics have proved as an appropriate mechanism to guide creative-oriented processes. The definition of rules based on previous experience and well-known practices allows reusing procedural knowledge, reducing the relevance of the design experience.

The definition of the heuristics is based on the review of the literature about SA-oriented design, visualization, and GDTA as described in Sects. 2 and 3, as well as the application of these concepts during the design of control system interfaces. In particular, the heuristics have been defined following a systematic approach:

- After reviewing the literature on SA-oriented design, principles related to the design of operational systems were collected [4, 5]. As mentioned before in Sect. 3.1, these principles were analysed and filtered, considering only those principles related to the design of the user interface. Similarly, the most widely accepted visualization design principles (see Sect. 3.2) were selected.
- Secondly, and taking into account the GDTA method, the main goals of the design process of control systems were highlighted. For each of these goals, the literature on visualization design was considered to identify a set of experienced-based design rules. For instance, related to the elicitation of supported tasks, taxonomy of high-level visualization task [1] was reviewed, identifying such tasks about the review of great pieces of information and the recognition of unexpected situations. Based on these references, the first draft of the heuristic was created.
- Finally, the description of the heuristic was carried out. These descriptions were based on the principles selected on the first stage of the process. In case of not obtaining a coherent and consistent description underpinned by the principles, the heuristic was withdrawn.

4.2 Heuristics for Cognitive Task Analysis

The heuristics defined cover three purposes of the task analysis process: (1) the elicitation of visualization-supported tasks, which is devoted to identify those relevant tasks to the visualization design; (2) the identification of information requirement to the task at hand, which is focused on gathering relevant information from users to the task at hand; and (3) the characterization of such information requirements, which is related to characterize the information requirement attributes. Following are the heuristics presented according to the purpose to which they are referred. With the goal of illustrating them, they will provide an example in the power transmission domain for each heuristic. The goal of power transmission operators is to get an efficient, safe, and sustainable power transmission. With such an aim, operators must manage on real-time large volumes of multidimensional data streams, for which extensive visualization are used. A summary of theseheuristics is provided in Table 1.

The Elicitation of Visualization-Supported Tasks

This first group of heuristics is intended to characterize those operators' tasks whose performance may be enhanced by the use of visualizations. Accordingly, and based on the taxonomy of high-level visualization tasks previously mentioned, a set of high-level abstract goals shared by those visualization-supported tasks has been compiled. This set of high-level abstract goals is classified into three categories: (1) The management of data spread across multiple sources. SA within operational environments involves being aware of what is happening across many aspects of the environment; (2) The monitoring of a large number of potential events. Achieving good SA in operational environments is based on understanding what the data and cues perceived

Table 1. Heuristics summary

The elicitation of visualization-supported tasks	
H1	*Overview tasks.* Tasks that involve the acquisition of a general qualitative awareness of one aspect of some data, preferably in a very short period of time
H2	*Attention sharing tasks.* Tasks that involve multiple pieces of information that must be processes simultaneously
H3	*Pattern recognition tasks.* Tasks that involve the extraction of patterns from data
H4	*Cause and effect tasks.* Tasks that involve an understanding of what assumptions have gone into creating data and thus affected the outcomes inferred
The identification of information requirements to the task at hand	
H5	*Significant information.* Information sources that are relevant to the operator's task at hand
H6	*Priority of the information.* The importance assigned to such information according to the operators' task at hand
H7	*Relationship between pieces of information.* Potential relationships among the pieces of information
H8	*Modes of obtaining information.* How the operators obtain the required information to the task at hand
The modeling data stage	
H9	*Data attributed characteristics.* Data attributed must be defined to properly perform visual mappings
H10	*Structural relationships among data.* Structural relationships existing among data
H11	*Volume of data handling.* The amount of data that must be handled to the task at hand

mean in relation to relevant goals and objectives; and (3) The recognizing of patterns in information. To achieve SA, the operators try to establish correlations among data in order to comprehend what is its significance. Relying on these categories, the heuristics defined are:

- **H1. Overview tasks.** It is necessary to characterize those tasks that involve the acquisition of a general qualitative awareness of one aspect of some data, preferably acquired in a very short period of time.

  In the electrical grid domain, the operator should be able to comprehend the current condition of the grid infrastructure at any given point in time. Thus, an overview of the various attributes of alarms is needed. An example of this overview would be the display of the distribution of the number of active alarms on a specific grid area or the typology of alarms that is contributing most to the failures.

- **H2. Attention sharing tasks.** It is necessary to identify those tasks that involve multiple pieces of information that must be processed simultaneously.

  In the electrical grid domain, a grid operator must concurrently perform planned operations over the grid infrastructure and monitor the grid status in order to both detect and register potential incidents. Hence, managing potential incidents is a task of interest from the viewpoint of the design of SA-oriented visualizations.

- **H3. Pattern recognition tasks.** It is necessary to characterize those tasks that involve the extraction of patterns from data. These tasks are related to the requirement of both integrating and prioritizing the data to achieving comprehension of the current situation.

  An abnormal situation can lead to an avalanche of alarms, which grid operators need to interpret in order to identify both its origin and seriousness. Therefore, handling alarms may take advantage of the capabilities provided by SA-oriented visualizations.

- **H4. Cause and effect tasks.** It is necessary to characterize those tasks that involve an understanding of what assumptions have gone into creating data and thus affects the outcomes inferred.

  During an avalanche of alarms, operators must project the grid infrastructure status and the likely effects of their own actions. These two tasks are potential candidates from the viewpoint of the SA-oriented visualization design.

The Identification of Information Requirements to the Task at Hand

Since the last purpose of visualization is to display information that matches the processing characteristics of the human visual system, performing GDTA for designing visualizations should involve not only the identification of the cognitive tasks related to operators' goals but also the information required to carry out these tasks. Accordingly, the following heuristics are defined in order to guide the requirement gathering about relevant aspects of this information from the viewpoint of visualization:

- **H5. Significance information.** It is necessary to ask for only those information sources that are relevant to operators' task at hand. Additional information may be distracting and makes the task more difficult.

  While an operator must be aware of both planned operations over the grid and the status of different electrical assets for monitoring tasks, the operator does not need to know the number of customers of the utility. In this way, questions about which pieces of information are more relevant for carrying out monitoring tasks must be formulated.

- **H6. Priority of the information.** A different priority level exists in the information. Hence, it is necessary to ask for the importance assigned to such information according to the operators' task at hand.

  Alarms are the essential mechanisms used to interpret and correct abnormal situations over the grid instead of monitoring power values. Thus, questions about which information has more priority or relevance to manage abnormal situations must be conducted.

- **H7. Relationship between pieces of information.** It is necessary to characterize the potential relationships among the pieces of information.

The information provided by the field personnel is essential to carry out safe planned operations over the grid. Such information must be provided in relation with infrastructure devices. Accordingly, questions about any relationship existing between the information provided by external actors and other pieces of information managed by primary actors must be formulated.

- **H8. Modes of obtaining information.** It is necessary to characterize how the operators obtain the required information to the task at hand. Operators may need to explore the information space in order to obtain the needed pieces of information.

Operators may navigate across several static lists of alarms in order to gain understanding about the status of a fragment of the grid affected by an incident. Thus, questions focused on how the operators retrieve the required information to perform their tasks must be conducted.

The Characterization of Information Requirements
The purpose of this last group of heuristics is to guide the definition and detail of the tasks previously identified. This effort leads to the characterization of their information requirements. Accordingly, this characterization will serve as the input for designing SA-oriented visualizations:

- **H9. Data attributed characteristics.** It is necessary to characterize the data attributed characteristics in order to perform visual mappings properly.

Monitoring the grid status is mainly based on the information supplied by SCADA systems. Therefore, the design of visualization requires the knowledge of the number of dimensions of this data and the type of values. In this case, SCADA systems produce multidimensional and alphanumerical data.

- **H10. Structural relationships among data.** It is necessary to characterize the structural relationships existing among data.

Based on structural relationships among alarms such as time or topological relationships among electrical assets, operators may be capable of understanding the seriousness of the problem. Accordingly, it is necessary to make the type of existing relationships among alarms explicit in order to design effective visualizations.

- **H11. Volume of data handling.** It is necessary to characterize the amount of data that must be handled to the task at hand in order to determine the visual scalability required.

During abnormal situations, the number of alarms registered doubles, which may hinder the achievement of SA by operators. Thus, it is necessary to identify the number of alarms that operators must handle to diagnose a problem. This number of alarms will be dependent on the operational situation.

5 Conclusions

Embedding knowledge into digital representations is a well-known mechanism for increasing the cognition of the operator and a manner of easing the performance of operating tasks. In that way, most operation centres are comprised of a set of technological devices that deploy digital representations about the system to operate. It means that operators are mainly in contact with the control system they operate via the information provided by these digital representations. In particular, the use of visualizations has been highlighted as an essential artefact to support both the understanding of the operators about the system and the performance of appropriate actions. Similarly, SA is considered as the most important factor that determines the performance of the operators. SA involves being aware of what is happening in the system to operate and how these facts could impact immediately and in the near future. Unfortunately, in spite of their mutual arrangement and relation, there is a lack of design artefacts that lead the definition of visualization specially conceived to provide SA. SA-oriented design methodologies are focused on identifying such labours that must be fulfilled by the operator, leaving aside which information should be managed to perform those labours or which of them could be better accomplished by the use of digital representations. Besides, the criticality of the operational environments hinders the application of the usual interactive design techniques such as prototyping. Thus, the definition of prescriptive artefacts comes up as an essential requirement to address the design of SA-oriented visualizations.

One of the most important activities in design, in general, and in SA-oriented design, in particular, is the inquiry process. The definition of rules based on previous experience and well-known practices allows reusing procedural knowledge, reducing the relevance of the design experience. The review of literature related to SA-oriented design and GDTA, and the application of both concepts during the design of control system interfaces has allowed us to identify a set of tasks that may take full advantage of visualization power. In particular, tasks such as overview tasks, attention sharing tasks, pattern recognition tasks, and cause and effect tasks have been identified as the most significant visualization-supported tasks to provide SA. Additionally, a set of guides about what kind of information and which dimensions should be collected to design appropriate visualizations has been defined. Dimensions such as the significance of the data, its priority, relationship, and modes of obtaining information are necessary to ensure that extra features not required by the task at hand are included by these visualizations.

Operational environments, as critical working settings, can be regarded as a very procedural environment, in which the operators perform their tasks in keeping with well-known procedures and protocols. Accordingly, the specification in advance of the operational goals is competently achievable. Nonetheless, there are unexpected and unusual situations, situations defined as crisis situations, which cannot be completely specified in advance. Consequently, our approach can be considered as an appropriate solution to define such visualizations that assist regular operational conditions. Even so, since during crisis situations the operation is basically based on the ability, experience, and training of the operators, moving the digital representation to the background, this limitation barely restricts the usefulness of our solution.

Further work will lead to the application of these heuristics to other different operational domains for refinement or refutation. Subsequently, these heuristics will be extended to address the application of SA-oriented design principles. Such principles provide a blueprint for considering SA aspects into designs but its proper application is also mainly dependent on the designer's experience. As a second step, the limitation of our approach to crisis situations will be faced. In particular, other cognitive engineering frameworks, such as the Cognitive Work Analysis (CW) [14] or the Work-Centered Design (WCD) [3], should be analysed to identify the keys of building systems that facilitate SA in unexpected situations. The final aim of our work is to define a design framework that addresses the human-centered visualization paradigm in operational environments.

Acknowledgments. This work has been supported by the ENERGOS Project, funded by the Centre for Industrial Technological Development (CDTI) of the Ministry for Science and Innovation of Spain.

References

1. Amar, R., Stasko, J.: A knowledge task-based framework for the design and evaluation of information visualizations. In: IEEE Symposium on Information Visualization (Infovis), pp. 143–149 (2004)
2. Card, S., Mackinlay, J., Shneiderman, B.: Readings in Information Visualization. Morgan Kaufmann, San Francisco (1999)
3. Eggleston, R.G.: Work-centered design: a cognitive engineering approach to system design. In: Proceedings of the Human Factors and Ergonomics Society, pp. 265–269 (2003)
4. Endsley, M.R.: Design and evaluation for situation awareness enhancement. In: Proceedings of Human Factors Society 32nd Annual Meeting, Santa Monica (1988)
5. Endsley, M.R.: Toward a theory of situation awareness in dynamic systems. Hum. Factors **37**(1), 32–64 (1995)
6. Endsley, M.R., Bolté, B., Jones, D.G.: Designing for Situation Awareness. Taylor & Francis, New York (2003)
7. Endsley, M.R., Bolstad, C.A., Jones, D.G., Riley, J.M.: Situation awareness oriented design: from user's cognitive requirements to creating effective supporting technologies. Hum. Factors Ergon. Soc. Annu. Meet. **47**, 268–272 (2003)

8. Greitzer, F.L., Schur, A., Paget, M., Guttromson, R.T.: A sensemaking perspective on situation awareness in power grid operations. IEEE Power and Energy Society General Meeting Conversion and Delivery of Electrical Energy in the 21st Century. IEEE, Pittsburgh (2008)
9. Kerren, A., Ebert, A., Meyer, J.: Human-Centered Visualization Environments. Springer, Berlin (2006)
10. Mackinlay, J.: Automating the design of graphical presentations of relational information. ACM Trans. Graph. 5(2), 110–141 (1986)
11. Munzner, T.: A nested model for visualization design and validation. IEEE Trans. Vis. Comput. Graph. 15(6), 921–928 (2009)
12. Norman, D.: Things That Make Us Smart: Defending Human Attributes in the Age of the Machine. Perseus Books, New York (1993)
13. Rothenberg, D.: Alarm Management for Process Control. Monumentum Press, New Jersey (2009)
14. Tversky, B., Morrison, J.B., Betrancourt, M.: Animation: can it facilitate? Int. J. Hum.-Comput. Stud. 57(4), 247–262 (2002)
15. Wassink, I., Kulyk, O., van Dijk, E.M.A.G., van Veer, G.C, van der Vet, P.E.: Applying a user-centred approach to interactive visualization design. Trends in Interactive Visualization. Advanced Information and Knowledge Processing. Springer, London (2008)
16. Zhang, J., Johnson, K.A., Malin, J.T.: Human-centered information visualization. In: International Workshop on Dynamic Visualization and Learning, Tubigen (2002)

Cognitive Ergonomics in Visualization

Michael Raschke[(✉)], Tanja Blascheck, and Thomas Ertl

Institute for Visualization and Interactive Systems, University of Stuttgart,
Universitätsstrasse 38, 70569 Stuttgart, Germany
michael.raschke@vis.uni-stuttgart.de
http://www.vis.uni-stuttgart.de

A key factor to assure success of a visualization technique is how efficiently users perceive information using this visualization technique. This efficiency is strongly correlated with visualization parameters which we will summarize in the following with the term *cognitive ergonomics*. In this chapter we will motivate the reader to study cognitive ergonomics in visualization using an interdisciplinary approach. This interdisciplinary approach is based on *eye tracking data visualization*, *ontology based visualization models*, and *cognitive simulations*. Figure 1 shows the chapter structure, and the interdisciplinary approach we suggest.

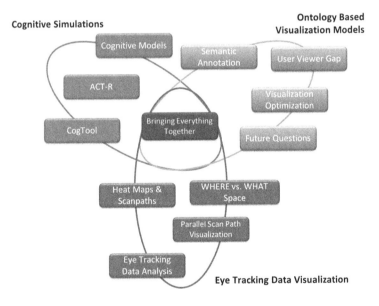

Fig. 1. This chapter presents an interdisciplinary approach to study cognitive ergonomics in visualization based on eye tracking data visualization, ontology-based visualization models, and cognitive simulations.

Many user experiments have been conducted to study perception of visualization techniques. Apart from measuring accuracy rates and completion times, eye

A. Ebert et al. (Eds.): HCIV Workshops 2011, LNCS 8345, pp. 80–94, 2014.
DOI: 10.1007/978-3-642-54894-9_7, © IFIP International Federation for Information Processing 2014

tracking experiments provide an additional technique to evaluate visualizations. Due to eye tracking devices becoming cheaper, eye tracking is a promising approach to study visualization parameters that are relevant for cognitive ergonomics. The results of eye tracking experiments allow researchers to investigate scan paths of eye fixations on the stimulus. Thereby, researchers can measure which areas on the stimulus have been focused on in which order, by which participants, and with how many fixations. Overall, eye tracking metrics allow evaluating cognitive stress by statistically analyzing fixation durations, distributions, and sequences, or cognitive workload by studying changes of pupil size of participants.

Besides using statistical algorithms to compare eye tracking metrics, visualization techniques allow to visually analyze fixation durations, distributions and sequences of several participants at one glance. However, only state of the art visualization techniques are usually used, such as scan path or heat map visualizations (cf. Fig. 2). For this reason, we are motivating readers to develop further visualization techniques for eye tracking data analysis in the first part of this chapter. We will analyze the structure of eye tracking data, and the visual analysis process of eye tracking results from an information visualization pipeline perspective. This systematic approach will help visualization developers to find new visualization techniques for graphical representations of eye tracking data. We will conclude this part with the presentation of the parallel scan path visualization technique which we have developed following this systematic approach.

Today, the development of visualizations is mostly driven by a technical perspective. The main goal of visualization research is to visualize as many data points in real time on high resolution screens as possible. However, there are now tendencies towards a user-centered design of visualizations. The user-centered design takes effects into account such as perception of graphical representations and cognitive workload. The second part of this chapter demonstrates how this user-centered design paradigm can be applied in a visualization scenario. In this scenario we annotate visualizations with semantic information to allow viewers to customize their visualizations.

The discussion of cognitive ergonomics is strongly related to the question if metrics such as fixation durations, distributions, and sequences can be modeled and then be simulated? If this question can be answered positively, the high effort which is required for the preparation, and conduction of eye tracking experiments could be reduced. In the future, interesting visual tasks and visualization parameters could be selected in advance by running a simulated experiment without conducting any experiments with real participants. This approach is mainly inspired by the successful application of cognitive simulations in human computer interaction (HCI) research. The third part of this chapter will give a brief motivation for using cognition simulations to test visualization designs. Therefore, we will discuss interesting aspects of CogTool from HCI, and the cognitive simulation framework ACT-R.

Finally, we will conclude the chapter by bringing together approaches, concepts, and techniques presented in this chapter to formulate a road map to study cognitive ergonomics of visualizations in future work.

1 Eye Tracking Data Visualization

To study the readability, efficiency, and cognitive workload of visualizations, controlled experiments, usability tests, longitudinal studies, heuristic evaluations, or cognitive walkthroughs can be performed [1]. Standard metrics to evaluate visualizations are accuracy rates and completion times. Since the recording of eye movements became easier during the last decade, many user study designers additionally use eye tracking techniques. Eye tracking data provides information about eye movements of a participant during a user experiment. In most cases the participants' fixation positions on the screen, the fixation durations, and the sequence of fixations on the stimulus (in the following scan path) is of interest.

Usually, the goal of eye tracking experiments is to find common eye movement patterns. One approach is to use visualizations which show the eye movements of several participants in an appropriate way to support finding common structures. Classic techniques to do this are heat maps and traditional scan path visualizations (cf. Fig. 2) [2]. Enhancements to these classic techniques have been presented by Aula et al. who developed a non-overlapping scan path visualization technique [3]. Another technique is used by eSeeTrack which combines a time line and a tree-structured visual representation to extract patterns of sequential gaze orderings. Displaying these patterns does not depend on the number of fixations on a scene [4]. If areas of interest are available, transition matrices [5,6] or string editing algorithms can be used [7–9]. A relatively new approach is presented by Andrienko et al. [10]. In their work, the authors discuss the application of visual analytics techniques for the analysis of recorded eye movement data. As a follow-up work, Burch et al. demonstrate how visual analytics techniques can be used to analyze an eye tracking experiment [11].

One example of an eye tracking study in visualization research is the comparison of different types of graph layouts such as radial, orthogonal, and traditional by Burch et al. [12]. Another example is the eye tracking experiment by Huang

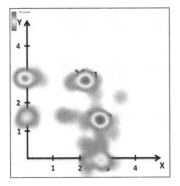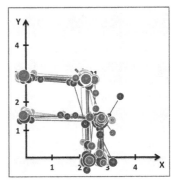

Fig. 2. Most prominent visualization techniques for eye tracking data: Heat maps are time aggregated density based representations (left), scan paths are line based visualizations.

et al. Their results show that graphs are read following a geodesic-path tendency. As a result, links which go towards the target node are more likely to be searched first [13]. Another experiment by Kim et al. investigates the influence of peripheral vision during the perception of visualizations [14].

However, fundamental questions of using eye tracking to test the cognitive ergonomics of visualizations remain. The most important issue about using eye tracking techniques to measure cognitive ergonomics is the question, if the recorded eye movements reflect mental processes, what often is called the "Eye-Mind Hypothesis"? We think, that this question cannot be answered with a definite "yes" or "no", and refer to the literature [15,16]. Our opinion is, that the answer depends on the complexity of the visualization, the visual task and the required mental processes. Another relevant point for visual analysis of eye tracking data is, that scan paths can have completely different shapes for different participants performing the same task. The question of how these different eye movement patterns could be compared with each other is still not sufficiently answered. However, we think that new visualization techniques for eye tracking data can bring benefit to scan path comparison.

In the following sub chapters, we will analyze the structure of eye tracking data from the visualization pipeline perspective to motivate the reader to develop further visualization techniques. In a second sub chapter we will present the parallel scan path visualization technique as a result of this analysis.

1.1   New Visualization Techniques for Eye Tracking Data

The visualization pipeline defines four steps for deriving a graphical representation from raw data. In the original work of Naber and McNabb these four steps are: data analysis, filtering, mapping, and rendering [17]. In the following, we will formulate a concept for developing new visualization techniques for visual eye tracking data analysis.

Step 1: Analysis of Eye Tracking Data
Current eye tracking software systems generate large amounts of data representing the output of eye tracker sensors. The most important types of the data sets are: *various types of timestamps, fixation point information for left/right/both eye(s), pupil size for left and right eye, software meta data.*

Step 2: Filtering
The raw data is filtered depending on research questions which will be answered using the new visualization technique. Usually, usability researchers are interested in: *timestamp of a fixation, fixation coordinates on the screen,* and *validity of this fixation.* Handling a large number of fixations can be impractical. To alleviate this effect, *areas of interest* (AOI) can be defined to group fixations (Fig. 3).

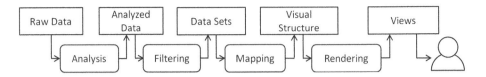

Fig. 3. The visualization pipeline defines four steps for deriving a graphical representation from raw data. We applied the model of the visualization pipeline on eye tracking data to systematically develop our parallel scan path visualization technique.

Step 3: Mapping

The data selection from step two has to be mapped to geometrical shapes. At first, we have to choose a visualization concept. Even though it seems to be too simple, we can visualize eye tracking data with one dimension using a number line. In this visualization scenario one number line could represent the temporal characteristics of this data. If we want to visualize more information about participants' eye movements on a screen, two dimensional diagrams can be used. For example, heat map and scan path visualizations use Cartesian coordinate systems to display the positions of the eye movement elements. We can get inspirations from visualization collections like http://www.visualcomplexity.com or http://infosthetics.com/ to find an adequate visualization technique.

Besides geometrical dimensions of visualizations, colors can indicate additional characteristic of the eye tracking data. Scan paths from different participants can be distinguished using a color table, or can be colored differently when intersecting with areas of interest. Alternatively, interesting characteristics of the eye movements, like high eye movement frequencies, can be displayed using color gradients. Other data dimensions can be mapped to different types of symbols.

Step 4: Rendering

Finally, the filtered and mapped data is rendered to the screen. Thereby, existing rendering libraries for information visualizations can be used.

1.2   Parallel Scan Path Visualization (PSP)

As a result of our analysis we have developed the parallel scan path visualization (PSP) technique [18]. This visualization uses areas of interest. It maps gaze durations and fixations to vertical axes. The top left picture of Fig. 4 shows a sketch of the PSP visualization, where three areas of interest are defined and are mapped to three vertical coordinate axes. The leftmost axis indicates time, starting from the bottom of the diagram with the start time of the eye tracking recording. The orientation of the parallel scan path visualization is arbitrary. In the following we use a vertical time axis from bottom (start of the eye tracking recording) to top (end of the eye tracking recording) as introduced in the original work. The horizontal axis displays all selected areas of interest as independent values. Saccades between areas of interest are indicated with dashed lines. Ascending lines indicate fixations outside given areas of interest.

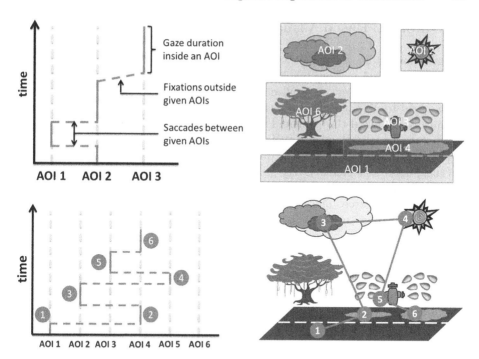

Fig. 4. The PSP visualization maps fixation durations inside areas of interest and single fixations to vertical axes (top left). The leftmost vertical axis indicates time. Thereby, areas of interest (top right) are mapped to vertical coordinate axes in the diagram (bottom left). The corresponding traditional scan path visualization is shown at bottom right. Both the PSP visualization and the traditional scan path visualization show an exemplary scan path for the question "Why is the road wet?".

Key feature of the **parallel scan path visualization (PSP)** is the visualization of eye movements of many participants in a single visualization with a parallel layout containing various levels of detail, such as fixations, gaze durations, eye shift frequencies, and time.

Figure 4 top right shows an example stimulus together with AOIs of an experiment where participants had to answer the question "Why is the road wet?". Figure 4 bottom left shows one fixation sequence using the parallel scan-path visualization, Fig. 4 bottom right the traditional scan path visualization of the same fixation sequence. A fixation sequence could be to first focus on the road (1), then on the puddle (2), on the cloud (3), on the sun (4), and on the fire hydrant (5). Finally, the attention would move to the puddle again (6). Using the PSP visualization changes of participant's attention can be studied by following the fixation sequence line in the visualization.

2   Ontology Based Visualization Models

Visualizations often don't have a unique meaning. They can be interpreted differently by several viewers due to different start conditions of their interpretation, such as cultural or intellectual differences. Also a different context of use can lead to different interpretations of the information which is represented graphically. To avoid these misunderstandings this chapter describes a method to annotate visualizations and their graphical elements with semantic information[1]. We annotate visualizations on two levels: the *visualization concept level* and the *graphical elements*. Every graphical element represents a piece of graphically encoded information. We propose to link every graphical element with a semantic web resource. This concept will allow viewers to customize their visualizations and thus, to close the user viewer gap discussed by Norman [20].

Graphical representations often don't have a unique meaning. This chapter describes a method to avoid these misunderstandings. Therefore, we propose to annotate visualizations on the *visualization concept* level and on the *graphical elements* level. Finally, we will show how this annotation will allow users to individually optimize their visualizations.

Our literature research has shown that one of the most applications of annotated visualizations is to better find graphical elements inside a visualization [21]. Only few approaches deal with the question how semantic annotations can improve the understanding of visualized information. For example, Janeck and Pu show how annotations can be used to find related information about the presented graphics [22]. Other approaches use annotations to allow a semantic filtering [23] or an intelligent zooming [24].

2.1   User Viewer Gap

Norman has described how the designer of a visualization transfers information into a graphical form for the viewer (cf. Fig. 5) [20]. The designer creates a *design model* of the visualization. The user conveys a *user model* from the visualization. This user model is based on the interpretation of the graphical elements, their shapes, colors, and spatial relations. In an ideal case the design model is equivalent to the user model. The designer can achieve this equivalence by paying attention to the task, requirements of the visualization, and by adapting the visualization to the user's skills. A user viewer gap emerges from a deviation from the two mental models of the designer and the viewer. This leads to a misunderstanding of the visualized information.

---

[1] We firstly presented this concept during the workshop "Interaktion und Visualisierung im Daten-Web (IVDW 2011)" (Interaction with and Visualization of Data in the Semantic Web) at the Informatik 2011 conference [19].

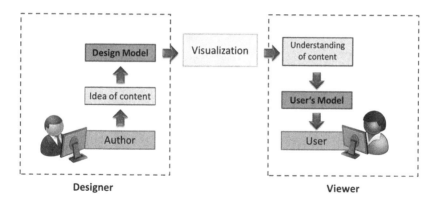

Fig. 5. Different mental models from the visualization designer, and the visualization viewer can lead to misunderstandings of the visualized information.

2.2 Interaction Model for a User Centered Visualization Optimization

We propose to use resources from domain ontologies, and resources from graphical ontologies of the semantic web for the semantic annotation of the visualization concept, and the graphical elements. The designer as well as the viewer both use semantic web resources for the user centered optimization. The annotation with domain ontological information describes the meaning of the graphical elements. References to graphical ontologies define the restrictions and dependencies of the properties of graphical elements, and of the visualization concept. Graphical ontologies allow the designer and the viewer to find alternative graphical elements with the same meaning which can replace an existing graphical element in a visualization. The interaction model is divided into two parts, one for the visualization designer and one for the visualization viewer.

Visualization Designer
The visualization designer annotates both graphical elements and the visualization concept with resources from domain ontologies and resources from graphic ontologies (cf. Fig. 6 left side). Every graphical element is assigned one or more URIs (Unified Resource Identifier).

Visualization Viewer
The visualization viewer can explore the visualization using the assigned annotations (cf. Fig. 6 right side). The viewer can replace graphical elements or change the visualization concept. Dependencies and restrictions of the ontologies guarantee a simultaneous persistence of the meaning of the visualization and its graphical elements.

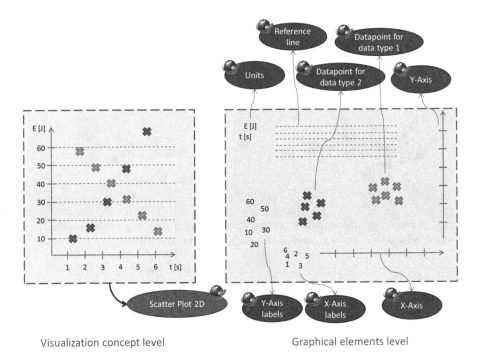

Visualization concept level   Graphical elements level

Fig. 6. We propose to annotated visualizations on two levels: the *visualization concept level* (left) and the *graphical elements* level (right).

2.3   Future Questions

The annotation concept seems to be very simple and useful. However, we identified the following questions for future work during the implementation of our prototype that are crucial for a successful implementation of the concept:

– As described in Sect. 1.1 the visualization process can systematically be divided up into several steps. The last step of every visualization presentation is the rendering step. Thereby, the rendering is always based on parameters such as the geometrical layout, shapes, and colors from the steps before. These parameters are defined by the visualization designer. During the implementation we asked ourself how a renderer which is based on semantic information could look like? What are important input parameters from the semantic models to the renderer algorithms? How can a visualization layout be described in a semantic model?

– We developed a WIMP (Windows, Icons, Menus and Pointer) prototype, where different visualization concepts and graphical elements could be chosen via pull down menus. Due to that, the prototype provided a very simple interaction concept, the question remains how more powerful HCI concepts can be used to improve the user center optimization of visualizations?

- One important drawback of our ontology based concept is, that there does not exist a well defined comprehensive ontology for visualizations and their graphical elements. How could an ontology look like? What are important semantic elements of a visualization? What are their relations? One starting point could be the VISO ontology [25].
- And finally, what are other possible applications of semantic annotated visualizations?

3 Cognitive Simulations

Cognitive simulation frameworks provide a promising simulation technique to study formalized cognitive processes during the perception of visualizations. In general, cognitive scientists who are using cognitive simulations aim at using results of psychological experiments to develop models for mental processes which are processes by these simulation frameworks. Cognitive simulations are used to model a wide field of human behavior from problem solving, planning, learning, knowledge representation over natural language processing, perception, expert systems, psychological modeling, to robotics, and human computer interaction. This section motivates using the simulation framework ACT-R in visualization research to model visual search, and the perception of graphics. This section concludes with a brief presentation of results from the successful application of ACT-R in the HCI simulation tool CogTool.

> This section presents the basic concept of the cognition simulation framework ACT-R and motivates for using this framework to study aspects of cognitive ergonomics in visualization.

3.1 Brief Introduction to the Adaptive Control of Thought-Rational Simulation Framework (ACT-R)

ACT-R is a modular cognitive architecture, using a production system to operate on symbolic representations of declarative memory[2] [26]. In its core the ACT-R system comes with a visual module for the identification of objects in the visual field, a manual module for hand control, a declarative module for retrieving information from the memory, and an intentional module for the current action goals and intentions. All modules are coordinated through a central production system, which can respond to a limited amount of information in the buffers of the visual, manual, declarative, or goal module. This central production system can recognize patterns in these buffers, and make changes to theses buffers. The buffers form one of the fundamental parts of the ACT-R framework, and are noted to cortical regions.

---

[2] ACT-R is available at http://act-r.psy.cmu.edu/ together with a large number of articles, conference papers, examples, and the programming documentation.

The ACT-R architecture divides knowledge up into two categories: *declarative knowledge* and *procedural knowledge*. The declarative knowledge represents factual knowledge. For example, declarative knowledge describes what the parts of a bicycle are. Declarative knowledge is processed with so called *chunks*. The procedural knowledge describes actions, for example how parts of a bicycle have to be used in order to drive it. Procedural knowledge is describe by *production rules*. Pattern matching algorithms allow the production system to find appropriate production rules for declarative knowledge chunks in the retrieval buffer considering a given *goal* in the goal buffer.

The framework is mainly written in a LISP dialect, and uses several modules which represent different brain areas. The modules are connected via buffers. Information between the modules is exchanged trough these buffers. ACT-R uses several metrics to measure cognitive activities. These metrics allow the comparison of the simulation results with results from psychological experiments or fMRI images. A comfortable graphical user interface allows to set up all simulation parameters, and to view the simulation results.

Additional to the built-in visual module of ACT-R Salvucci et al. have developed the "Eye Movements and Movement of Attention" (EMMA) module [27]. This ACT-R module is used to calculate fixation positions during processing a visual search task. EMMA extends the built-in visual module by taking into account effects of fixation frequencies and foveal eccentricity when encoding visual objects. EMMA can predict timings and positions of when and where eyes move, and hence serves to relate high-level cognitive processes with low-level eye movement behavior.

3.2   CogTool - Simulation of Human Computer Interaction

Besides the application to model basic intelligent capabilities, cognitive simulation frameworks are used as a basis to model human computer interaction. One example of a tool which models human computer interaction processes is *CogTool*[3] which is based on ACT-R [28]. CogTool provides a framework to design user interface prototypes, and to test their usability. Thereby, CogTool models the execution of prescribed human computer interaction steps, and presents simulation detail results such as timings for vision processes, eye movements, cognition, and manual actions such as hand movements (cf. Fig. 7).

CogTool describes the graphical user interface of applications by *frames* which are views of an application (this could be a dialogue or a complete window). Changes between different frames are called *transitions* which describe interactions leading to a transition. Standard transitions are keystrokes or mouse actions. Therefore, CogTool uses an enhanced keystroke level model (KLM) [29]. Perception and visual search is modeled via EMMA. CogTool provides operators for eye movement preparation, eye movement execution, vision encoding, system

---

[3] CogTool is an open source project released under LGPL. Executables, documentary, examples, and source code is available at: http://cogtool.hcii.cs.cmu.edu/.

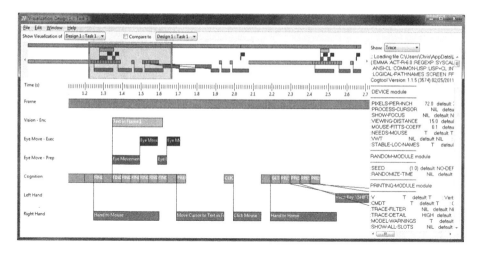

Fig. 7. CogTool visualizes interaction tasks in a time line diagram. Each row of the time line diagram represents a category of perceptual, cognitive, or motor activity such as vision, eye movement preparation, eye movement execution, cognition, and motor activities of the hands.

wait, cognition, key presses, cursor moves, mouse clicks, and simple hand movements. These operators are lined up in parallel. For example, the user can move the mouse and can think in parallel. The computation of the duration times of the single operators is done via ACT-R. Thus, duration times are not fix like in the KLM model. They can be different depending on their point in time during the interaction process.

4   Bringing Everything Together - Roadmap to Study Cognitive Ergonomics of Visualization

In contrast to HCI, modeling of visual search strategies is not yet a widespread tool for evaluating visualization with respect to their cognitive ergonomics. Analogue to arguments in HCI research by John et al. [28], we believe that the cost of constructing models of visual tasks, even simple ones, is perceived to be too high to justify the advantages of modeling visualization tasks.

We think that by combining results from eye tracking data analysis, semantic models, and cognitive simulation frameworks the cost of constructing cognitive models and running simulations of visualization perception can be reduced.

Once valid models are available the overall effort for conducting user experiments can be reduced by running simulated pre-studies. To reach this goal, we propose to develop a simulation tool similar to CogTool in visualization research. Figure 8 shows a sketch of how the three presented topics can be combined. Eye tracking is used to analyze scan paths from user studies. This analysis is done both with respect to the fixation distribution on the screen (*WHERE space*) and

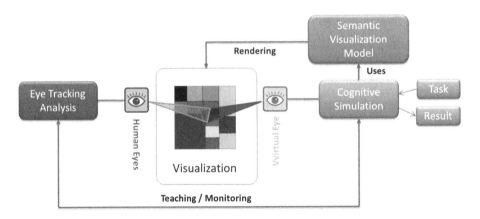

Fig. 8. We propose to use results of eye tracking experiments in the *WHERE* and *WHAT* space to formulate cognitive models for simulating visual search strategies.

with respect to the semantic structure of the scan paths (*WHAT space*). The analysis in both spaces leads to results in two different directions: first, time durations of different visual tasks, and common visual search strategy patterns of participants; second, a model for knowledge processing of visual elements by the temporal order of focused semantic entities, their relations, and meanings. Based on these two results, ACT-R or other cognition simulation frameworks can be used to simulate cognitive and perceptual processes that lead to visual search strategies.

> We propose to use results of eye tracking experiments in the *WHERE* and *WHAT* space to formulate cognitive models for simulating visual search strategies. These simulations will lead to a better understanding of visualization parameters leading to optimize cognitive ergonomics of visualizations.

We conclude this chapter with the following remarks and questions formulating a road map to study parameters of cognitive ergonomics in visualization:

1. Most visualization techniques as well as the parallel scan path visualization technique allow to analyze eye movements in the WHERE space; they graphically represent participants' scan paths on the screen. We proposed to annotate graphical elements of a visualization with semantic information. Using this annotation the "WHAT" space of scan paths can be studied.
2. To study the WHAT space, a sufficient visualization technique of semantic attention, and declarative knowledge processing has to be developed.
3. We proposed to use results from eye tracking experiments in the WHAT and WHERE space to formulate both a cognitive model of visualization perception, and to simulate visual search strategies. How could such a model look like? What are the development strategies for such as model? Would it be

based on a KLM approach with operators [29] or on a declarative knowledge processing simulation? Would it be possible to combine both approaches?

Acknowledgements. We would like to thank our students for their contribution: Tanja Agapkin, Christoph Bergmann, Xuemei Chen, Alex Duscheck, Christian Dittrich, Tobias Eikmeier, Stephan Engelhardt, Dominik Herr, Paul Hummel, Michael Kircher, Andreas Neupert, Hannes Pfannkuch, Sven Plohmer, Nico Ploner, Edwin Püttman, Oliver Schmidtmer, and Stefan Strohmaier (in alphabetical order).

References

1. Tory, M., Staub-French, S.: Qualitative analysis of visualization: a building design field study. In: Proceedings of the 2008 Workshop on BEyond Time and Errors: Novel evaLuation Methods for Information Visualization, pp. 1–8 (2008)
2. Spakov, O., Miniotas, D.: Visualization of eye gaze data using heat maps. Electron. Electr. Eng./Elektronika ir Elektrotechnika 2(74), 55–58 (2007)
3. Aula, A., Majaranta, P., Räihä, K.-J.: Eye-tracking reveals the personal styles for search result evaluation. In: Costabile, M.F., Paternó, F. (eds.) INTERACT 2005. LNCS, vol. 3585, pp. 1058–61. Springer, Heidelberg (2005)
4. Tsang, H.Y., Tory, M., Swindells, C.: Eseetrack-visualizing sequential fixation patterns. IEEE Trans. Visual Comput. Graph. 16(6), 953–62 (2010)
5. Ponsoda, V., Scott, D., Findlay, J.M.: A probability vector and transition matrix analysis of eye movements during visual search. Acta Psychol. 88(2), 167–85 (1995)
6. Goldberg, J.H., Kotval, X.P.: Computer interface evaluation using eye movements: methods and constructs. Int. J. Ind. Ergon. 24(6), 631–45 (1999)
7. Privitera, C.M., Stark, L.W.: Algorithms for defining visual regions-of-interest: comparison with eye fixations. IEEE Trans. Pattern Anal. Mach. Intell. 22(9), 970–82 (2000)
8. Duchowski, A.T., Driver, J., Jolaoso, S., Tan, W., Ramey, B.N., Robbins, A.: Scanpath comparison revisited. In: Proceedings of the 2010 Symposium on Eye-Tracking Research and Applications (ETRA), pp. 219–226 (2010)
9. Heminghous, J., Duchowski, A.T.: iComp: a tool for scanpath visualization and comparison. In: Proceedings of the 3rd Symposium on Applied Perception in Graphics and Visualization, pp. 152–152 (2006)
10. Andrienko, G.L., Andrienko, N.V., Burch, M., Weiskopf, D.: Visual analytics methodology for eye movement studies. IEEE Trans. Vis. Comput. Graph. 18(12), 2889–98 (2012)
11. Burch, M., Andrienko, G.L., Andrienko, N.V., Höferlin, M., Raschke, M., Weiskopf, D.: Visual task solution strategies in tree diagrams. In: Proceedings of IEEE PacificVIS 2013, pp. 169–176 (2013)
12. Burch, M., Konevtsova, N., Heinrich, J., Höferlin, M., Weiskopf, D.: Evaluation of traditional, orthogonal, and radial tree diagrams by an eye tracking study. IEEE Trans. Vis. Comput. Graph. 17(12), 2440–8 (2011)
13. Huang, W., Eades, P., Seok-Hee, H.: A graph reading behavior: geodesic-path tendency. In: Proceedings IEEE PacificVIS 2009, pp. 137–144 (2009)
14. Sung-Hee, K., Zhihua, D., Hanjun, X., Upatising, B., Yi, J.S.: Does an eye tracker tell the truth about visualizations?: findings while investigating visualizations for decision making. IEEE Trans. Vis. Comput. Graph. 18(12), 2421–30 (2012)

15. Just, M.A., Carpenter, P.A.: A theory of reading: from eye fixations to comprehension. Psychol. Rev. **4**(87), 329 (1980)

16. Anderson, J.R., Bothell, D., Douglass, S.: Eye movements do not reflect retrieval processes. Psychol. Sci. **15**(4), 225–31 (2004)

17. Haber, R., McNabb, D.A.: Visualization idioms: a conceptual model for scientific visualization systems. In: Nielson, G.M., Shriver, B., Rosenblum, L. (eds.) Visualization in Scientific Computing, pp. 74–93. IEEE Computer Society Press, Los Alamitos (1990)

18. Raschke, M., Xuemei, C., Ertl, T.: Parallel scan-path visualization. In: Proceedings of the 2012 Symposium on Eye-Tracking Research and Applications (ETRA), pp. 165–168 (2012)

19. Raschke, M., Heim, P., Ertl, T.: Interaktive verständnisorientierte Optimierung von semantisch-annotierten Visualisierungen. INFORMATIK 2011: Informatik schafft Communities; 41. Jahrestagung der Gesellschaft für Informatik e.V. (GI) (2011)

20. Norman, D.: Some observations on mental models. In: Gentner, D., Stevens, A.L. (eds.) Mental Models, pp. 7–14. Lawrence Erlbaum Associates, Hillsdale (1983)

21. Ferecatu, M., Boujemaa, N., Crucianu, M.: Semantic interactive image retrieval combining visual and conceptual content description. Multimedia Syst. **13**(5–6), 309–22 (2008)

22. Janecek, P., Pu, P.: Searching with semantics: an interactive visualization technique for exploring an annotated image collection. In: Meersman, R. (ed.) OTM-WS 2003. LNCS, vol. 2889, pp. 185–96. Springer, Heidelberg (2003)

23. Kalogerakis, E., Moumoutzis, N. Christodoulakis, S.: Coupling ontologies with graphics content for knowledge driven visualization. In: Proceedings of the IEEE Virtual Reality Conference (IEEE VR'06), pp. 43–50 (2006)

24. Patel, D., Sture, O., Hauser, H., Giertsen, C., Groller, E.: Knowledge-assisted visualization of seismic data. Comput. Graph. **33**(5), 585–96 (2009)

25. http://www-st.inf.tu-dresden.de/smtvis/blog/. last Accessed 20 Aug 2013

26. Anderson, J.R., Lebiere, C.: The Atomic Components Thought. Lawrence Erlbaum Associates, Hillsdale (1998)

27. Salvucci, D.D.: A model of eye movements and visual attention. In: Proceedings of the Third International Conference on Cognitive Modeling, pp. 252–259 (2000)

28. John, B.E., Prevas, K., Salvucci, D.D., Koedinger, K.: Predictive human performance modeling made easy. In: Proceedings of the SIGCHI Conference on Human Factors in Computing Systems, pp. 455–462 (2004)

29. Card, S.K., Moran, T.P., Newell, A.: The keystroke-level model for user performance time with interactive systems. Commun. ACM **23**, 396–410 (1983)

Perception or Pixels – Designing a Visual World from the User's Point of View

Els Rogier, Gerrit C. van der Veer[(⊠)], Laura Benvenuti,
and Teresa Consiglio

Open University the Netherlands, Heerlen, The Netherlands
gerrit@acm.org

Abstract. User centered design would benefit from a dedicated environment, where the designer can focus on the application domain. Our current main domain is design for adult learning. We show how user centered interaction design may require a flexibility that often is not supported in commercially available digital learning environments. Based on design ideas that emerged during observing our students, supporting their needs for learning resources and our actual teaching we developed prototype learning facilities that fit the "human size".

Introduction: Designers Build Bridges Between Worlds

Designers use their professional expertise to apply it on the domain they are designing for. The next section will elaborate on this for our case. Designers need tools and a design environment, in order to implement their design decisions. If these are not available, designers have to invest in additional types of expertise, or they have to cope with a suboptimal context.

Applying design to the domain of adult and distance learning requires a choice for a design paradigm. Designing electronic learning support may be approached from two sides:

- Choosing or adapting an (existing) learning environment or building one based, based on a general view on what is the best way to support learning (as intended by the "client of design", which could be an educational authority, or the intended the learners). The actual learning content may subsequently be inserted and its presentation format and the related interaction possibilities will have to fit the functionality provided by the environment.
- Analyzing the multiple types of learning activities that the intended learners might want to perform. How to enable or support these will depend on each learner's individual background regarding knowledge in the learning domain, preferences for presentation and interaction, and the actual context of learning that includes location (e.g., at home, in a bus), time available (a day, 10 min), and available resources (books at hand, a peer in the same room). Based on this analysis design patterns may be found or developed that support the activities. In this case the next step will be to identify or develop an electronic learning environment that facilitates the provision of these patterns.

A. Ebert et al. (Eds.): HCIV Workshops 2011, LNCS 8345, pp. 95–123, 2014.
DOI: 10.1007/978-3-642-54894-9_8, © IFIP International Federation for Information Processing 2014

We decided to choose for adaptation to the individual and momentary needs and the learning context of the learners (symbolized by 'perception' in our title, rather than for the application of standard commercially available learning environments and their rigid templates (the 'pixels' in our title). That is what the main section of this chapter is about for our case, where visualizing our design ideas is the main challenge. We will not aim at a complete overview of all possible learning activities and all possible ways of presentation and interaction. We will choose a sample of activities that we often encounter in our teaching practice in the domain of interaction design, and show various ways of supporting them in our practice of blended learning that we discovered useful for our adult students. So far we did not aim at a complete set of guidelines. What we are developing in the first place are design patterns for support of individual learning activities of adult learners in blended learning situations in specific context.

In this chapter we will first discuss the multidisciplinary character of user centered design, followed by a description of our students and the content domain of learning. Next we will discuss the commercially available electronic learning environments that were available in our teaching context.

For our research approach we choose action research. We will argue for this choice and describe the process.

Next we will provide examples of learning activities, and the various ways to support these, that we analyzed, tried, and assessed. Finally we will provide conclusions and point to a research agenda.

User Centered Design is a Multidisciplinary Expertise

User centered design requires theoretical understanding, knowledge of techniques, experience with tools, and general design skills, in the domain of application. If the application is user-system interaction, the domain requires expertise from: Cognitive Psychology, Software Engineering, Industrial/Interaction Design and, depending on the context of use, Cultural Anthropology, Ethnography, or Organizational Design. In an ideal world designing is team work where the team owns all different types of expertise.

Our current case considers the domain of adult learning: we teach our students the various aspects of theory, concepts, tools and techniques of human-centered design, and we ourselves practice the expertise of designing Internet based learning resources. This allows students, independent of location, context, or time, to find and use learning resources. These resources need to optimally fit unpredictable learning situations. Learners might need their learning activities to be supported, context dependent for different types of devices (smart phones, laptops, Wii, wall size screens, e-book-readers [2, 3]) communicating through many different modalities, e.g.:

- The system output to the learner through spoken or readable text (in some cases with voice over), still pictures (2D, 3D), video (sound could be synchronous and authentic to the video, or an expert's comment to the video, or a studio audience's reaction to the video, or a suggested learner's reaction, ...) etc.
- The learner's input to the system through voice, pointing in 2D or 3D, typing and mouse handling, body movements, ...

The current state of technical opportunities that are available for our students mainly consists of some kind of computer (most of the time mobile) with a screen, and internet availability depending on the context. Consequently, we focus on visual design with pointing and gestures and sound as the common available basics.

Learners should be able to interact with these supporting systems in a way that fits the "human size". This includes supporting human ways of reading, scanning, pointing, and a system's way of reacting to learner behavior that is "naturally" perceivable, noticeable, and acceptable. And these aspects require a system behavior that should fit both: human perception, and culturally determined expectations and meaning (of colors, turn taking, location, reading direction, etc.).

Our Students and Their Learning Topics

The students that we have been working with are living in many different countries: Germany, Belgium, Romania, China, Spain, the Netherlands, and Italy. They are all University level students, some in the last phase of a Bachelor, many in a Masters study or even in a post Master curriculum [4, 10, 23].

Their background, or the official label of their curriculum varies between Cognitive psychology, Ergonomics, Computer science, Information sciences, User system interaction, Artificial intelligence, or Architecture and design.

Many are at the age of "traditional" university students, some are adults, often in a University that focuses on adult education. In general, the courses we teach are taken by students who are genuinely interested. Consequently, hardly anybody ends with a "fail", though some (max 10 %) decide to withdraw. From our experience, all our student groups should be considered "adult" as far as learning intention and behavior is concerned.

The names of our courses vary: Cognitive ergonomics, Human information processing, Visual design [14, 28], Service Design [10, 27], Task analysis and task modeling [11], Design for cultural heritage, etc.

In all cases, we provide an introduction to the domain of the course and discuss just a sample of the relevant concepts, techniques or tools, after which we require our students to each study several of the remaining items in these categories, and teach these to each other. After each student presentation we provide a reflection on the presentation, mainly underscoring the good points, and, whenever needed, providing additional information (e.g., things we missed from the student's presentation). We record all presentations, put our own (portioned in 10-minute mini courses) on a dedicated YouTube channel, and provide the students' ones on website that is open only for the current student group. All our courses include as a main part real hands on experience of the approach, the techniques and tools. In each case we ask them to analyze and design for a real live need of a real (local) client in that we carefully select based on size and content of the project and on possibility of the client to be available for the students during the course.

Commercially Available Platforms are Conservative

We teach for students that we cannot supervise "full time", because we are traveling teachers and many of our students are not living close to the location where we happen to deliver our tuition. Our learning situation can be characterized by the concept of "blended learning" where we sometimes have face to face meetings, sometimes teach through the internet, and frequently provide learning opportunities through electronic learning environments.

A blended learning approach combines face to face classroom methods with computer-mediated activities to form an integrated instructional approach. In the past, digital materials have served in a supplementary role, helping to support face to face instruction. For example, a blended approach to a traditional, face to face course might mean that the class meets once per week instead of the usual three-session format. Learning activities that otherwise would have taken place during classroom time can be moved online. There is no consensus on a single agreed-upon definition for blended learning and, in addition, the terms "blended," "hybrid," and "mixed-mode" are used interchangeably in current research literature [25]. Pennsylvania State University defines blended learning as a combination of face to face classroom methods with computer-mediated activities to form an integrated instructional approach [20].

Most of the universities where we provide our courses do in fact have their preferred or prescribed electronic learning environment. We discovered that four rather divers learning environments were regularly used:

- Blackboard [5] – commonly used to provide lecture presentations, exercises for homework, and exams, to upload homework in a dropbox, and to form student discussion groups, and a chat facility can be provided. Streaming video can be added through mashup-modules.
- Elluminate Live [16] – a communication tool that includes integrated voice over IP and teleconferencing, chat, quizzes and polls, and the use of multiple webcams. There are visualization tools and shared whiteboard facilities for uploading documents and controlled sharing of writing rights. The teacher can plan as well as record the meeting.
- Adobe Connect [1] – based on Adobe Flash, this environment supports video meetings where multiple webcams can be used, presentations may be given, and documents can be uploaded and shared with controllable writing rights. Like the previous environment, sessions can be recorded. Different from, Elluminate there is no tool for planning and no requirement to have the teacher fix meeting times in advance, so each participant can enter the environment and work there whenever needed.
- Smartschool [24] – a learning environment that is developed, and extensively used, in Belgium (Flemish) educational institutes. It is mainly focused on administrative management of education and exchange between institutes and teachers, and it contains an electronic learning environment that allows exchange of learning content.

We were supposed to use these and we tried. We found ourselves confronted with rules, requirements, restrictions, and impossibilities that made us stop spoiling our time.

We decided to build our own learning environments, mainly in a Moodle environment, which allows us to provide open access and with a Creative Commons license as well as to use (with appropriate attribution) others' resources under that license. Creative Commons (CC) is a nonprofit organization that enables the sharing and use of creativity and knowledge through free legal tools. The CC copyright licenses provide a simple, standardized way to give the public permission to share and use creative work — on conditions of the user's choice. CC licenses allow easy change of copyright terms from the default of "all rights reserved" to "some rights reserved." Creative Commons licenses are not an alternative to copyright. They work alongside copyright and enable you to modify your copyright terms to best suit your needs [13].

Moodle is a Course Management System (CMS), also known as a Learning Management System (LMS) or a Virtual Learning Environment (VLE). It is a Free web application that educators can use to create effective online learning sites [21].

Action Research

The development of our electronic learning environments is based on growing understanding during practical use. We aim at supporting our students' authentic learning needs.

For our research approach we choose for action research, which, according to the British Open University [9] is characterized as "Any research into practice undertaken by those involved in that practice, with an aim to change and improve it. It is therefore, a process of enquiry by you as a practitioner (an OU tutor in this case) into the effectiveness of your own teaching and your students' learning. Action research is about both 'action' and 'research' and the links between the two. It is quite possible to take action without research or to do research without taking action, but the unique combination of the two is what distinguishes action research from other forms of enquiry."

According to Carr and Kemmis [8] action research is simply a form of self-reflective enquiry undertaken by participants in social situations in order to improve the rationality and justice of their own practices, their understanding of these practices, and the situations in which the practices are carried out. Bogdan and Biklen [7] define action research as the systematic collection of information that is designed to bring about social change.

According to Ferrance [17] there are numerous reasons to choose Action research as the basic paradigm for investigations in practical educational context:

- it allows, and in fact requires a focus on school issue, problem, or area of collective interest;
- it naturally includes a form of teacher professional development;
- it is based on, as well as stimulates, collegial interactions;
- it provides participants the potential to impact school change;
- it is based on reflection on own practice;
- it supports improved communication on the phenomena investigated.

We decided on joining this choice.

Examples

Adult learners might want to perform a multitude of different types of activities. We will in this chapter only describe a sample that illustrates those that are most common in the learning domain that we consider, e.g.:

- Get a definition;
- Get an explanation;
- Get theoretical background material related to a definition;
- Get a well prepared example;
- Construct their own example;
- Practice a skill;
- Attach a personal note to received or constructed material
- Highlight parts of material
- Attach a note to be shared with other learners;
- Attach a note intended to share with a teacher or expert;
- Discuss a topic with one or more others (synchronously or asynchronously).

With our electronic learning environment we intend to support this type of activities. In many cases the activities are to be expected, though we are regularly prompted by our students. Based on our experience in teaching we design support and we provide this during the next course where we expect it would be appreciated. Our observation of the resulting student behavior, the learning results, and the students' comments (unsolicited as well as triggered) teaches use what to keep and what to adapt. That is how we learn. The current chapter provides an overview of work in progress.

For the above illustrative set of basic learning activities that we need to support we will show examples of how to support these. If relevant we also discuss the context for which alternative representations seem to work best.

Example 1. Get a Definition

Students will, and do need definitions of concepts. They will ask for this during face to face lectures, and they turn out to look for them in their electronic learning environment. Depending on the context (being in a quiet home or in a noisy bus) they might prefer a different presentation mode. Figure 1 shows a video capture of a lecture. The definition is visible on the screen where a PowerPoint slide is displayed. The professor is standing next to the screen explaining the definition. We found that students preferred this representation in the learning environment in case they had attended the actual class previously: they reported it helped them to remember and supported a more thorough understanding.

Figure 2 shows and alternative where the definition is presented (silently) in a scrollable text that is followed by a more elaborated explanation of the definition. This kind of representation can be easily accessed from either a regular computer or a (smaller) mobile device. Some students that did not attend an actual class preferred this in order to study in depth and make notes.

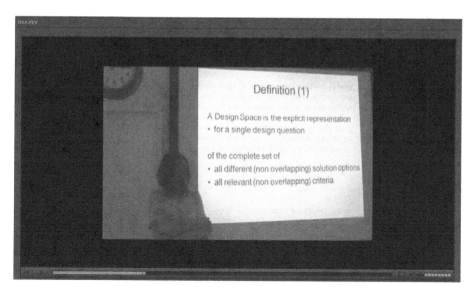

Fig. 1. Definition as given by a teacher using a slide and life discussion

Definition
What is a Design space?

A Design Space is the explicit representation
- for a single design question

of the complete set of
- all different (non overlapping) solution options
- all relevant (non overlapping) criteria.

So it is not a design question about how to solve the big problem, but it is a design question for each separate question where you make a decision about. We represent the design space and we try to find out all the different solutions that we define as different solutions that don't overlap. If there are solutions that do overlap, then you have to be more precise in making it more clear. Suppose you can either choose A or B or A plus B. A+B is different from A and A+B is different from B, this means that we now have three different choices. These are the non-overlapping solutions and then you have to compare all these solutions, taking into account all relevant criteria.
The criteria should also be formulated in such a way that they don't overlap. One criteria might be 'It shouldn't be too expensive'. Another one could be 'It shouldn't take too much time'. Don't make

Fig. 2. Definition followed by explanation, in a scrollable text that fits on PC screens as well as on mobile phones

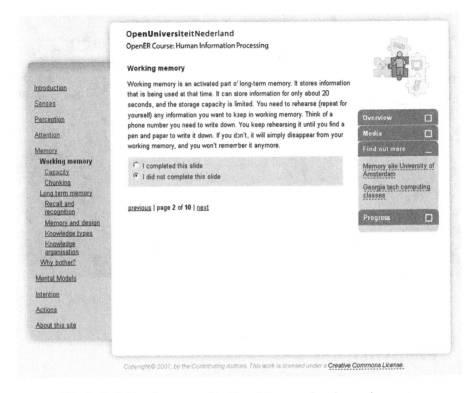

Fig. 3. Definition incorporated inside a full course learning environment.

Figure 3 is from an online course on human information processing [19]. The definition of working memory is displayed within a text. Extra information about the definition is available in different ways: in following pages, as well as in pointers to "external" sources that will pop up in a new window. This visual structure will work best on a laptop or PC screen, though it allows for scattered short learning periods like the other alternatives: a student can mark for each page if he considers he studied this page or not. This pattern is preferred by students who take a course and at their own pace without any face to face meetings. They will often return to the text later and go to additional resources.

Finally, Fig. 4 shows a slide that was used during a face-to-face lecture where the teacher explains in greater detail. The slide does not formally state it as a definition but is one nonetheless. This type of slides can also be used as stand-alone learning material or can be accompanied by voice over. Some students use this to refresh their understanding and in that case, the voice over explanation may provide additional support if needed and if the use of sound is feasible in the actual context.

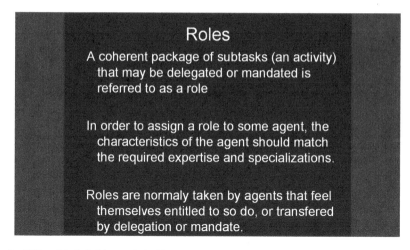

Fig. 4. Slide with definition, originally used in class, and subsequently provided as standalone definition resource with optional voice over explanation

Example 2. Get an Explanation

Explanations, in our learning domain, are mostly about a concept (most of our students in fact appreciate to be able to have both, a definition, and an explanation of concepts that are core in the learning domain), a phenomena, or a tool.

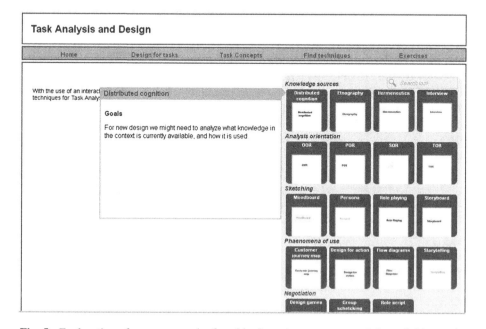

Fig. 5. Explanation of concepts can be found by hovering a concept and then clicking on it.

Figure 5 is a screenshot from a website on task analysis and design [12]. It shows the screen at the moment that the mouse is moved over the square labelled "Distributed cognition", at which event a rectangle pops up that explains the goal for which the labelled tool or technique could be used. Different concepts (tools and techniques for task analysis) are presented on the right side and when hovering over them with the mouse a short explanation is shown. This allows quick scanning a structure of unfamiliar terms, as indicated by the labels that group the concepts: Knowledge sources; Analysis orientation; Sketching; Phenomena of use; and Negotiation. As the structure itself is relevant for comparison and choice, a relatively large part of the screen is needed to display this.

If, after orientation based on the short explanation, a learner wants to learn about the details, a click on the rectangle makes the pop-up screen changes to provide a choice of 5 tabs that allow information to be studied in detail: the type of problem that could be solved by applying the tool or technique; how to apply this; examples of the use; an exercise to trying out; and pointers to more information.

Learners will choose which tab(s) to open depending on how they estimate the information to be relevant for their actual aim in studying the material. If they will come back to a concept later they have different possibilities to refresh their understanding. Re-reading examples might help them most since this refers to application in

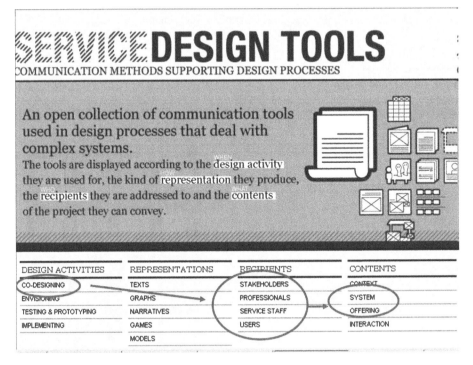

Fig. 6. Slide showing Roberta Tassi's website [22] overlaid with a dynamic visual representation on how to find relevant tools

a realistic case. If this strengthens the applicability for the actual moment, they might subsequently go to the "how" tab that provides them with detailed guidelines.

Tools and techniques, in our domain of interaction design, are never used in isolation. Their applicability in relation to the phase of design, the context, and the type of problem to be solved, need explanation as well. As an example we refer to the open source website created by Tassi [22]. This site is a learning resource for service design, intended to be used stand alone, though we have actually used it extensively in blended learning courses. We discovered it does help learners to explain the system and structure of the tools and techniques in relation to the process and context, as well as to have learners work through an actual design process (designing for a real client). We discovered it makes sense to support the process by providing an explanation of the use of this website, to which end we used a presentation in a face to face session of which Fig. 6 shows the main slide.

This slide in fact combines two layers of explanation: the original representation is taken from the service design tool collection [22], where the text of the main page itself gives an explanation of what the website is about. In our lectures, as well as in our website for each course on service design, we showed this slide that (in dynamic red graphics) highlights and a shortly explains, our suggestion for using the resources in that website. A voice over is an option for the individual student who cannot attend class.

From our online course on Human Information Processing, that is supposed to be studied in a free time schedule and without any contact with a teacher or with peer students, Fig. 7 presents how students get an explanation on why they should bother about perceptions. The explanation is supported by a relevant picture, as it turned out to make the phenomenon much more easy to understand and remember. Learners in general commented that this worked just fine for them. The amount of explanation was considered just enough to understand without any other support or possibilities to discuss with others during the actual reading. Still, for who would ever wants more, we provide a possibility to "find out more" which will bring the learner to additional explanations from sources that differ from the actual lecture.

Example 3. Get Theoretical Background Material Related to a Definition
Even if a definition seems enough (or is considered so in a certain context by a teacher) individual students might well feel a need to know more. Especially in the case of fully stand alone online courses, learners appreciate the possibilities to find additional material which may well stem from other websites.

Figure 8 is a screenshot from the online course of human information processing, where the definition of a concept (Working memory) is provided. The figure shows the screen after the learner just hit the blue box at the right hand side that says "Find out more". At this event, in the blue box there appears a section in which the student can find background links from other locations related to the definition presented on the central stage. In this case these are additional definitions and theoretical background on them from different trusted sources, i.e., from the "Memory" site of the Cognitive Psychology department of the University of Amsterdam, and the Computing classes site of Georgia Tech.

Fig. 7. Explanation with words and a picture

Clicking on these URLs will open a new window that displays the relevant material on those sites. Learners will often first look at what material might be available for further reading and only in a second round come back and go to these resources.

Example 4. Get a Well Prepared Example

Definitions, explanations, and additional pointers, often are not enough for some, or even most, of the learners. Examples allow them to reason about the concept, the phenomenon, or the technique, and try out their understanding by interpretation in practice. In a physical classroom or laboratory, examples may well be samples of the actual phenomenon. Students can be walked through a process (a design, an experiment, the observation of behaviour) and experience the process in real time accompanied by explanations and by questions that trigger understanding. In an electronic environment we may provide a simulation or suggest the experience by a proxy.

Figure 9 is a screenshot from the online course of human information processing. On the right side in the blue box is a section "Try it". This is a well prepared example illustrating the text on the centre stage. In this example the user can do a test that allows to understand the written material better. The phenomenon to be understood is attention, the test in "Try it" is a case where the actual attention is manipulated by the text "you must count how many times this red ball bounces on the 4 sides of the

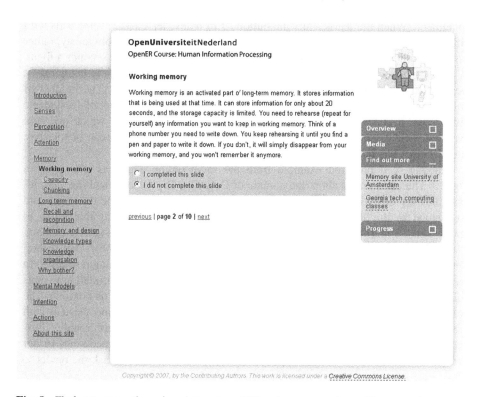

Fig. 8. Find out more through pointers to additional resources that will appear in a new window.

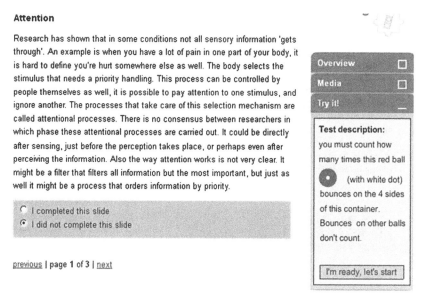

Fig. 9. An example that is experienced as a game, illustrating the issue

container". When the learner hits the button "I'm ready, let's go" several balls with different colours start to bounce along with the red one. That one is, obviously, rather easy to follow and the bounces may be counted. However, after a few seconds a figure of a brown monkey, with the same size as the balls, appears and starts bouncing as well. After the monkey disappears (after 15 s) the test stops in 5 s. The number of bounces is asked and then the learner is asked about the monkey. 9 out of 10 students did not see it at all. Now they are suggested to repeat the test, at which occasion everybody notices the monkey, and they all understand the phenomenon of selective attention that has been discussed in the main page.

Another well prepared example from the same online course is illustrated in Fig. 10. The main text is about the domain of Cognitive Psychology, and the "Try it" examples are developed to show remarkable phenomena that can be described and understood in this domain. The student can do several experiments that allow to understand the reason for going into dept regarding the theoretical part of the domain.

The experiment in this figure illustrates the "Stroop" effect that shows that several dimensions of an incoming stimulus may trigger different and conflicting responses. In the original Stroop test there is a page with individual words that are printed in various colors. The reader has to mention the colors of the words as quickly as possible. The next page contains color names, printed in different colors that are inconsistent with the word. The time needed to name the printing colors suffers considerably, illustrating the effect of conflicting input dimensions on information processing. In our version of the Stroop effect we use only words printed in black, and ask the reader to

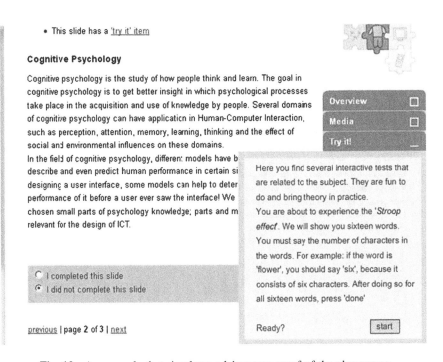

Fig. 10. An example that simulates a laboratory proof of the phenomena

mention the number of letters. Our second page only contains words that label a number ('one', 'two', 'three', 'six', etc.), which allows the learner to experience the same phenomenon without violating copyright rules.

Finally, we present an example of a concept from a visual design pattern collection. Figure 11 shows how a pattern is applied. The example contains pictures, text and links to find out more about the example. The way to browse the pattern examples and to explore the knowledge on them is in fact analogous to the concept explanation pattern that we illustrated in Fig. 5: hovering over the pattern icon reveals only a visual representation of the pattern, clicking on the icon provides the pop-up as shown in Fig. 11 where the learner, by choosing one of the tabs, may find the basics of the visual design pattern; an elaborated example from a real website; the forces in the current design space that would support or discourage the use of this pattern; how the pattern may be applied, and a systematic overview of when and why to apply it.

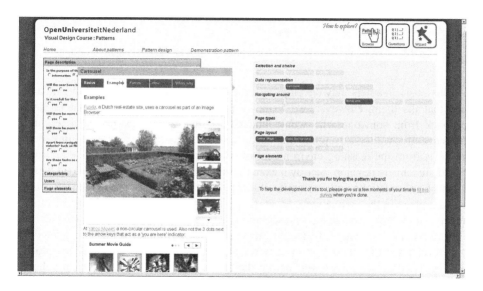

Fig. 11. A visual design pattern example.

Example 5. Construct My Own Example

For many learners the construction of their own example is the ultimate proof of understanding. In this case, some feedback is almost always needed. In courses with face-to-face possibilities, this can be scheduled or provided on request.

Figure 12 shows two pictures that a student made during a course in Italy. The student presented his work to the teacher and other students in a slide presentation. A picture of the prototype that the student designed was drawn in a natural context to explain the new prototype and the changes from the previous design. The first of the student's pictures illustrates how users of a current type of remote control might have problems reading the labels of the multiple buttons and needed time to discover what button to press. The second picture shows a new prototype remote control with only a few (considerably larger and shaped) buttons that would allow quick scanning and quick user action.

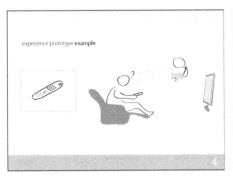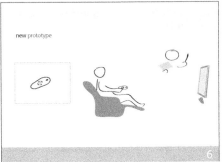

Fig. 12. Two pictures from a student's presentation to show changes in design

Obviously, learners may develop this type of examples wherever they are and any time that fits them. However, we found in practice that they mostly want to have feedback from someone who would understand, like a peer learner or a teacher. Consequently, we try to support this need even for blended learning situations. Figure 13 is from the learning environment of a course on service design. We actually trigger students to develop their own examples and provided facilities to upload these. A list of presentations with examples students made themselves are displayed at the relevant place in the course website. Participants in the course can review how other students in their class made their presentation and view the examples they constructed.

In a recent case where we taught this course, the (Chinese) students triggered a new development for their learning environment, requesting the possibility to upload their intended presentations well before the face-to-face meeting in order to collect feedback from their peers prior to "submitting" it to the teacher's comments.

Example 6. Practice a Skill

Students need, and want, to demonstrate their knowledge. Even though this is not a main goal in any of the courses we teach, nor a main goal of any of the learners that visit our electronic learning environments. A fact, however, is that students differ regarding their competence and we discover they are happy to try themselves and to learn from each other. A teacher may be of help in this case.

In order to aim at systematically improving presentations (whenever needed, depending on the culture and level of the students) we have developed a process of selecting those student presentations that we consider exemplary for the quality, structure, content, or even performance. We publish a short list of "remarkable" presentations and we suggest students to especially consider the video recordings of these and we give each student team in the course the assignment to write a brief report on those selected recordings stating why each of these is excellent.

Fig. 13. Students developed presentations to share with each other, sometimes prior to officially presenting it to the teacher

In the slides in Fig. 14 the exercise is explained. Students are encouraged to learn from each other and therefore are asked to look at good examples of fellow students. On purpose we ask them to view the presentation videos on a small screen, in order to avoid the viewers to focus on content details. We generally experience a striking improvement on the aspects that we aim at and mention in the exercise.

Occasionally students are unable to attend. A student that was unable to physically attend the class on the day of the presentation asked, and received permission, to do his presentation at home in front of a video camera. His presentation was highly rated by his peers as well as by the teacher.

But face-to-face meetings are also taken as an opportunity to practice relevant skills. Figure 15 shows a picture from a Chinese student who really wanted to learn how to present the work he prepared. He developed his own ideas to do so, combining a prepared slide show on the screen with notes and schedules drawn on a flipchart during his presentation. He wanted the presentation to be videotaped so that people could give feedback and allow him to learn from it.

Example 7. Attach a Personal Note to Received or Constructed Material
In our blended learning courses students are frequently asked to upload material.

Students sometimes spontaneously add a personal note uploading their homework. Other students or the teacher who receives this could be triggered to respond to in the same way. Figure 16 shows an example, where both the student and the teacher (that is the one who is answering in this example) need to be aware whether the conversation is private between the two of them, or between a well specified design team, or open for reading as well as reacting by the whole course group. Our learning

10. June 6, example presentations	as announced last week:
in order to prepare your team presentation to the client,	examples are provided to study, from a youtube channel, to be viewed on iPhone, smartphone,
study some examples from your own class, on a smartphone,	so each team should have access to one
and describe what you learned from these.	
presentations to study	**write what you learned**
Federico Cossu – see how he addresses the people in the room	Each team should deliver a 2 page report: for each of these examples:
Antonella Sechi – see how she keeps the room listening, even when reading from notes	• what is the most useful aspect, • why is this good for the final presentation • how can your team use this,
Francesco Frulio – see how he feels free to speak and uses gestures	Deliver the report by email to Selene and Gerrit at June 7, 13:00,
Alessandro Fadda – sheets are well readable	seluras@gmail.com gvv@ou.nl

Fig. 14. Suggested peer presentations to improve presentation skills

Fig. 15. Voluntary trial presentation intended to collect feedback

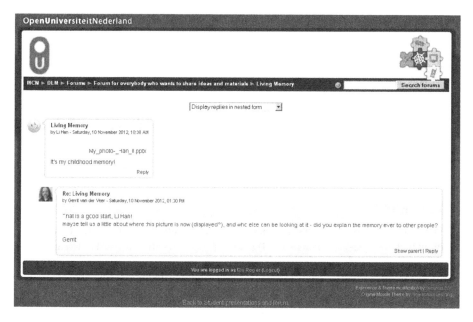

Fig. 16. Personal notes may well be part of a learning environment

environments now allow each of these, and we find in most cases the students choose the "open for the whole class" mode.

Example 8. Highlight Parts of the Material

When learning material has to be structured and the structure is complex, it may often only fit on large screens (laptops, PCs). In that case learners tend to read in their "normal" reading habit – e.g., from left to right and from top to bottom in European and Chinese current cultures. Any complex (e.g. 2D) representations might make the student miss some relevant features.

Figure 17 is an example of a visual pattern wizard [15] for website design. Through different questions the learner may explore what visual patterns could be suitable for the website they are designing. At the left hand students may, first of all, choose for one of four different design space categories, each with multiple variables:

- Page descriptions, which allow, but not enforce, choices between

  - Purpose of the site: information or entertainment?
  - Size of text to read (long or short)?
  - Number of pages of the site (more than 30 pages or not)?
  - Number of pages with actual content (15 or less)?
  - Interaction tasks other than navigation (e.g., form filling, file upload)?
  - Tasks that need a sequence of subtasks?

- Categorisation of the site structure

  - Meaningful sections?
  - Hierarchy of depth more than 2?

- Icons to support categorization?
- Content continuous with categorization?

• User characteristics

- Mainly experienced internet users?
- More than ten events a year interesting for users?
- Desktop only or mobile use as well?
- Are there user polls or review questions to be answered by users?

• Page elements

- Icons used for menus in the pages?
- (Large) tables?
- Photo journals?

Each time a learner answers a question in the left side box, or deletes an answer (which makes the question unanswered) (Fig. 17 top), an arrow towards the right side box dynamically starts to appear and move, and some patterns lighten up (Fig. 17 middle part). After that a back arrow (Fig. 17 bottom) indicates that the changing configuration of feasible patterns is in fact related to the answers of the questions that the user just gave, and which may be revised.

The moving arrows in the previous example turned out to help notice that something new has appeared on the right side as a result of what is going on by the learner's tentative choices at the left.

In the courses that we build ourselves, we may apply any highlighting technique that fits the purpose. However, we will often use relevant and open source available learning recourses if they fit our students' needs. During a course where cultural diversity [26] was an issue, we wanted to explain how to use the website from Hofstede [18] and what kind of information you could find on it. Therefore, in preparing a lecture, the teachers connected live to the website and used these for a demonstration while his screen and his comments were recorded. The mouse pointer is highlighted to allow the viewer to see what elements the teacher is attending to and pointing at. This dynamic representation (Fig. 18) supported learners to follow the teacher's attention and to understand the actual use as demonstrated. Viewing a recorded video capture of the session turned out to be appreciated as well as providing the intended learning.

In a course on design for cultural heritage, pictures are shown of personal item that are considered family heritage. The type of pictures, in this case, do not match well with dynamic visualisation of attention support, and require careful study without disturbance of esthetic aspects. In a discussion on such an item one or more specific parts may need to be considered, like the year 1883, or the name indication MAK (in this case the name of the young women who embroidered this in the indicated year) in the example of Fig. 19. Trying out in practice showed us that the temporary indication of which part we are referring to by using a not confusing shape and color (in this case a red circle) helps to clearly focus attention. When that is reached the attention support can be removed and the meaning of the detail may be discussed, experienced, and appreciated. In this case, dynamics turn out not to be needed (and even to be considered irritating) to draw attention.

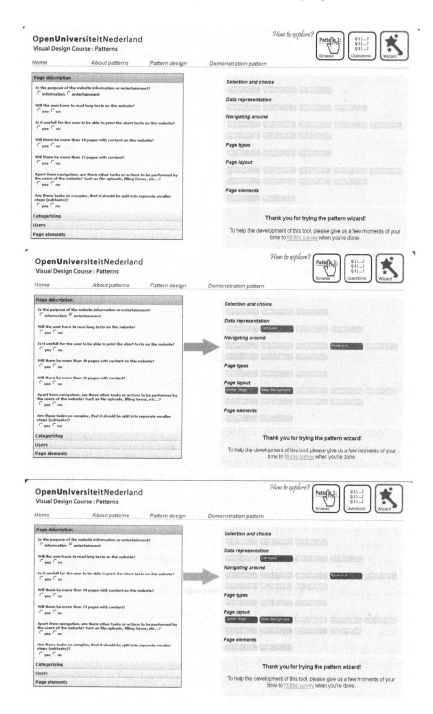

Fig. 17. Successive views of a dynamic support to attention to new information on the right hand side that is the result of checking options at the left.

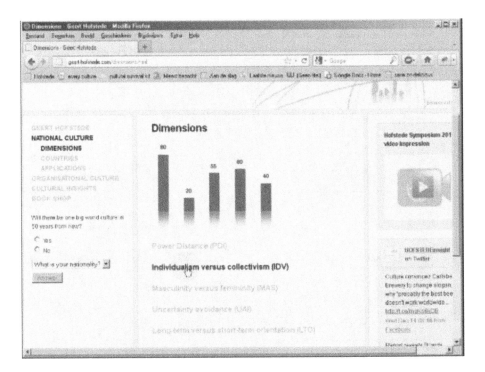

Fig. 18. Dynamic highlighting of the teacher's pointer, combined with a voice over explanation

In our courses there are often various different elements and phenomena that occasionally require attention to be drawn. The previous examples show, respectively, how to support attention to the effect of student actions (as discussed with Fig. 17) and how to focus attention of students to join the teacher's focus. However, there are many situations in electronic learning environments where there are opportunities that learners might miss. Screens often cannot be just plain and simple, and multiple options for interaction need to be provided at the same time. In that case reactions to mouse over may help the learner find out (or remember) there are interaction possibilities available. Figure 20 shows 2 phases from interaction with the design pattern wizard [15] where attention to relevant parts is triggered by dynamic highlighting on mouse over, through a red exclamation mark and a thought cloud.

Example 9. Attach a Note to Be Shared with Other Learners

Sharing ideas with peers is common practice in face-to-face learning situations. In the Moodle learning environment that we often use as a platform for our design there is an option for a learner to share work, ideas and materials with others. The result is posted in a discussion topic. Other students and teachers can read and reply on the message. Obviously, this facility needs to be known and triggered, like Fig. 21 illustrates, where our learning environment administrator fount out there was a need to alert students. She posted a message that started the actual use that was apparently not obvious for a new class of students.

Fig. 19. Simple static way to draw attention to a detail that could easily be missed. After attention has been established, the pointer should be removed to allow acceptable experiencing of the esthetics.

Once students are aware of this functionality they turn out to use it and they want others to receive the message, to react and to collaborate. In fact students in a group will use the board for purely social purposes as well. Figure 22 is a snapshot from the creation of a topic "Pictures" on a discussion board used during a course we gave in China. A student wanted to share pictures taken during the last class with the rest of her classmates. She adds a note telling people what to do in case they cannot open the file. As you may read, the teacher was triggered to react as well, with a personal not to thank for the nice initiative.

Example 10. Attach a Note Intended to Share with Well Defined Others
In some cases our students wanted to be very precise on whom to share their notes with. Sometimes our courses draw over 100 students and in such a case the teacher is supported by tutors, about 1 per 30 students. Tutors support the students in providing facilities, additional learning resources, and when there are communications problems with uploading homework or preparing presentations because English is not the first language of the students. Tutors are available even when the teacher is only present at scheduled times (e.g., Only 2 day during each fortnight). In teaching such relatively large groups, we found out there may well be a wish for several levels of intimacy. Students feel the need to share some communications only with the teacher or tutor; or only between their design team, or between the team and the tutor, or with the whole class.

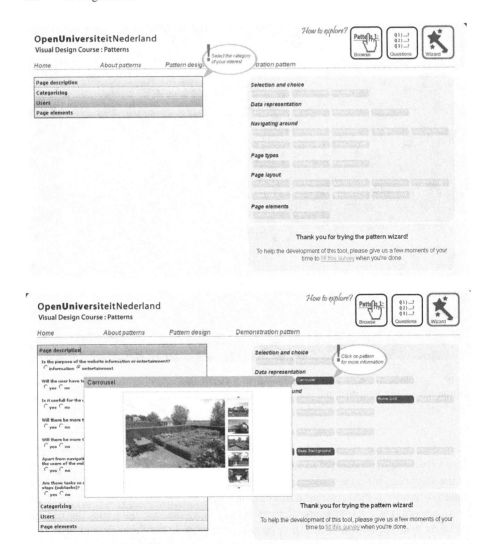

Fig. 20. Dynamic highlighting to draw attention to possibilities

Figure 23 shows a design sketch, not yet implemented, of a web environment for this type of context [6]. The "sticky notes" suggest informal messages the student can choose to keep private or to share. With the create group button, a person or new group of people can be added. In the current example, each student can choose to keep the notes private or make them general or share them with "UtrechtSC", his group of computer science students at the University of Utrecht. Also, the sketch indicates that each note can have a PDF attached, allowing the sharing of documents that have a more formal state compared to a sticky note.

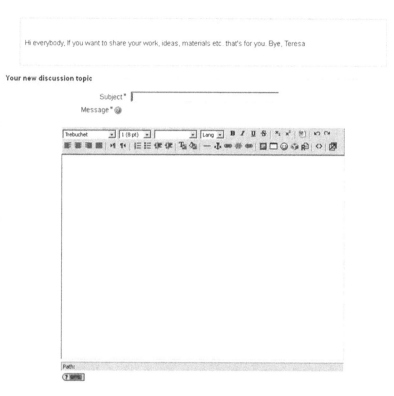

Fig. 21. A triggering message to show students how to upload and share notes

Fig. 22. A personal note and some help in case the zip file cannot be opened

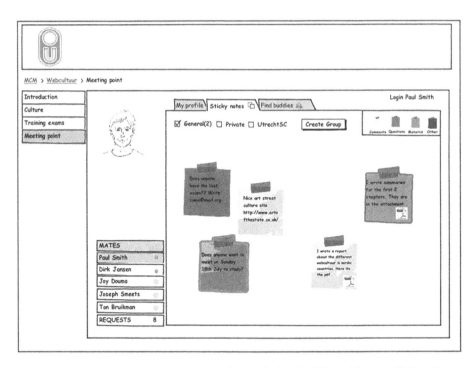

Fig. 23. Prototype (not implemented yet) of note sharing facilities with a specified audience

Fig. 24. A series of discussion topics created by students right after a series of presentations

Example 11. Discuss a Topic with One or More Others
Students often ask for possibilities to discuss issues with their peers beyond the possibilities in the face-to-face meetings. If privacy is not considered an issue (which we found out is clearly culture dependent), Moodle allows acceptable functionality. Figure 24 shows how we are able to provide this in our Moodle based electronic learning environments. On the right side of the screen several discussion topics are listed. Students and teachers can react on these topics or start a new discussion topic.

Design Requires a Supporting Environment
After design follows implementation, for which different types of expertise are needed to implement an actual product or service. A design team should be aware of the characteristics, possibilities and restrictions that the design environment is providing. The current commercially available products that we were supposed to use (e.g., Blackboard, Elluminate, Smartschool, and Adobe Connect) present us with problems. The guiding principles and concepts for visual design in these electronic learning environments are a mismatch to our learner centered didactic approach and to our students' learning objectives. In contrast, open source environments like Moodle offer more flexibility and allow us to develop our own extensions, to profit from the creations of our colleagues and to combine successful ideas. In practice, many educational institutes have yet to learn to trust and rely on open source solutions where an active community is replacing the commercial business model for managing risks.

This means we are confronted with limitations in the visual facilities of digital learning environment that hinder the support of learners in a way that fits the "human size" of this type of user. In many cases the system imposes, by design, restrictions to who is the boss of a screen's real estate: where can we put a question, a video, a button to press, or how can we specify our own animation. On the other hand, most designers of learning support are not eager to focus on pixels and to reinvent a wheel for which they do not have the expertise.

Commercially provided learning environments should be re-developed to allow designers to do their job in a proper way, possibly by freely applying Open Source based solutions. On the other hand, Open Source environments should (be developed to) acquire a state of acceptability for educational institutes that allow both designers and learners access to state of the art solutions.

Conclusions
Our experiences and the ideas we developed are based on supporting blended learning, for adult students in many countries, in the domain of interaction design. Our students are highly motivated and well aware of the restricted opportunities and time available for them.

We base our teaching, as well as the design of our learning environments, on what we learned during teaching. Our adult learners turn out to set their own learning goals. In addition, they are learning in a large and unpredictable variety of contexts and time slots. They will try to learn wherever they can access learning resources, and they choose to aim at learning goals that fit the availability of time.

Our design knowledge is developing during practice; hence we choose action research as our paradigm. Experiments for our type of learners and our type of learning domain are not possible and would not make too much sense.

In order to optimally support learning, we started by identifying learning activities, trying out how to support them, assessing the result in practice as far as practice allows assessment. In many cases the assessment is subjective: students let us know, or do not complain, and if we were lucky half of them answered short questionnaires.

We are in a situation where we are allowed to teach our courses in different settings and different educational cultures in many countries as far apart as Europe and China. This helps us to find out what our growing understanding is worth. Still we are currently in the process of identifying design patterns to support a growing set of learning activities, taking the context (location, available time, opportunities to contact peers and teacher, available hardware and platform) as well as the individual learner's state (educational background, domain knowledge, actual need) into account.

We are working on it. The current chapter provides the examples that help us to consider further research, where we are aware of the need to combine our action research with the experiences of our colleagues, who, hopefully, be as open as we try to be in sharing.

References

1. Adobe Connect. http://www.adone.com/products/adobeconnect.html (2013). Accessed 21 Aug 2013
2. Benvenuti, L., Hennipman, E.J., Oppelaar, E.J., Cruijsberg, B., van der Veer, G.C., Bakker, G.: Experiencing and learning with 3D virtual worlds. In: Spector, J.M., Ifenthaler, D., Isaias, P., Kinshuk, Sampson, D. (eds.) Learning and Instruction in the Digital Age, pp. 191–204. Springer, New York (2010)
3. Benvenuti, L., van der Veer, G.C.: Practice what you preach: experiences with teaching 3D concepts in a virtual world. In: Hai-Jew, S. (ed.) Virtual Immersive and 3D Learning Spaces: Emerging Technologies and Trends, pp. 45–53. IGI-global, Hershey (2011)
4. Benvenuti, L., Rogier, E., van der Veer, G.C.: E-learning in a distance learning curriculum: a workplace approach. In: Proceedings of the European Conference on Cognitive Ergonomics 2012 (ECCE 2012), ACM Digital Library (2012)
5. Blackboard. http://www.blackboard.com (2013). Accessed 21 Aug 2013
6. Blanco, M.M., van der Veer, G.C., Benvenuti, L., Kirschner, P.A.: Design guidelines for self-assessment support for adult academic distance learning. In: Hai-Jew, S. (ed.) Constructing Self-Discovery Learning Spaces Online: Scaffolding and Decision Making Technologies, pp. 169–198. IGI Global, Hershey (2012)
7. Bogdan, R., Biklen, S.K.: Qualitative Research for Education, p. 223. Allyn and Bacon, Boston (1992)
8. Carr, W., Kemmis, S.: Becoming Critical. Education, Knowledge and Action Research. Flamer, Lewes (1986)
9. Coats, M.: Action research, a guide for associate lecturers. Centre for Outcomes-Based Education. Open University, Milton Keynes (2005)
10. Consiglio, T., van der Veer, G.C.: Designing an interactive learning environment for a worldwide distance adult learning community. In: Dittmar, A., Forbrig, P. (eds.) Designing Collaborative Activities - Proceedings of ECCE 2011, pp. 225–228. ACM Digital Library, New York (2011)

11. Consiglio, T., van der Veer G.C., de Moel, N.: Learning resources for task analysis. In: Proceedings of the BCS HCI 2012 Workshops HCI Educators: 1–4, Electronic Workshops in Computing. ewic.bcs.org (2012)
12. Consiglio, T., van der Veer G.C.: Task analysis and design. terconsi.it/taskanalysis/ (2013). Accessed 27 March 2014
13. Creative Commons. http://creativecommons.org/about (2013). Accessed 21 Aug 2013
14. De Moel, N., van der Veer, G.C.: Design pattern based decision support. In: Dittmar, A., Forbrig, P. (eds.) Designing Collaborative Activities - Proceedings of ECCE 2011, pp. 93–96. ACM Digital Library, New York (2011)
15. De Moel, N.: Visual design patterns. patternwizard.nl/pattern/wizard (2013). Accessed 21 Aug 2013
16. Elluminate. http://www.elluminate.com/Services/Training (2013). Accessed 21 Aug 2013
17. Ferrance, E.: Themes in Education. Action Research. LAB, Brown University, Providence (2000)
18. Hofstede, G.: National culture dimensions. geert-hofstede.com/dimensions.html (2013). Accessed 21 Aug 2013
19. Oppelaar, E.J., van der Veer, G.: Human information processing. http://www.opener2.ou.nl/opener/hip (2013). Accessed 21 Aug 2013
20. PennState. http://weblearning.psu.edu/blended-learning-initiative/what_is_blended_learning (2013). Accessed 21 Aug 2013
21. Rice, W.: Moodle 2.0 E-Learning Course Development. Packt Publishing Limited, Birmingham (2011)
22. Tassi, R.: Service design tools, www.servicedesigntools.org/, nc-by-nd cc licence (2009)
23. Rogier, E., van der Veer, G.C.: Designing education for people's understanding and experience. In: Dittmar, A., Forbrig, P. (eds.) Designing Collaborative Activities - Proceedings of ECCE 2011, pp. 229–232. ACM Digital Library, New York (2011)
24. Smartschool. http://www.Smartschool.be (2013). Accessed 21 Aug 2013
25. Torrisi-Steele, G.: This thing called blended learning – a definition and planning approach. Res. Dev. High. Educ. **34**, 360–371 (2011)
26. van der Veer, G.C.: Culture centered design. In: Marti, P., Soro, A., Gamberini, L., Bagnara, S. (eds.) Facing Complexity - Proceedings CHItaly 2011, pp. 7–8. ACM Digital Library, Austin (2011)
27. van der Veer, G.C., Consiglio, T., Benvenuti, L.: Service design - a structure for learning before teaching. In: Marti, P., Soro, A., Gamberini, L., Bagnara, S. (eds.) Facing Complexity - Adjunct Proceedings CHItaly 2011, pp. 144–147. ACM Digital Library, Austin (2011)
28. van der Veer, G.C., Verbruggen, C.: Teaching visual design as a holistic enterprise. In: Ebert, A., Dix, A., Gershon, N.D., Pohl, M. (eds.) HCIV (INTERACT) 2009. LNCS, vol. 6431, pp. 163–172. Springer, Heidelberg (2011)

Patterns in the Clouds - The Effects of Clustered Presentation on Tag Cloud Interaction

Johann Schrammel[1](✉) and Manfred Tscheligi[2]

[1] CURE – Center for Usability Research and Engineering, Vienna, Austria
schrammel@cure.at
[2] ICT&S Center, University of Salzburg, Salzburg, Austria

Abstract. Tag clouds have become a frequently used interaction technique in web-based systems. Recently, different clustered presentation approaches have been suggested to improve usability and utility of tag clouds. In this paper we describe a modified layout strategy for clustered tag clouds and report the findings of an empirical evaluation of automatically clustered tag clouds with 22 participants for both specific and general search tasks. The evaluation showed that automatically clustered presentation performs as well as alphabetic layouts in specific search tasks and that clustered presentation is an improvement over random layout for general search tasks. Clustered tag cloud presentation also was preferred by a majority of users for general search tasks. High quality of the clustering was mentioned as key variable for usefulness of the approach in the qualitative interviews with the users.

Introduction

Since the first introduction of tag clouds different means to further enhance their usefulness have been proposed. Suggestions for modifications were directed towards the utilization of additional display properties for encoding more data dimensions [15], the optimization of the layout algorithms [17], adaptation of sorting strategies (e.g. alphabetically versus importance-based) [13], or the combination of tags with graphical elements [9]. A specifically popular direction of research has been along the lines of clustering and displaying tags along their semantic meaning, and different approaches have been suggested [2, 3, 5].

Only few empirical evaluations exist assessing the expected advantages, and were they are available they did find no or only minor advantages [7, 11]. We think that these rather discouraging results are partly due to shortcomings in the used clustering methods and presentation approaches of semantically clustered tag clouds. Typically the used methods are not optimized for the most relevant tasks and context situations.

Another critical element regarding the usefulness of clustering approaches for use in tag cloud display is the quality of the automatically calculated clusters. Evaluations of human-made clusters based on hand-picked data have shown very promising results for usage of clustered approaches [7]. Results for methods that use automated clustering however have been much less convincing [11]. The quality of the clustering

A. Ebert et al. (Eds.): HCIV Workshops 2011, LNCS 8345, pp. 124–132, 2014.
DOI: 10.1007/978-3-642-54894-9_9, © IFIP International Federation for Information Processing 2014

algorithm and whether the resulting clusters are understandable for humans seem to be of major importance with regard to the usefulness of clustered presentation approaches.

Also, the type of task a user is working on has been shown to be a main influence on whether an interface solution is perceived well by users or not [13]. Therefore in our work we address both specific and general search tasks.

In our work we want to answer the question whether similar results as with hand-made clusters could be achieved with realistic data and state-of-the-art clustering algorithms. We developed a rectangular clustered layout approach and evaluated it in the context of specific and general search tasks. In the next sections we present related work, the study design and the evaluation results.

Related Work

Visual Features of Tag Clouds

The importance of visual features of tags within tag clouds for attention has been researched recently, and results from different authors [1, 10] show that font size, font weight and intensity prove to be the most important variables. Regarding the importance of tag position reported empirical findings are not as concise. Whereas [1] found no influence of tag position other researchers [7, 10, 11] report that tags in the upper-left quadrant receive more attention than tags in the lower-right quadrant. Tag clouds and information seeking tasks.

Sinclair et al. [13] compared the usefulness of tag clouds against search interfaces for general and specific information seeking tasks and concluded that tag clouds are especially useful for non-specific information discovery as they can provide a helpful visual summary of the available contents and its relevance. Similarly, comparing the visualization of search results using tag clouds in contrast to hierarchical textual descriptions Kuo et al. [9] found that users were able to answer overall questions better when using tag clouds. Regarding specific search tasks however both studies showed disadvantages for tag clouds. Using eye tracking data to analyze the effect of introducing search results overview in the form of a tag cloud Gwizdka and Cole [18] found that a results overview in form of a tag cloud helps a user to become faster and more efficient.

Layout of Tag Clouds

Halvey and Keane [4] investigated the effects of different tag cloud and list arrangements comparing the performance for searching specific items. The setup included random and alphabetically ordered lists and tag clouds. Clustered presentation was not part of their setup. They found that respondents were able to more easily and quickly find tags in alphabetical orders (both in lists and clouds).

Rivadeneira et al. [10] compared the recognition of single tags in alphabetical, sequential–frequency (most important tag at the left-upper side), spatially packed (arranged with Feinberg's algorithm, for more information see www.wordle.net) and list-frequency layouts (most important tag at the beginning of a vertical list of tags). Results did not show any significant disparity in recognition of tags. However, respondents could better recognize the overall categories presented when confronted with the vertical list of tags ordered by frequency.

Hearst and Rosner [6] discuss the organization of tag clouds. One important disadvantage of tag cloud layouts they mention is that items with similar meaning may lie far apart, and so meaningful associates may be missed.

Semantic Tag Clouds

Hassan-Montero and Herrero-Solana [5] proposed an algorithm using tag similarity to group and arrange tag clouds. They calculate tag similarity by means of relative co-occurrence between tags. Likewise, Fujimura et al. [3] use the cosine similarity of tag feature vectors (terms and their weight generated from a set of tagged documents) to measure tag similarity. Based on this similarity they calculate a tag layout, where distance between tags represents semantic relatedness. Another very similar approach is proposed by [2].

Semantic approaches have been evaluated recently by different researchers. Schrammel et al. [11, 12] evaluated a semantic layout approach that places related tags together but does not explicitly calculate and present groups of tags. They report that semantic layouts can provide minor advantages, and that it was difficult for users to identify and understand the layout strategy.

Lohmann et al. [7] studied a clustered layout were groups of similar tags were placed together and indicated by border lines and background shading. They report advantages of the clustered layout for general search tasks. However, as they used a manually constructed tag corpus and provide no details on how the clustering was calculated the question remains whether these results can be replicated with realistic data and unsupervised clustering algorithms.

Research Questions

In detail we wanted to answer the questions how automatically clustered tag layouts affects search time, the perception of tag clouds as well as the subjective satisfaction of the users after interacting with the tag clouds both when searching for a specific tag and when performing searches for tags that belong to a specific topic. We compare three layout strategies: alphabetic (the currently most used approach), random (to be able to see if clustered presentation provides any improvement over no structure at all) and automatically clustered.

Study Materials and Participants

Tag Corpora. As a basis for our work we decided to use data from del.icio.us, as this site allows everybody to tag and that the site employs a blind tagging process i.e. the users cannot see which tags where used by other users during the tagging process. In detail our work is based on a large data sample that was downloaded from 'del.icio.us' by Yusef Hassan-Montero, who thankfully provided us with the data. The data originally was collected for research described in detail in [5]. Data was crawled by means of an automatic crawler during October 2005 and contains 218,063 URLs tagged with 242,349 tags by 111,234 users.

Clustering. To calculate tag similarity we used a well proven method known as Jaccard coefficient. Similarity between tags is measured by the intersection divided by the union of the sample set. Based on this similarity measure clusters of tags where calculated using the bisecting k-means approach. For a discussion of different clustering approaches and their pros and cons see Steinbach et al. [14]. The clusters were calculated using the CLUTO-Toolkit provided and described by [8]. Basically the N-dimensional similarity matrix of tags was used as an input for the clustering algorithm. The target number of clusters to calculate was specified as 20. This number was chosen to form clusters of about five tags, which informal pre-test showed to be a good size for clusters.

Tag Selection for Test Content. Six different tag content sets were needed to guarantee that participants worked with a new content set in every condition. To construct the different tag content sets the 600 most useful tags according to the improved selection mechanism described by [5] were chosen from the delicious data set. Tags where then divided into three groups according to their frequency of use. This later one is used to decide on the size of the item in the tag clouds. The three different groups were not of equal size, as this would result in an unaesthetic and inefficient use of tag clouds.

Tag Cloud Composition. Next, each of these three tag collections was divided into groups of six items to form the basis for the different needed tag clouds. Tags where assigned to groups starting from the tags with the highest value for usefulness continuing to the lower values (again based on [5]). Then the tags of these groups were assigned randomly to the six test content sets. With this procedure we could ensure both that (a) all tag clouds have the same number of big, medium and small tags and that (b) the items of the different tag clouds are of similar quality and usefulness.

Tag Cloud Design. In contrast to [5] who place each cluster in a new line or [3] who translate semantic distance into screen distances we decided to keep the typically used rectangular layout of tag clouds. The reason for this approach is its efficiency with regard to screen real estate, and the advantages regarding readability and scanability. Furthermore this design layout eases implementation.

To mark the different clusters color-coding was used: each tag within a cluster was underlined with the same color. To avoid disconnecting clusters spatially in case of line-breaks tags were placed in the tag cloud in a zig-zag-manner (i.e. one line was filled in the normal reading direction left-to-right with tags, and the next from right to left). Clusters were also separated from each other by additional blank space to enhance immediate perceptibility of clusters. The placement approach also reflects the similarity between clusters and not only between tags. Clusters that are placed near

(a)   Alphabetic

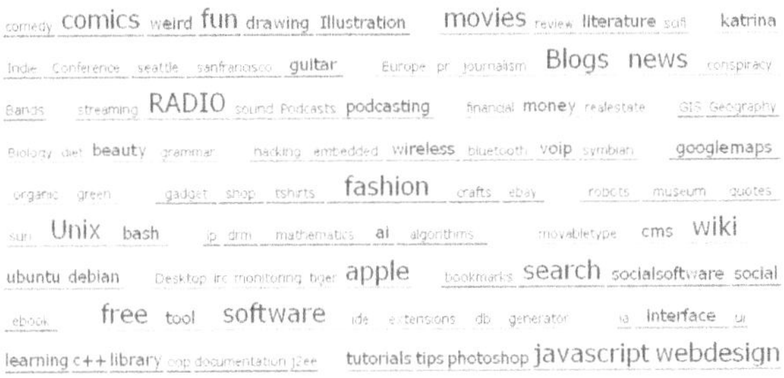

(b)   Clustered

Fig. 1. Example content displayed in alphabetic and clustered layout condition

each other are more similar than clusters with great distance between them. Figure 1(b) shows an example from the set of constructed clustered tag clouds.

Participants. 22 user (17 male, 5 female) participated in the evaluation. Average age of participants was 31.9 years (Min: 25, Max: 53). All of them had normal or corrected to normal vision. All participants had a technical background (because of the used tag corpora from delicious which contains many technical terms) and were intense users of web technologies

Experiment One: Finding Specific Tags

The first experiment was designed to test how clustered tag layout influences search time and subjective evaluation of task difficulty when searching for a specific tag within a tag cloud. The task for the test participants was to find a predefined tag within a tag cloud as fast and accurately as possible.

The tag to be found was shown on the screen, on clicking 'Next' a tag cloud containing the target word appeared on the screen. The target word was also shown below the tag cloud. After locating the target tag participants had to click on it to proceed to the next task. Search time and clicked tag was logged.

For each layout condition twelve search tasks for different targets within the same tag cloud where performed. Target tags where evenly distributed across the three font sizes. We controlled for evenly distributed target position across the four quadrants of the clouds used in each condition, as prior research showed that tag position can have relevant influence [7, 10]. Presentation order of layout during the test procedure was systematically varied to counterbalance possible order effects.

Effects of Tag Cloud Layout on Search Time

Repeated Measures Analysis of Variance showed a significant influence of the layout condition on search time ($F_{2,42} = 61.48$, $p < 0.000$). Post-hoc analysis using paired-samples t-tests with Bonferroni-corrected alpha levels showed that the alphabetic layout is significantly faster than random ($t_{21} = -12.4$, $p < 0.000$) or clustered ($t_{21} = -10.3$, $p < 0.000$) layout. There is no significant difference between random and clustered layout ($t_{21} = 0.0$, $p = 0.33$). Average search times are shown in Table 1 below.

Table 1. Mean search times in seconds for the three layout strategies for specific searches (Experiment One) and general searches (Experiment Two)

	Alphabetic	Clustered	Random
Specific search (Exp. One)	3.7 s	13.3 s	14.6 s
General search (Exp. Two)	18.6 s	17.1 s	22.0 s

Experiment Two: Finding Tags Related to a Specific Topic

In the second part of the study the task of the participants was to find a specific tag that belongs to a pre-defined category. The categories were selected manually by the researchers. Special care was given that only unambiguous categories were used. Table 2 below provides examples of tasks for the selected categories for the tag cloud shown in Fig. 1. All categories were verified by informal testing with colleagues of the authors with regard to their understandability and unambiguousness.

For every tag cloud three categorical search tasks were defined that contained multiple (two or three) relevant tags that were grouped together by the clustering algorithm into one cluster. Similarly, two categorical search tasks were defined that also contained two tags, but where the clustering algorithm had placed these tags into different clusters. Furthermore ten tasks were specified, where only one correct target tag existed. Again special care was given that these target tags where evenly distributed across all quadrants in the alphabetic, random and in the grouped tag cloud layout. Table 2 below shows example tasks for all three task categories.

Table 2. Example tasks for general search in Experiment Two

Category	Task	Solution
Multiple tags in same cluster	City in the USA	Seattle, Sanfrancisco
Multiple tags in different clusters	IT-Enterprise	Sun, apple, ebay
Only one target	Name of a continent	Europe

Effects of Tag Cloud Layout on Search Time

Repeated Measures Analysis of Variance showed a significant influence of the layout condition on search time ($F_{2,42} = 3.37$, $p = 0.044$). Post-hoc analysis using paired-samples t-tests with Bonferroni-corrected alpha levels showed that the clustered layout is significantly faster than the random layout ($t_{21} = 2.6$, $p = 0.017$). Even though mean search time for clustered layout is 1.5 seconds faster than for alphabetic this difference is not statistically significant ($t_{21} = 0.96$, $p = 0.349$). Based on information from the qualitative interviews we think this is due to the very high variation in the data which is caused by cases were test persons did overlook a tag and had to scan the tag cloud for very long time.

User Preferences

After conduction of the experiment users were asked to state their preference for a layout strategy both when searching for a specific tag and when trying to achieve an overview on a web page. All except one participant preferred alphabetic layout for the specific search. For gaining orientation and overview a majority of users preferred the clustered layout (15) over alphabetic (4) or random (3) layout strategies.

Qualitative Comments of Users

After each experiment users were briefly interviewed regarding their subjective impression regarding the clustered presentation approach. The general impression can be summarized as positive. Most participants really liked the approach for orientation tasks and general searches. Almost everyone also mentioned having been irritated and confused by some arbitrary looking clusters or 'wrong' placements of tags. Another negative aspect mentioned was the additional cognitive cost for understanding the meaning of a cluster. Few participants were irritated by the colors used to mark the clusters.

Discussion and Conclusion

Clustered tag cloud layouts seem to have the potential to improve search performance and satisfaction for general search tasks. However, our results (especially from the qualitative interviews) also show that state-of-the-art clustering mechanisms still produce artifacts that are difficult to understand by the users, and that counteract the possible usefulness of the approach. Application of clustered approaches therefore is only recommended in case sufficient quality of the clustering can be ensured. Results for specific searches show - as expected - that clustered presentation is only suited for application contexts were the main goal of the users is to gain an overview, and were searching for specific contents is secondary.

We could show that clustering tags in tag clouds is feasible in realistic settings i.e. using real data and applying state-of-the art clustering algorithms, and produces satisfactory results that are welcomed by users for general searches.

In future we plan to work on tackling the problems arising from suboptimal clusters. We want to explore the effects of only marking clusters with high internal homogeneity, and to use machine learning based categorization approaches to be able to also label found clusters.

References

1. Bateman, S., Gutwin, C., Nacenta, M.: Seeing things in the clouds: the effect of visual features on tag cloud selections. In: Proceedings of Hypertext and Hypermedia 2008, pp. 193–202. ACM Press, New York (2008)
2. Berlocher, I., Lee, K., Kim, K.: TopicRank: bringing insight to users. In: Proceedings of SIGIR 2008, pp. 703–704. ACM Press, New York (2008)
3. Fujimura, K., Fujimura, S., Matsubayashi, T., Yamada, T., Okuda, H.: Topigraphy: visualization for large-scale tag clouds. In: Proceedings of WWW 2008, pp. 1087–1088. ACM Press, New York (2008)
4. Halvey, M.J., Keane, M.T.: An assessment of tag presentation techniques. In: Proceedings of WWW 2007, pp. 1313–1314. ACM Press, New York (2007)
5. Hassan-Montero, Y., Herrero-Solana, V.: Improving tagclouds as visual information retrieval interfaces. In: Proceedings of InfoSciT (2006)
6. Hearst, M.A., Rosner, D.: Tag clouds: data analysis tool or social signaller? In: Proceedings of HICSS (2008)
7. Lohmann, S., Ziegler, J., Tetzlaff, L.: Comparison of tag cloud layouts: task-related performance and visual exploration. In: Gross, T., Gulliksen, J., Kotzé, P., Oestreicher, L., Palanque, P., Prates, R.O., Winckler, M. (eds.) Human-Computer Interaction-INTERACT 2009. LNCS, vol. 5726, pp. 392–404. Springer, Heidelberg (2009)
8. Karypis, G.: CLUTO - a clustering toolkit. Technical Report #02–017, November 2003
9. Kuo, B.Y., Hentrich, T., Good, B.M., Wilkinson, M.D.: Tag clouds for summarizing web search results. In: Proceedings of World Wide Web 2007, pp. 1203–1204. ACM Press, New York (2007)
10. Rivadeneira, A.W., Gruen, D.M., Muller, M.J., Millen, D.R.: Getting our head in the clouds: toward evaluation studies of tagclouds. In: Proceedings of CHI 2007, pp. 995–998. ACM Press, San Jose (2007)
11. Schrammel, J., Leitner, M., Tscheligi, M.: Semantically structured tag clouds: an empirical evaluation of clustered presentation approaches. In: Proceedings of CHI '09, pp. 2037–2040. ACM, New York (2009)
12. Schrammel, J., Deutsch, S., Tscheligi, M.: The visual perception of tag clouds - results from an eye tracking study. In: Proceedings of Human-Computer Interaction - INTERACT 2009, 12th IFIP TC 13 International Conference, Uppsala (2009)
13. Sinclair, J., Cardew-Hall, M.: The folksonomy tag cloud: when is it useful? J. Inf. Sci. **34**(1), 15–29 (2008)
14. Steinbach, M., Karypis, G., Kumar, V.: A comparison of document clustering techniques. In: Grobelnik, M., Mladenic, D., Milic-Frayling, N. (eds.) KDD-2000 Workshop on Text Mining. Boston (2000)

15. Waldner, M., Schrammel, J., Klein, M., Kristjansdottir, K., Unger, D., Tscheligi, M.: FacetClouds: exploring tag clouds for multi-dimensional data. In: Proceedings of the Graphics Interface Conference, pp. 17–24 (2013)
16. Lee, B., Riche, N.H., Karlson, A.K., Carpendale, S.: Sparkclouds: visualizing trends in tag clouds. IEEE Trans. Vis. Comput. Graph. **16**(6), 1182–1189 (2010)
17. Kaser, O., Lemire, D.: Tag-cloud drawing: algorithms for cloud visualization. In: Proceedings of Tagging and Metadata for Social Information Organization (WWW 2007)
18. Gwizdka, J., Cole, M.: Does interactive search results overview help?: an eye tracking study. In: CHI '13 Extended Abstracts on Human Factors in Computing Systems (CHI EA '13). ACM, New York, pp. 1869–1874 (2013)

Building Bridges:
Non-formal Modeling
(ECCE 2011)

Non-formal Techniques for Early Assessment of Design Ideas for Services

Gerrit C. van der Veer[1](✉) and Dhaval Vyas[2]

[1] Open University The Netherlands, Heerlen, The Netherlands
gerrit@acm.org
[2] Queensland University of Technology, Brisbane, Australia

Abstract. Designing systems for multiple stakeholders requires frequent collaboration with multiple stakeholders from the start. In many cases at least some stakeholders lack a professional habit of formal modeling. We report observations from student design teams as well as two case studies, respectively of a prototype for supporting creative communication to design objects, and of stakeholder-involvement in early design. In all observations and case studies we found that non-formal techniques supported strong collaboration resulting in deep understanding of early design ideas, of their value and of the feasibility of solutions.

In Early Stages of User Centered Design Flexibility Is Required

In user centered product design a strong tradition exists of starting from a task model, subsequently developing a detailed design model (often structured along functionality, dialogue, and representation), model based prototyping and evaluation, ending in formal specifications [6].

However, since increasingly design efforts focus on services (i.e., opportunities which often will be new including the context of use), the stakeholders of the new service are unable to precisely formulate and formalize their needs, ideas, and the context of the envisioned service [8]. Sommerville [4] points to the need of flexible requirements elicitation techniques, both for single user type situations in the phase of feasibility study, and for the current service context: stakeholders often do not know what they need, do not agree, and requirements change during the analysis.

Sommerville's elicitation techniques are viewpoint oriented, but the problem is how to identify future viewpoints. Stakeholders most of the time are not able to be explicit on what they need in relation to a new system that will change the context of use. Moreover, stakeholders often have different roles that result in different points of view on the requirements for a new system. And as soon as the concepts of a new system develop requirements change.

Ethnography alone does not work since any design aims at a new system that will be different from the existing system and which will change the structure of the related community of practice. In addition, we need to consider that not only the requirements but also the context will change through putting the novel services in practice. An obvious solution is the use of scenarios to envision, in collaboration with the stakeholders, how a new system may be used in practice.

A. Ebert et al. (Eds.): HCIV Workshops 2011, LNCS 8345, pp. 135–149, 2014.
DOI: 10.1007/978-3-642-54894-9_10, © IFIP International Federation for Information Processing 2014

Designers use their professional expertise to apply it on the domain they are designing for. Designers need tools and a design environment, in order to implement their design decisions. If these are not available, designers have to invest in additional types of expertise, or they have to cope with a suboptimal context. And all the time they need to communicate, with their colleagues in a design team and with stakeholders. Visualizing design ideas often is a main challenge. Keeping track of ideas, both for the individual designer and for the team, is another. Finally, when communicating with stakeholders, these need to be supported to understand, as well as to contribute their own ideas too.

That is what the last section of this paper is about. IT supported services are new, and in many cases are meant to be new, stakeholders will only have vague ideas if at all, and mostly have no clue about other stakeholders, about differences in context and culture, nor about relevant functionality and opportunities. The traditional and well grounded tools and techniques are not sufficient for this emerging domain of design.

We will illustrate our observations and emerging approach by providing illustrations from ethnographic studies of design practice in academic design contexts, after which we will discuss two case studies in design education where we were able to introduce some new elements in the situation and to observe and analyze (again, in an ethnographic way) the outcomes, featuring: (1) co-design merging ethnography with rough prototyping; and (2) bootstrapping service design techniques in collaboration with stakeholders.

Ethnographic Impressions of Student Design Practices

We will first illustrate some observations from a series of ethnographic studies reported in [7] that triggered our interventions in the case studies that will be discussed below. We had the opportunity to observe work in progress in several industrial design studios in polytechnics and to follow projects of design students. Observations 1–5 are from two different Industrial Design Departments in Dutch Polytechnics (in total 6 teams of 3–5 students).

These students worked in teams, as was required by their supervisors, and as seems standard in current industrial design practice. Their teachers did not stress specific design methods or the use of specific tools and techniques. In almost all cases it was the final design and the story told with it that was subject to assessment, quite similar to what clients of design tend to look for.

Our focus was on the process, on the techniques and tools applied and on the artifacts and representations created and used during the process. We detected several phenomena that seem "natural" for (student) design studios, which we like to share:

Observation 1. Exploration Utilizes Multiple Media and Multiple Types of Behavior

Students talk, gesture, sketch, and scribble (sometimes most of these at the same time, see Figs. 1 and 2).

Observation 2. The Environment Will Be Dressed to Support

Our designers develop a creative ecology that they need to get inspired. To a certain extend this is personal and kept kind of private (Fig. 3), but there seem a strong need for a shared environment developed and used as a team (Fig. 4).

Fig. 1. Communication through a complex of channels

Fig. 2. Communication using artifacts and gestures

Fig. 3. Private work environment

Fig. 4. Shared team design environment

These environments are for "just be inspired" (Fig. 5) or to create artifacts like personas to share understanding (Fig. 6), and they join each other in adding annotations. Ongoing projects required shared awareness of what has been considered (Figs. 7(a) and (b)). The physical space is used to develop structure, to compare and understand development, and to develop and share visions and concepts.

Fig. 5. Elements in the environment considered to inspire

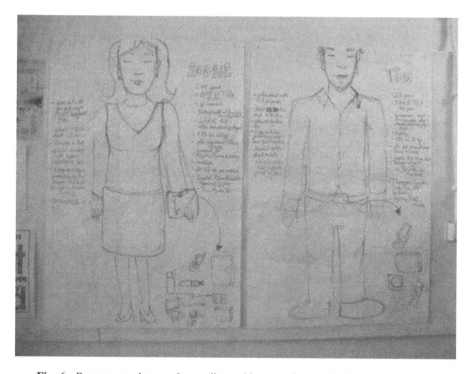

Fig. 6. Personas to share understanding, with annotations added by team members

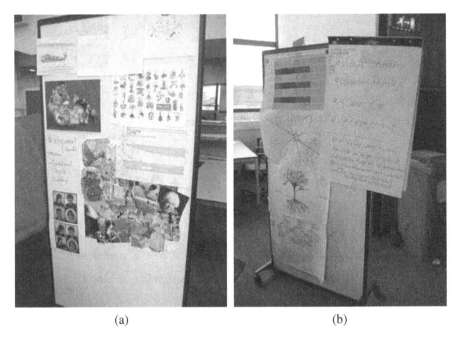

(a)   (b)

Fig. 7. Poster boards created to maintain shared awareness

(a)   (b)

Fig. 8. Spontaneously developed performances to communicate meaning

Observation 3. Communication May Develop into Impromptu Performances
On several occasions we identified communications that went far beyond single gestures, where a performance was staged to communicate the meaning of concepts or interaction with artifacts (Figs. 8(a) and (b)).

(a)   (b)

(c)

Fig. 9. Physical space used create structure; to understand development; and to share inspiration

(a)

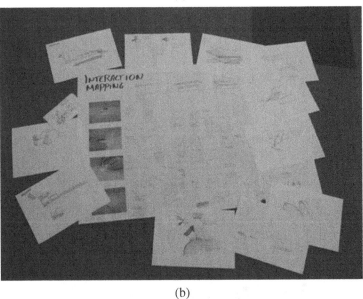

(b)

Fig. 10. Collaborative physical activities to develop shared understanding

Observation 4. The Use of Physical Space

Space is used to develop structure (Fig. 9(a)) by moving artifacts around; to compare and understand development (Fig. 9(b)) by observing physical configurations of representations of a developing concept, and to develop and share inspiration by moving around poster boards with representations (Fig. 9(c)).

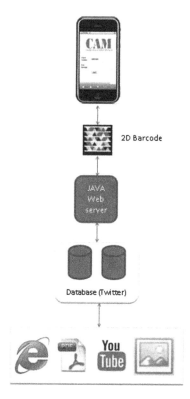

Fig. 11. Architecture of CAM

Observation 5. Physicality of Collaboration

Collaboration often is a physical activity, like group sketching (Fig. 10(a)) or adding and configuring annotations with sticky notes (Fig. 10(b)).

Two Case Studies

In the case studies reported next, we tried to support the design process, by on purpose providing a simple prototype concept that might physically as well as conceptually enrich the design ecology (case study 1) or by pointing to tools and techniques that in fact are supposed to trigger enrichment of the design ecology (case study 2). Case study 1 was performed in a Design faculty in a German University, including 3 design teams of 4 students each. Case study 2 was performed in an Italian University in the Faculty of Architecture and Design, with 5 teams of 3–4 students. In both cases, we never mentioned or hinted at the actual phenomena that we just discussed, we just provided a simple tool, or we just suggested our design students to consider the various tools for their design projects.

Case Study 1: from Ethnography to Prototype Use

Team work is characteristic for industrial design. Teams are often multidisciplinary. Collaboration on design is often not a purely verbal activity. State of the art ICT seems to provide intriguing tools for motivated teams. Based on our prior ethnographic work

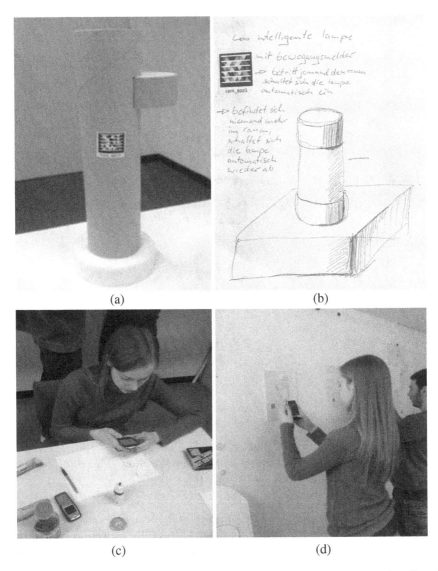

(a)   (b)

(c)   (d)

Fig. 12. Tagged mock-up and sketch; tweeting information to a tagged object; and reading the tweet log of a tagged object.

in design studios and with student design teams [7], we developed a simple tool, CAM (Fig. 11, from [8]).

CAM stands for "cooperative artifact memory". It is in fact a prototype that currently runs on an iPhone. Cam uses 2D barcodes that can be stuck to any physical object, whether 2D (e.g., anything on paper) or 3D (e.g. mockups and physical prototypes). See Figs. 12(a) and (b) where design team members decided to tag their design artifacts. The iPhone can be aimed at a tagged object and the barcode will be read. Each tagged object has its own digital profile on the internet, associated with a

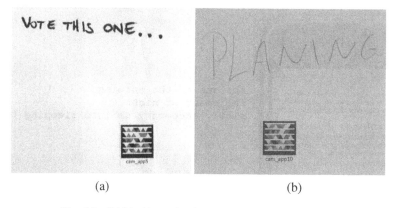

(a)   (b)

Fig. 13. CAM objects for decision making and planning

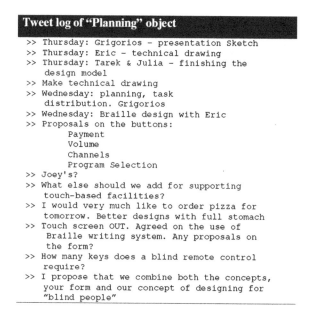

Fig. 14. Tweet log of "planning" object (translated from German. Time runs from below

twitter account. A JAVA web server has been developed to communicate through a Twitter API, to add information to any tagged object by sending a tweet to them (Fig. 12(c)), and to read the tweet log of each object (Fig. 12(d)).

We found three different teams of design students not only tagged and communicated to (a) 3-D mock-ups; (b) sketches, textual descriptions on paper, and combinations of these; but also (c) abstract references, like an empty sheet of paper only marked with, e.g., "vote on this", or "Planning" (Figs. 13(a) and (b)). Subsequently these became related to a history of tweets on votes and opinions about a proposed

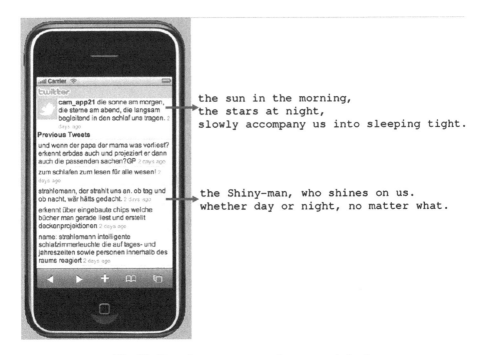

Fig. 15. Two short poems tweeted to a tagged sketch

design decision, resp., a history of tweets regarding a planned process and its actual deviations and updates (Fig. 14).

Another surprising way of using CAM was the opportunity to express emotions and aesthetics: e.g., a sketch for a night lamp triggered several "poems" by different "authors" (originally in German, Fig. 15).

In general, the tryout of CAM learned us that non-formal contributions to design were appreciated and we consider this a potential support for collaboration and shared creativity. Discovering new opportunities and functionality just "happened", though the tool seemed to systematically trigger certain new types of functionality in the design ecology, including abstract reference objects, and a stage for esthetical and emotional creations and performances.

Case Study 2: Bootstrapping Service Design Techniques

When developing a brand new course on service design, there were no course books available, and only a single repository for techniques [5]. Our students, worked in design teams for real clients to develop services with many different types of stakeholders outside the clients' business with clearly different corporate and geographical cultures (e.g., in tourism industry).

We pointed the students to Tassi's repository as well as to Hofstede and Hofstede's website [3] and to the Cultural Survival Kit [1], as well as to design documents from the UK Government and to our visual design pattern wizard [2]. We additionally introduced them to the design approach by Tassi [5].

Fig. 16. Co-design with stakeholders

Fig. 17. 3-D mock up (rough prototype) presented to, and discussed with, various different stakeholders

We asked our students to study these sources and to teach each other the different techniques and tools. During the design process we challenged them to decide for each phase which of the tools and techniques offered were relevant. The students' progressing projects showed how the various different non-formal techniques were applied to a co-design approach where different types of stakeholders (e.g., hotel owners, tourist information providers, and visitors; see Fig. 16) collaborated in generating ideas, e.g., group sketching. We also found non-formal techniques being applied for assessing concepts before any services were actually implemented, like rough prototyping with 3D mock ups (Fig. 17), unpredicted initiatives that were accepted and actually supported by the stakeholders.

Conclusions

Based on previous ethnographic studies we identified several phenomena of non-formal techniques applied in the early design phases of requirements elicitation, modeling and early assessment: the use of multiple types of communication, the relevance of design ecology, the possibility for impromptu creativity and performance, the use of physical space and the physicality of collaboration.

In two case studies with design students we provided two different potential supports for these phenomena, resp. a prototype system CAM to allow communication through design artifacts, and a set of techniques and tools that might be considered at will and taught by the design students to their peers.

The resulting design processes showed how these interventions spontaneously led to the students' choice of applying these facilities to support or create some of the afore mentioned phenomena.

We did not prove these interventions are the sole cause of the effects observed, but they certainly seem to help in providing a design ecology where the phenomena develop in a natural way, where students as well as stakeholders dare to embark on creative and multimodal behavior, communicate and collaborate on design meaning and create and maintain awareness of the process.

Our observations and case studies concerned University design student teams in several European countries (The Netherlands, Germany, Italy). Because we have experienced teaching Design in several other European countries (Spain, Romania, Belgium) we dare expect the phenomena we observed during ethnography and case studies) are typical for European student design teams. We are currently teaching design in a University in China, which will be an opportunity to validate our understanding for a rather different cultural context. Still, we should also validate our analysis for design outside of the University situation. Ethnographic observations, as well as case studies in industrial design practice will have to be a next step.

References

1. Cultural Survival Kit http://wiki.morevm.org/index.php/Main_Page (2011)
2. de Moel N., van der Veer G.C.: Design pattern based decision support. In: Dittmar, A., Forbrig, P. (eds.) Designing Collaborative Activities - Proceedings of ECCE 2011. ACM Digital Library, pp. 93–96 (2011)

3. Hofstede G., Hofstede G.J.: www.geerthofstede.nl (2011)
4. Sommerville, I.: Integrated requirements engineering: a tutorial. IEEE Softw. **22**(12), 16–23 (2005)
5. Tassi R.: Servicedesigntools. www.servicedesigntools.org/repository (2009). Accessed June 2010
6. Van Welie, M., van der Veer, G.C.: Groupware task analysis. In: Hollnagel, E. (ed.) Handbook of Cognitive Task Design, pp. 447–476. Erlbaum, Inc., Hillsdale (2003)
7. Vyas, D.M., Heylen, D.K.J., Nijholt, A., van der Veer, G.C.: Collaborative practices that support creativity in design. In: Proceedings of the Eleventh European Conference on Computer-Supported Cooperative Work - ECSCW. pp. 151–170, Springer, Berlin (2009)
8. Vyas, D.M., Nijholt, A., Heylen, D.K.J., Kroener A., van der Veer G.C.: Remarkable objects: supporting collaboration in a creative environment. In: Bardram, J. (ed.) 12th ACM International Conference on Ubiquitous Computing, pp. 1–4. ACM, New York (2010)

We Need Non-formal Methods Based on Formal Models in Interaction Design

Andreas Maier and Steffen Hess[✉]

Fraunhofer Institute for Experimental Software Engineering IESE,
Kaiserslautern, Germany
{andreas.maier,steffen.hess}@iese.fraunhofer.de

Abstract. According to our experience, early collaboration with non-expert stakeholders aimed at designing interaction in a user-centered way is mandatory if the goal is a great user experience. We have found that insistence on formal modeling when collaborating with non-experts leads to insufficient results. Therefore, we propose a user-centered approach in order to enable collaboration and communication among expert and non-expert stakeholders. This non-formal approach should be based on a formal model, which also builds the common ground for discussions between all involved project stakeholders.

1 Introduction

1.1 Motivation

Well-designed and usable human-computer interaction (HCI) is a key factor for successful software products. Offering a large number of features is no longer sufficient for achieving success on the market. We observe stronger interest in usability and user experience factors in the decisions people make regarding particular products in the same class of devices (e.g. iPhone vs. other smartphones, iPod vs. other MP3 players). Users expect good usability and want to enjoy a great experience when interacting with the system. But what makes an interaction a great experience? What are the elements of a great HCI? Which dependencies exist between these elements? How do we design such an interaction? These are the questions we want to answer in order to improve the results of interaction design and contribute value to the HCI community. To do so, we developed a formal interaction model, which shows the most important elements of HCI and their dependencies. This model is called MAInEEAC (Model for Accurate Interaction Engineering, Enhancement, Alteration, and Characterization) and is introduced briefly in Sect. 2. Since we are aware of the fact that a model is not applicable to conversations between expert stakeholders and non-expert stakeholders, we also created and use the non-formal interaction design method mConcAppt, which is built on MAInEEAC and tailors HCI elements to the given context in which an HCI is designed. During this article, we refer to experts as experts in terms of software development. After the description

A. Ebert et al. (Eds.): HCIV Workshops 2011, LNCS 8345, pp. 150–164, 2014.
DOI: 10.1007/978-3-642-54894-9_11, © IFIP International Federation for Information Processing 2014

of MAInEEAC, we describe our interaction design method in Sect. 3. Section 4 sums up the advantages of our approach. The article closes with a conclusion and an outlook on future work.

1.2   Our Model-Based Interaction Design Approach

In contrast to purely formal model-based approaches or the strict performance of formal methods, we apply a user-centered design approach [6], which combines the advantages of both formal models and non-formal methods. In this approach, we involve non-expert stakeholders as early as possible, since only potential operators of the system under development know what constitutes a great experience in their context. When non-expert stakeholders are involved, experts use formal models to work effectively and efficiently: Every expert has a formal conceptual model of the target system in mind when designing an interaction [7], in this case a formal model for interaction design. With the help of this model, the experts are aware of every element of HCI and every dependency between elements. In conversations with non-expert stakeholders, the experts are able to ask for all relevant information regarding HCI, trace the development of the HCI, and find conflicting specifications immediately by matching the conceptual model to the non-expert stakeholders mental models of the system [ibid.]. To prevent non-expert stakeholders from being confused, the expert does not show the formal model to them, but only uses it as preparation and for post-processing. With the formal model in mind, the experts can describe a particular HCI on a very detailed level. They can easily show interaction elements and dependencies, can facilitate communication between stakeholders involved in the development process, and close the gap between interaction designers and end users. The non-formal method is used for eliciting, analyzing, and specifying requirements, prototyping HCI according to the elements given by the formal model, and validating the interaction design.

2   MAInEEAC - A Model for Interaction Engineering, Enhancement, Alteration, and Characterization

As the underlying model of our user-centered interaction design approach, we developed MAInEEAC - Model for Accurate Interaction Engineering, Enhancement, Alteration, and Characterization [4]. This model is view-based and currently consists of ten views, six of which we present in detail in this report. These six views are most relevant for this approach and build the formal basis of the non-formal method. The four views we do not describe in this report represent even more details of HCI and are mainly interesting for researchers in this area, currently. They deal with characteristics of users, with the process of information perception and its details, respectively, and with different types of interactions.

2.1   General Overview

Figure 1 gives an overview of the interaction flow as described in MAInEEAC. This basic and coarse overview conforms to the unanimous view on HCI taken by almost every area dealing with HCI. Triggered by an Intention, the Human initiates an action on the Input Interface of the system. The System processes the given input and delivers a system reaction via its Output Interface. The Human again perceives this as a reaction to his Intention and evaluates if the perception is appropriate. In any case, this perception might affect the subsequent Intentions. This short description shows the basic concept of our model. As mentioned above, this view is common sense in the field of HCI. The concepts follow the Gulf Model published by Donald Norman in 1988 [8]. The distinct feature of MAInEEAC is that it is not restricted to the general overview shown in Fig. 1, but shows all aspects in detail as well. It enables the different roles involved in system development to work with only one model. MAInEEAC represents the system in great detail, without being system-centered. In fact, it is interaction-centered, emphasizing the human at the same time. Cognition is not an explicit element in MAInEEAC, but implicitly covered by Perception, which covers the recognition, interpretation, and evaluation of information. Media and Modalities are well-defined distinct elements of HCI, both with an exact meaning: Media are representation forms of information, while Modalities are the concrete usages of human senses to perceive information. The user interface and possible system outputs are decomposed in order to describe HCI in even greater detail. Overall, MAInEEAC enables us to describe an interaction with a system without having to use another model. We decided on using a view-based representation of the model to emphasize certain aspects of HCI. The following sections describe the most important aspects of MAInEEAC, including detailed views on its basic components (human action, system, system action, and interaction).

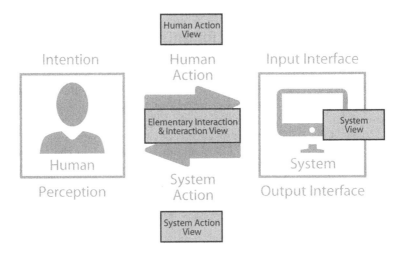

Fig. 1. MAInEEAC - general overview

2.2 System View

The System View describes the system side during HCI (see Fig. 2). MAInEEAC does not treat the System as a black box like many other HCI models do [8,9]. The System components highly influence HCI and thus are shown in the same detail as Human elements and elements of the Interaction itself. In general, we define System as a complex object based on software that fulfills a function by processing input and creating output. Systems in the application area of MAINEEAC might be PCs, industrial machines, handhelds, home appliances, consumer electronics, etc. Each System consists of a number of devices. A Device is a technical aid which acts as interface for transmitting information from human to system and/or from system to human. Furthermore, devices are all parts of the system, no matter if these parts are actually used for the interaction or not (e.g. an electric shutter being controlled with the system). A device acting as Input Interface transmits information from human to system (e.g., keyboard, PC-mouse, touch-screen, microphone, and digitizer), whereas a device acting as Output Interface transmits information from system to human (e.g., screen, loudspeaker, and braille-display). A System communicates with its environment through its User Interface, which presents the aggregation of all Input Interfaces and Output Interfaces. The important fact we show with this distinction between device, input interface and output interface is that input and output might take place on different devices and even at different locations during HCI. Every Input Interface is characterized by the Usage Types it offers. A Usage Type specifies how an Input Interface is used concretely to transmit information to a system (see also Sect. 2.2 for a further clarification). Furthermore, an Input Interface may give Direct Input Feedback which comes straight from the Device without the use of any Medium (for example, the sound that occurs when pressing a button on a mouse or keyboard). When a Device acts as an Output Interface, it gives Application Feedback and might give Indirect Input Feedback in addition. Both are transmitted via a Medium: Indirect Input Feedback is a reaction to the usage of the Input Interface to confirm the systems correct understanding of the

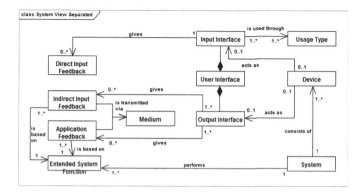

Fig. 2. System view

humans action, for example, highlighting of a selected menu item transmitted via the Medium graphic. It is always based on a System Function. The complete decomposition of system actions and detailed descriptions of each possible system action is represented in Sect. 2.4.

2.3   Human Action View

The Human Action view (see Fig. 3) describes the way the Human accomplishes his Intention on the Input Interface of the System. In MAInEEAC, this accomplishment is called Human Action and involves the whole activity performed by a Human to transmit information to a System. Every activity might be influenced by the Environmental Context in which the activity takes place. For example, the Human might not want to transmit information to the System via speech when he is in a noisy environment or he might want to interact with the System from a distance when his environment is a huge warehouse. The Environmental Context is an attribute of Human Action and thus has to be specified when using MAInEEAC. Each Human Action consists of at least one Action Method, which specifies the action of the Human. It comprises generic human movements according to original human abilities. We distinguish four types of action methods: 1. Fine Motor Skills (e.g., typing, writing, moving an object, pressing an object) 2. Gross Motor Skills (e.g., gesturing, walking, jumping) 3. Facial Expressions (e.g., smiling, grinning, frowning) 4. Vocal Utterances (e.g., speaking, whispering, shouting) Furthermore, a Human Action always has a Method Type, which specifies if the action is uni-methodical or multi-methodical. If there is only one kind of Action Methods, the type is uni-methodical. If there are at least two Action Methods, the Method Type is multi-methodical. When performing the Human Action, every Input Interface features different Usage Types that

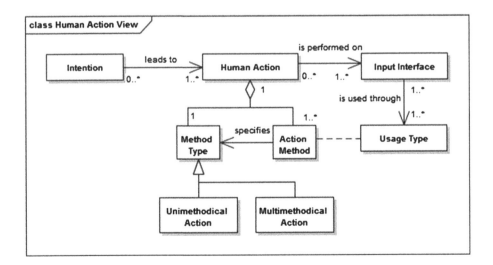

Fig. 3. Human action view

specify how an Input Interface is exactly used to transmit information to the System. For example, pressing object as an Action Method is underspecified. There is a set of concrete movements being performed within a Human Action. It makes a big difference whether one presses the left or the right mouse button or whether someone performs a single or a double click. In addition, the Usage Type concretely specifies the Action Method. For example, if the Usage Type of the Input Interface is single left click, the Action Method is determined as pressing object. When characterizing an interaction with MAInEAAC, the elements Action Method, Usage Type, and Input Interface influence each other. When an Action Method is determined, the possible Input Interfaces and Usage Types are deduced from that Action Method. If, for instance, the Action Method Speaking is determined, the number of Input Interfaces possible for sound input is low and the possible Usage Types are restricted to that Action Method. The Action Method in conjunction with the Usage Type restricts the number of possible Input Interfaces even more. With respect to the Usage Type, the same holds for the Action Method in conjunction with the Input Interface. The Usage Type determines the Action Method and restricts the number of available Input Interfaces to those that offer the specified Usage Type and allow for performing the deduced Action Method. For example, when the Usage Type Natural Speech is selected, Speaking is automatically determined as the Action Method. The list of Input Interfaces is restricted to different microphones like desktop microphone, handheld microphone, wearable microphone, etc. When we decide on a particular Input Interface, the Action Method as well as the Usage Type are restricted at the same time. When Input Interface and Usage Type have been determined, the Action Method is deduced from those. This does not hold for the determination of the Input Interface and the Action Method: When the Input Interface and the Action Method have been determined, we still have a choice regarding the Usage Type. For example, when we decide on microphone as Input Interface and natural speech as Usage Type, Speaking is automatically determined as the Action Method. When we leave the Usage Type open and decide on an Action Method from the class Vocal Utterance, we can still decide on which Usage Type to apply.

2.4 System Action View

The System Action view (see Fig. 4) describes the way the System reacts to the Human Action and the transmission of information from the System to the Human. The System Action is a composition of Direct Input Feedback, Indirect Input Feedback, Application Feedback, and System Function. Direct Input Feedback is feedback the Human gets directly from the Input Interface, i.e., not via any Medium. Example: the physical resistance of a keyboard stroke or the sound when pressing a key on a keyboard or a PC mouse. In contrast to this, Indirect Input Feedback is input feedback the Human gets via a Medium as a reaction to his usage of an Input Interface. It is the System Action on a humans action to confirm the systems correct understanding of that action. Indirect Input Feedback is always based on a System Function and can be influenced by a designer.

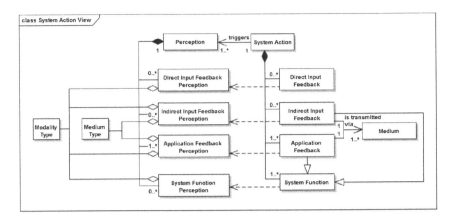

Fig. 4. System action view

Examples: bordering of an icon that the mouse cursor points to or highlighting of a selected menu entry. A System Function is a System Action that is performed automatically by the System as a reaction to an external trigger. An external trigger may be, for example, a Human Action, a call from an external system, or an environmental context change. A System Function does not necessarily address a Human directly, but recognizes events, interprets and manipulates data, and plans and initiates Application Feedback and Indirect Input Feedback. A System Function cannot be influenced by an interaction designer. Examples: an internal change in the system state, working hard disk drives, control of external but system-related objects (e.g., lights). From an interaction-centered point of view, a System Action is given when at least one Application Feedback exists. Furthermore, an arbitrary number of the other elements can be included. The rationale for this composition is that Application Feedback directly refers to the humans Intention. Without feedback to the Intention, we are not able to fulfill an Elementary Interaction. For example, if a user performs an action on a user interface and only receives the feedback that his input was successful, we do not refer to this as an Elementary Interaction. The user always has to perceive the part of the System Action that belongs to his Intention in order to complete an Elementary Interaction. This part is the Application Feedback. Depending on the Environmental Context in which the System Action takes place, the System Action might be influenced by that context. For example, the System Action might be to transmit information to the Human by means other than sound when the environment is noisy, or to show relevant information to a particular person when it detects that that person is near. The System Action triggers a humans Perception, which is composed according to the System Action. Because of this segmentation, we can trace which Perception is triggered by which kind of System Action. For each kind of Perception, a Modality Type is specified that determines if the Perception is unimodal or multimodal. Unimodal perception is given when exactly one Modality is used to perceive the part of the System

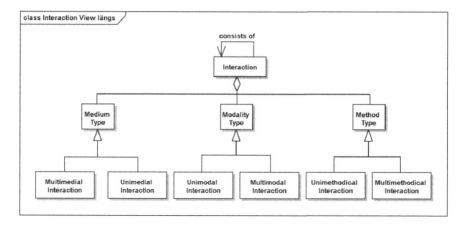

Fig. 5. Interaction view

Action. In multimodal perception, at least two different Modalities are used. In addition to that, for Indirect Input Feedback Perception and Application Feedback Perception, a Medium Type is specified that determines if the Perception is unimedial or multimedial. This is necessary for those two types because they are the only ones that are transmitted via a Medium. If one Medium is used for transmission, the medium type is unimedial; if at least two different Media are used, the medium type is multimedial.

2.5 Interaction View

The interaction view (see Fig. 5) gives a holistic overview of the views described so far and emphasizes the build-up of an Interaction. An Interaction consists of several Elementary Interactions. Furthermore, each Interaction consists of a Human Action that is initiated by an Intention and a System Action that triggers a Perception. This Perception either confirms or rejects the initial Intention. With the help of the interaction view, it is possible to describe an Interaction as a whole in a detailed manner, which can further be broken down by using more detailed views.

2.6 Elementary Interaction View

The Elementary interaction view (see Fig. 6) describes the composition of an Elementary Interaction and its specializations in detail. Furthermore, it is shown how an Elementary Interaction is constructed. Elementary Interactions are restricted to exactly one Human Action and one to many System Actions. Example: Typing text into a word processing application (Human Action) and perceiving the written text on a screen in order to check the correct spelling (text output as System Action). An Elementary Interaction always has three types, which specify how the Elementary Interaction takes place in detail. First, the Method Type

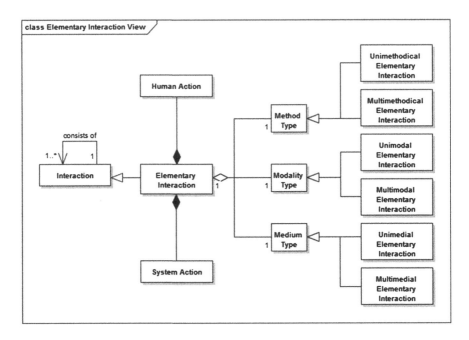

Fig. 6. Elementary interaction view

specifies if the Elementary Interaction is unimethodical or multimethodical. A unimethodical Elementary Interaction is an Elementary Interaction where the Human Action is unimethodical. A simple example is pressing a key on the keyboard in order to select a list item and visually perceiving the selected item. The attribute that is relevant for determining the Method Type derives directly from the Human Action; i.e., a unimethodical action remains unimethodical on the Elementary Interaction level, a multimethodical action remains multimethodical. Of course, in this simple example we have just one Action Method, namely pressing a key. A multimethodical Elementary Interaction is an Elementary Interaction where the Human Action is multimethodical. A simple example is pointing with a finger to an icon and saying open that and visually perceiving the opening application. In this example, two different action methods are used in parallel during the action, namely Gesturing and Speaking. Therefore, the Elementary Interaction is multimethodical. Second, the Modality Type specifies if the Elementary Interaction is unimodal or multimodal. A unimodal Elementary Interaction is an Elementary Interaction where Perception is unimodal. An example is requesting information from a speech dialog system on the phone and aurally perceiving the answers. A multimodal Elementary Interaction is an Elementary Interaction, where the Perception is multimodal. An example is requesting information from a speech dialog system on the PC and aurally as well as visually perceiving the answers. To determine the modality types, all Perceptions are subsumed and it does not matter which kind of Perception the modality derives from. Third, the Medium Type specifies if the Elementary Interaction is unimedial or multimedial. A unimedial Elementary Interaction is an Elementary Interaction where the Perception is unimedial. An example is using a command-based input shell (as in UNIX), perceiving only alphanumerical text. A multimedial Elementary Interaction is an Elementary Interaction where the Perception is multimedial. An example is using a GUI-based operating system (like Microsoft Windows) and perceiving alphanumerical text, graphics, animations, and icons during one single elementary interaction. To determine the Medium Type, each medium involved in Indirect Input Feedback Perception and Application Feedback Perception is considered. An Elementary Interaction always has to be characterized through the triple method type, modality type, medium type. For example, the Elementary Interaction of clicking the recycle bin icon on a MS Windows desktop to open the context menu is multimethodical (moving an object and pressing an object), unimodal (visual perception of the moving mouse cursor and the opening context menu), and multimedial (representation of information via the icon, text, and graphics within the context menu). An Elementary Interaction specified by only one or two of these types does not exist from our point of view.

3   A Non-formal Method Based on MAInEEAC

When collaborating with non-expert stakeholders in order to define an interaction concept for a particular software system, MAInEEAC as a formal model is not applicable in its original condition. Therefore, we have developed non-formal methods based on this formal model to facilitate this collaboration. After having accomplished a huge number of software engineering projects with interaction design activities, we have found that these methods, where stakeholders can speak freely, lead to more relevant information than strict formal and restricted approaches. One of these methods is the mConcAppt method [2,3,5], which is a method for the user-centered conception of mobile business apps. In this chapter, we focus on the part of mConcAppt that is relevant for the construction of the HCI.

3.1   Upfront Requirements Elicitation and Analysis

In this practical approach for mobile interaction design, we face typical challenges like short time to market, high user experience, and less focused user attention than with desktop systems. Furthermore, the user interface design is related to device, platform, and technology. It comprises upfront requirements elicitation and analysis in combination with an iterative interaction design (see Fig. 7). Both phases are conducted with close user involvement.

During the execution of mConcAppt, different kinds of artifacts are produced. Up-front requirements elicitation and analysis are mainly performed by means of a requirements elicitation workshop that involves end users as well as other project-relevant stakeholders (see Fig. 8). In addition, several requirements

Fig. 7. Brief overview of mConcAppt

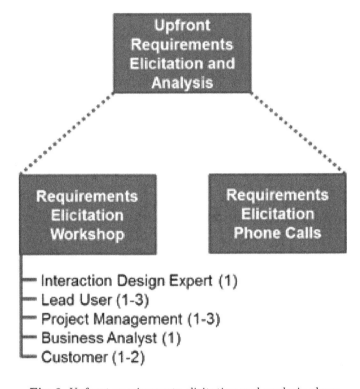

Fig. 8. Upfront requirements elicitation and analysis phase

elicitation phone calls or interviews might be performed in order to clarify information elicited in the workshop as well as to elicit further requirements. As a result from upfront requirements elicitation and analysis, the following artifacts are produced in close collaboration with non-expert stakeholders:

1. List of involved stakeholders
2. Stakeholder goals
3. Stakeholder description
4. Description of a user persona [1]
5. Description of the as-is situation
6. Problems in the as-is situation
7. Description of the to-be situation
8. Technical constraints
9. Exchanged domain data

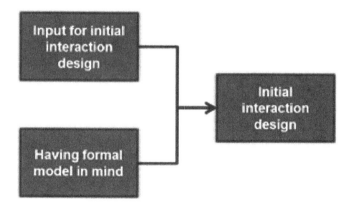

Fig. 9. Initial interaction design phase

Requirements and interaction design experts already have the formal MAInEEAC model in mind while eliciting and documenting those artifacts. From the list of involved stakeholders, the definite end users (cf. Human in MAInEEAC) are derived. Especially stakeholder goals elicited in combination with the description of the to-be situation will ultimately lead to the interaction created using the formal model. Already at this point in time, communication between the requirements engineer and the interaction designer is improved, since they both have a conjoint formal model in mind when discussing different aspects. All mentioned artifacts are used as input for the development of the initial interaction design, which will be described in the following chapter.

3.2   Iterative Interaction Design

The second phase during mConcAppt is the actual interaction design phase. Figure 9 shows that the artifacts elicited in the first phase and the formal model that the interaction designer has in mind are combined to create the interaction design. Therefore, interaction cases (see the example in Fig. 10) are created that structure the elicited to-be situation into a textual description using elements of the MAInEEAC model. During the textual specification of Interaction Cases, Action Methods, Usage Types, Input Feedback, and Application Feedback are defined. Using the interaction cases, the actual wireframes are assembled by combining exactly one Human Action and one System Action into one wireframe. In early iterations, wireframes are usually produced using paper prototypes and evaluated with real end users in a Wizard-of Oz setting. During those early evaluations and especially during later ones, when the prototype is already in a more mature state, the interaction designer benefits from having the formal model in mind when talking to the end user in order to check whether all recommended elements (e.g., giving Input Feedback at each Human Action) have been considered. In this phase, it might also beneficial to apply a co-design practice: interaction designers and end-users might create the interaction cases and wire-

Item	Description
ID	IC2: Track time
Usage Context	A business travel for multiple days. Meeting an industrial partner in Leipzig. The user is on his way to the hotel and uses the device while walking.
System Action 1	The system recognizes, that the user arrives at his destination and notifies him that the time of arrival is tracked (via notification center)
Human Action 1	The user taps the notification to directly open the app
System Action 2	The system opens the app and immediately shows the current trip itinerary and proposed time
Human Action 2	The user confirms the proposed time
System Action 3	The system provides feedback on confirmation to the user
Human Action 3	The user closes the app
Postcondition	Arrival time is persistently stored.

Fig. 10. Interaction case example

frames conjointly; this will probably minimize the effort necessary for reworks of the interaction design after it was evaluated by other end-users.

4   Advantages of Our Approach

The application of the approach we propose in this chapter bears a number of advantages: Non-expert stakeholders are not forced to worry about formal models, since expert stakeholders do not discuss formal models with non-expert stakeholders, but rather prepare their conversations with the help of the model. Due to the unrestricted and non-formal conversations, all stakeholders can speak freely and more relevant information is gathered than with strict formal and restricted approaches like workshops and interviews. During the conversation, the expert stakeholders know which information is missing and can describe and discuss the impact of decisions made collaboratively. But it is still the interaction designer who creates the final interaction design and the developer who implements the interaction. Benefits of our approach can also be found within the groups of expert stakeholders and non-expert stakeholders, where communications are facilitated, since a single model with a single terminology can be used. When single group members are familiar with or used to another terminology, both terminologies can be mapped very easily. Besides requirements engineers, interaction designers, and developers, visual designers, architects, business analysts, customers, and end-users will also benefit from this facilitation of communication. The requirements elicited, analyzed, and specified by these communications while applying the non-formal method can be traced to concrete interactions and their highly detailed elements. While the formal model represents the elements, the non-formal method assures traceability.

5   Conclusion

From our point of view, early collaboration with non-expert stakeholders is mandatory. This is done best by applying non-formal methods based on formal models. Insisting on formal modeling when collaborating with non-expert stakeholders leads to insufficient results, since non-expert stakeholders have to familiarize themselves with unusual formal models and unusual formal thinking instead of focusing on considerations about needs, wishes, and demands in terms of HCI. In this article, we presented our user-centered design approach for an interaction design based on our non-formal method mConcAppt, which follows our formal model MAInEEAC. Due to the early involvement of non-expert stakeholders, the software development process can be shortened and thus could be applied to a wide range of software development projects, especially to projects using an agile development approach. Such agile development approaches are often applied to mobile business applications, for example, which need a lightweight user-centered approach because of their special challenges. Formal approaches do not satisfy this requirement sufficiently. The approach can be applied to a large number of domains due to its flexibility and the formal structure in the background. The approach presented (MAInEEAC, mConcAppt and their interrelation) is based on best practices resulting from many projects in which we have designed interaction in collaboration with non-expert stakeholders, and is even supposed to enable semi-experts to design a wellconceived HCI. An example of the application of the approach in an actual project can be found in [1]. However, the approach is still evolving and work is in progress. We plan to integrate interaction-related aspects such as user experience and architecture in order to be able to cover a holistic view on HCI and to discuss all relevant aspects with non-expert stakeholders. We also believe that this approach is able to create new value through its capability to apply the co-creation practice. However, investigations of such effects by applying the approach were not conducted yet and remain an open issue to carry out as future work. Eventually, we hope to achieve a huge increase in interaction design quality with the help of our approach.

References

1. Cooper, A.: The Inmates Are Running the Asylum: Why High-Tech Products Drive Us Crazy and How to Restore the Sanity. Indianapolis, USA (1999)
2. Hess, S., Kiefer, F.: mConcAppt Methode - UX und Interaktionsdesign für mobile Business Apps in Usability Professionals Association, German Chapter: Usability Professionals 2012 Tagungsband. Konstanz (2012)
3. Hess, S., Kiefer, F.: Quality by construction through mConcAppt - toward using UI-construction as a driver for high quality mobile App engineering. In: QUATIC 2012 (2012)
4. Hess, S., Maier, A., Trapp, M.: Differentiating between successful and less successful products by using MAInEEAC - a model for interaction characterization. In: Jacko, J.A. (ed.) Human-Computer Interaction, Part I, HCII 2011. LNCS, vol. 6761, pp. 238–247. Springer, Heidelberg (2011)

5. Hess, S., Kiefer, F., Carbon, R., Maier, A.: mConcAppt - a method for the conception of mobile business applications. In: Uhler, D., Mehta, K., Wong, J.L. (eds.) MobiCASE 2012. LNICST, vol. 110, pp. 1–20. Springer, Heidelberg (2013)
6. International Organization for Standardization. ISO 9241–210:2010 - Ergonomics of human-system interaction - Part 210: Human-centred design for interactive systems (2010)
7. Norman, D.A.: Some observations on mental models. In: Gentner, D., Stevens, A.L. (eds.) Mental Models, pp. 7–14. Lawrence Erlbaum Associates Inc., Hillsdale (1983)
8. Norman, D.A.: The Design of Everyday Things. Doubleday, New York (1988)
9. Schomaker, L., Munch, S., Hartung, K.: A taxonomy of multimodal interaction in the human information processing system. Technical report, ESPRIT BRA, No. 8579 (1995)

Verbal Use Case Specifications for Informal Requirements Elicitation

Eliezer Kantorowitz[(✉)]

Technion – Israel Institute of Technology,
Technion City 3200 Haifa, Israel
kantor@cs.technion.ac.il

Abstract. Constructing a software system from poor specifications may necessitate costly repairs. We introduce the notion "satisfactory specifications" for quality specifications that do not require costly repairs. Satisfactory specifications may be produced by a Computer Supported Collaborative Work (CSCW) team incorporating all the relevant experts and the stakeholders. It is suggested that the CSCW team develops use case specifications, where its expertise is especially useful. Specifying in a natural language understood by all team members facilitates needed intensive cooperation between different team members. Compared to specifications formulated in formal terminology, verbal formulations in domain language represent a textual visualization. Translating the verbal specifications into formal UML diagrams provides a further graphical visualization. It is suggested that each specification is provided with a separate example for each kind of the possible situations. These examples may clarify meaning of poorly formulated specifications, facilitate identifying faults in formal specifications and employed for software debugging.

Keywords: Satisfactory specifications · Computer Supported Cooperative Work · CSCW · UML · Use case · Software specifications · Software requirements · Requirements elicitation · Human Factors · Verification · non-ambiguous · natural language · correct specifications · verbal specifications · formal specifications · behavioral study

Introduction

A common model of software system development begins with eliciting the requirements of the system, i.e. what the system is required to be able to do. Thereafter a system that meets the elicited requirements is specified. The specification of the system includes its structure and behavior as well as nonfunctional requirements such as the maximal permitted system size in bytes (called "foot print"). The specification process unearths sometimes further requirements. The requirement elicitation and system specification are therefore to some extend done simultaneously. The specifications are the basis for a later detailed design and construction of the system. If the requirements elicited in the beginning of the process are faulty, the constructed system will have the corresponding faults. The repair of such a faulty system typically involves high costs and unfortunate delivery delays. Getting the requirements right from the beginning is therefore an important goal. As a measure for achieving this goal, we introduce the concept of *satisfactory specifications*. Specifications are said to

A. Ebert et al. (Eds.): HCIV Workshops 2011, LNCS 8345, pp. 165–174, 2014.
DOI: 10.1007/978-3-642-54894-9_12, © IFIP International Federation for Information Processing 2014

be *satisfactory* when no major modifications are needed for producing a system that satisfies the intended users. Getting the specification right is, however, difficult to achieve. A study of the faults found in requirements of critical software systems [1] found 9.5 errors per each 100 requirements. This is a surprising high rate, as critical software is subject to an intensive verification and validation. It seems therefore that we have to work hard to produce satisfactory specifications. We discuss a number of known methods for requirement elicitation and specification development that we consider especially useful from a cognitive ergonomically point of view. Developing satisfactory specifications requires different kinds of expertise as well as knowledge of the needs of the users and customers of the specified system. It may therefore be a good idea to employ a *Computer Supported Cooperative Work* (CSCW) [2] team, including all those who may contribute to the creation, modification or removal of requirements (the *stakeholders*). Such a team may consider the system from the different points of view of the different stakeholders. Dan Beery [3] suggest including in the team persons that are not familiar with the problem domain. Such a person may ask questions that are out of the entrenched train of thoughts of the experts. In addition, the requirements elicited or omitted represent the priorities of the designers of the system. Such priorities can be negotiated in a CSCW team which includes the relevant stakeholders of the system.

A CSCW team may include software engineers, domain experts, potential users and mangers. Such a team is thus composed of persons of different professional backgrounds and of different human natures. A productive collaboration between such team members involves both behavioral and social challenges [4, 5]. These challenges have been the subject of many studies [2]. There are also difficulties in managing the large amount of data found in the requirements and specifications of real life systems. Validating the many different details of the system specification can be very important. Consider for example the case of the aircraft that failed to brake on landing in Warsaw airport in 1993 [6]. The essence of the cause of the accident, where two human were killed, is that the software for controlling the brake system was specified to be activated on landing, i.e. when the weight on each one of the two landing gears exceeded 12 tons. However due to side winds this happened on only one of the two gears. The paper [6] did not report whether the specification team included an experienced pilot (a domain expert) who may have suggested the inclusion of the side wind case in the specifications. Such a possible pilot member of the team should have carefully read the very large number of the aircraft specifications in order to detect this deficiency. The experience of this pilot may have been from the era, when the human pilot activated the brakes and they worked in any kind of wind. Our experienced pilot may therefore not have been aware of the effect off possible insufficient weight on one of the two landing gears. And not detected the side wind problem of the requirements. Could this problem have been detected by such a visualization means as storytelling? Possible not, as our story teller, i.e. the experienced pilot, was not looking for solutions for the side wind problem. Our pilot may have detected the problem by asking "is it possible that the brakes will not work?" To arrive at the side wind possibility requires out of the box thinking, where the non-expert member of the team may help. To determine whether the side wind is a real threat, the experienced pilot has to ask an aeronautical engineer to investigate the expected winds at landing situations and do the non-trivial computation of their effects on the landing gear weights. Such an investigation is time consuming and costly. The manger may not welcome these costs and delays. In addition our experienced pilot must admit that her/his air craft expertise is limited. The last problem was addressed in Weinberg's egoless programming approach [7], which is widely employed in current day's cooperative efforts, such as CSCW teams. Specifications developments by a CSCW team are, for example, are done in a friendly collegiate way. A team member may thus not be afraid of admitting lack of some expertise, as the overriding concern of the team is to come close to satisfactory specifications. The egoless honest approach is also needed in learned discussions in the CSCW team when attempting to clarify difficult problems, such as the above discussed example of whether the braking may not take place in some situations.

Use Case Specifications

Applications that are based on a well elaborated mathematical model may advantageously exploit this model. An example is the successful SQL database management systems, which employ the relational model. Today, some forty years after their introduction, the SQL model is widely employed, which is remarkable in fast evolving software world. In this paper we consider systems where some of the CSCW members may not be familiar with the use of formal methods. In these cases this paper suggests that after the validation of the elicited requirements, the CSCW team develops a verbal *use case specification* [8–10] of the system. Such specifications are widely employed in the industry. We explain why this kind of specification is especially useful in striving to satisfactory specifications. A *use case specification of a system* is the set of all its use cases [8]. Consider for example a library information system. The use case specification of this system may be composed of such use cases as "Lending a Library Book" (shown in Fig. 1), "Register a Library Book" and "Register a new Lender". A *use case* is a specification of the interactions between an external *actor* and the system that are required for accomplishing one particular application of the system, e.g. "Lending a book". An actor is either a human or different system. The interactions specified in the use case are implemented by software that may be called the *use case software*. Consider for example an actor that asks for data that are stored in a database. The use case software receives this request from the actor and conveys it to the *underlying system software* that manages the database. The use case software gets the requested database data from the underlying system software and conveys it to the actor. The use case specification does not specify the underlying system software. The underlying system software is specified advantageously after the completion of the use case specification, such that it interfaces to the already completed use case specifications. The specification of the underlying system software requires only software engineering knowledge and may therefore be produced by a software engineering team. The insights of domain expert members of the CSCW team are, on the other hand, essential for the specification of the use cases. Consider for example the design of a library information system. An experienced librarian (a domain expert) can provide needed information on the activities and problems of a library. This labor division between the CSCW team doing the use case specification and the engineering team specifying the underlying system software enables each team to work in an area where it is most useful.

> Identify the book by bar code reading.
> (Elapsed computer processing time should be less than 0.1 sec.)
> Identify the lender by bar code reading.
> (Elapsed computer processing time should be less than 0.1 sec.)
>
> Check if the lender is entitled to lend the book –
>   (Lending permission rules come here.)
>   (Elapsed computer processing time should be less than 0.1 sec.)
> Permit or reject the lending,
> EXCEPTION HANDLING   (what to do if :)
>   (The book is not registered in the database)
>   (The book bar code is corrupted)
>   (The book is not bar coded)
>   (The lender is not registered)
>   Etc
>   REQUIREMENTS IMPLEMENTED BY THIS USE CASE
>   ...

Fig. 1. Simplified specification of the use case called "Lending a Library Book", where some details are omitted. It includes nonfunctional requirements, such as "Duration of bar code processing < 0.1 s." Handling of exceptional cases and list of the elicited requirements that are implemented by this use case are also included.

This paper further suggests specifying the use cases in a natural language that is familiar to all CSCW team members. This should enable efficient collaboration between the different CSCW team members, which may be needed in clarifying difficult situations, such as the side wind example discussed in the previous section. Verbal use case specifications are employed in the industry using for example the instructions of [10]. This paper suggests that a use case specification should include all information related to the use case. Having all the information in one place may help the CSCW team members in understanding of difficult situations. Figure 1, which shows an example specification of the use case "Lending a Library Book", where some details are omitted. A use case specifies both the normal and the exceptional cases, e.g. what to do if the book is not registered in the database of the library. A use case specification should also specify *non-functional* requirements. As an example, it is required in Fig. 1, that the duration of the processing of the bar code reading should be shorter than 0.1 s. The purpose of this requirement is to provide the user of the system with the feeling of a fast responding system, i.e. a user experience purpose. This requirement is a "non-functional" one, because it is not about the functioning or non-functioning of a bar code reading, but about the duration of the reading. The use case specification should also provide a list the elicited requirements that the use case implements [11]. This enables a person that for some reason modifies the code of the use case software, to check that the modified code still implements the relevant elicited requirements.

It is suggested that after a thorough validation of the developed verbal use case specifications by the CSCW team, these specifications are manually translated to a formal UML specification [12–14]. UML was designed to support the software development process. It provides tools for visualization of the specifications and for some validations. There are UML tools for code generation and for test case generation [15]. UML tools regarding system dependability are discussed in [16]. UML tools for *Model Driven Software Engineering* are discussed in [17]. These powerful tools may be employed throughout the life cycle of the software for future extensions and modifications.

English Issues

In order to simplify the formulations in the following part of this paper, we employ the term "English" as an abbreviation of "Natural language, for example English". Summerville [18] lists a number of difficulties in writing natural language requirements specifications. One of the problems is that "Natural language understanding relies on the specification readers and writers using the same words for the same concept." This problem is avoided by many writers of mathematical proofs, scientific papers and commercial contracts, who succeed in conveying their messages in a clear and correct way. Writers of software requirements specifications face the same linguistic problems as the above mentioned writers and may therefore adopt their methods and be equally successful. We consider first an example of a mathematician writing a proof. Her intended readers are mathematician, who like herself, have been trained during their university studies to employ the by and large globally accepted vocabulary of mathematics and the English idioms employed in mathematical explanations. Before her paper is published, it is typically reviewed by three mathematicians who check both the correctness of the proof and the clarity of English explanations. Their improvement suggestions may then be incorporated in the published revised paper. By employing the by and large globally accepted mathematical vocabulary it is ensured that the author and her readers understand the concepts in the same way.

Consider now, for example, the writer of the requirements specifications of a library information system. Following the mathematician example, the requirement specification writer will employ the vocabulary of library science in the requirements that regard library issues and computer science vocabulary in the requirements that regard software issues. Similarly to the mathematical proof case, the requirements specifications should be thoroughly reviewed for their correctness as well as for their understandability.

The handbook [19] distinguishes between linguistic and software engineering ambiguities in requirements specifications. Software engineering ambiguity is when some specifications needed for the implementation of the requirements are missing. An example of such a software engineering ambiguity is found in Fig. 1 in the instruction "Identify the book by bar code reading". There exist however four different possible bar code standards and it is not specified which to employ. Such ambiguities may be normal at an early stage of the specification process, when some of the design decisions have not yet been made.

As regard the linguistic ambiguities, the manual [19] provides detailed instructions for producing precise formulation in English and avoiding *unintended ambiguities*, i.e. ambiguities not intended by the specification writer. The manual provides linguistic equivalents to mathematical formulations. Linguistic formulations may thus be as precise as mathematical formulations. This enables employing argumentations in English in mathematical proofs. In the following we compare some usability issues of formal and verbal specifications. The comparison will be illustrated by an example specification of a small restaurant (Figs. 2, 3 and 4).

> 1. The restaurant has two tables named table A and table B.
> 2. Each table can accommodate up to and including four diners.
> Examples:
>> Two dine on table A. Three dine on table B.
>> No one dines on table A. No one dines on table B.
>> Four dine on table A. Four dine on table B.
> Clarifying statement:
>> The restaurant can accommodate up to and including eight diners.

Fig. 2. Specification of a small restaurant formulated by the instructions of [19]

In order to avoid misunderstanding due to poor English formulations [19] suggest adding clarifying examples and explanations as illustrated in Fig. 2. We suggest an engineering praxis, where a separate example is provided for each kind of situation that may occur. The examples of Fig. 2 represent thus a "normal" situation and two "extreme" situations. These examples clarify for the reader the intents of the specification writers in each of the three possible situation kinds. These examples may also be employed by proof readers and specification validators for checking purposes. The specification of Fig. 2 could have employed the domain knowledge, that a table may be free (no diners), but we preferred to clarify this point by the second example.

Figure 3 illustrates how an example disambiguates an unintended ambiguity, which is due to a poor formulation of statement 2 of the specification. This statement 2 has the false interpretation marked as II, which was not intended by the specification writer. Examples one and three as well as the clarifying statement of Fig. 3 show that interpretation II is false. The unintended ambiguity of statement 2 in Fig. 3 contrasts with the efficient specification employed in Fig. 2, where the statement marked as 2 is intentionally ambiguous. It has 25 different correct interpretations, three of which are the three examples. In other words the single statement 2 specifies 25 possible situations. This is an example of the possible usefulness of ambiguities in natural languages.

1. The restaurant has two tables named table A and table B.
2. All the tables can accommodate up to and including four diners.
Examples:
  Two dine on table A. Three dine on table B.
  No one dines on table A. No one dines on table B.
  Four dine on table A. Four dine on table B.
Clarifying statement:
  The restaurant can accommodate up to and including eight diners.

Statement 1 of the specification can be understood in two ways:
  I. Each table can accommodate up to and including four diners.
  II. The two tables can together accommodate up to and including four diners.

The clarification examples show that I is the intended specification

Fig. 3. The restaurant of Fig. 2 specified with an unintended ambiguity in statement 2. The clarifying examples enable a disambiguation. The proof reader of this poorly written specification may detect the problem and improve formulation.

We shall now employ our restaurant specification for a brief illustration of the differences between verbal and formal specifications. Figure 4 is a formal specification of the same restaurant.

n – number of tables
a – number of diners on table 1
b – number of dinners on table 2
$n = 2$
$\{a \in Z : a \geq 0 \wedge a \leq 4\}$
$\{b \in Z : b \geq 0 \wedge b \leq 4\}$
  Examples
    $a = 2, \ b = 3.$
    $a = 0, \ b = 0.$
    $a = 4, \ b = 4.$
  Clarifying statement
    $a + b \, d \, 8$

Fig. 4. Formal specification of the restaurant specified in Fig. 2.

We suggest employing examples and clarifying statements even in the very simple specification of Fig. 4, as they may facilitate fast and correct understanding. Examples and clarifying texts may be very useful in complicated specifications, where the specification writer may err. Examples may also have an explanatory value for the reader. It is noted that writing and reading of long logical expressions in formal specifications are error prone processes [20]. This indicates that the deciphering of mathematical expressions involves a non-negligible cognitive effort. It is therefore recommended to employ only short expressions when possible. A further problem is that understanding a formal specification involves cognitively both a deciphering the mathematical expression and formulating it in the terminology of the domain. This contrasts with a verbal specification which readily expresses in the terminology of the domain. Whether the possible differences in the cognitive effort involved in manipulating formal and verbal specifications influence significantly the efficiency of the system specification process is difficult to tell without an elaborate experimental comparison. The training and experience of the specifications developers must be considered. Furthermore, formal specifications may in some cases be advantageously manipulated mathematically by computer programs.

Discussion and Future Research

This paper introduces the Satisfactory Specifications concept, which is defined as specifications that without major modifications enables production of a system that satisfies the intended users. The goal is thus to produce a quality specification such that costly repairs of the system and unfortunate delays are avoided. A CSCW team having the relevant experts and stakeholders has the insights needed for producing satisfactory specifications. However, even for a CSCW team, achieving satisfactory system specifications is a difficult task, especially when the system includes novel components that have not yet been tried, e.g. using a computer instead of a human for controlling the brakes of a landing air-craft. Analyzing such an unknown situation may require an intensive cooperative analysis by team members having different training and expertise. These members must understand and agree on the specifications that they develop. Therefore, if some of the members involved in the discussion are not familiar with formal specifications, the use of verbal specification seems to be the right thing. Alternatively the team members familiar with formal methods write the formal specifications and translate them into English for the members who are not familiar with formal specifications. This involves the risk that the translations do not convey some details correctly. A possible future behavioral study may compare these two specifications development processes. The paper suggests translating validated verbal specifications into standardized formal UML diagrams, which visualize the design and enables using UML tools, e.g. for validation and code generation. This approach exploits the advantage of both verbal and formal specifications.

In the discussion on whether to employ formal or verbal specifications, the value of the expressiveness of English is in our opinion not given sufficient weight. Providing this kind of expressiveness to an English like formal language [22, 23] may therefore be difficult. The problems of possible unintended ambiguities in English may be mitigated by using English correctly and by employing clarifying examples and explanations [19]. This paper suggests employing a separate example for each kind of the possible situations, e.g. a use case for solving a real quadratic equation may have a separate example for no roots, one root and two roots. The examples provided for a specification may therefore also be employed for debugging the software. These examples are also useful illustrations for persons wishing to understand the specification.

References

1. Ambrosio, A.M., Madeira, H., Silva, N., Véras, P.C., Vieira, M., Villani, E.: Errors on space software requirements: a field study and application scenarios. In: 2010 IEEE 21st International Symposium on Space Software Requirements Engineering, Software Reliability Engineering (ISSRE) (2010)
2. Grudin, J., Poltrock, S.: CSCW - computer supported cooperative work. In: Soegaard, M., Dam, R.F. (eds.) Encyclopedia of Human-Computer Interaction. The Interaction-Design.org Foundation, Aarhus, Denmark (2012)
3. Berry, D.M.: The importance of ignorance in requirements engineering: an earlier sighting and a revisitation. J. Syst. Softw. **60**(1), 83–85 (2002)
4. Grudin J.: Why CSCW applications fail: problems in the design and evaluation of organizational interfaces. In: CSCW '88 Proceedings of the 1988 ACM Conference on Computer-Supported Cooperative Work (1988)
5. Schmidt, K., Bannon, L.: Taking, CSCW seriously. Computer Supported Cooperative Work (CSCW) **1**, 7–40 (1992)
6. Hawkins, R.D., Habli, I., Kelly, T.P.: The principles of software safety assurance. In: 31st International System Safety Conference 2013 (2013)
7. Weinberg, G.M.: The Psychology of Computer Programming. Dorset House, New York (1971)
8. Jacobson, I., Christenson, M.P., Jonsson, P.G.: Overgaard Object-Oriented Software Engineering: A Use Case Driven Approach. Addison-Wesley, Reading (1992)
9. Cockburn, A.: Why I still use use cases. alistair.cockburn.us (2008-1-9)
10. Cockburn, A.: Writing Effective Use Cases. Addison-Wesley, Boston (2001)
11. Winkler, S., Pilgrim, J.: A survey of traceability in requirements engineering and model-driven development. J. Softw. Syst. Model. (SoSyM) **9**(4), 529–565 (2010)
12. Object Management Group: Catalog of OMG Modeling and Metadata Specifications. http://www.omg.org/technology/documents/modeling_spec_catalog.htm
13. Rumbaugh, J., Jacobson, I., Booch, G.: Unified Software Development Process, The Complete Guide to the Unified Process from the Original Designers. Addison Wesley, Reading (1999)
14. Lange, C.F.J., Chaudron, M.R.V., Muskens, J.: In practice: UML software architecture and design description. IEEE Softw. **23**(2), 40–46 (2006)
15. Abdurazik, A., Offutt, J.: Using UML collaboration diagrams for static checking and test generation. In: Evans, A., Caskurlu, B., Selic, B. (eds.) UML 2000. LNCS, vol. 1939, pp. 383–395. Springer, Heidelberg (2000)
16. Bernardi, S., Merseguer, J., Petriu, D.C.: Dependability modeling and analysis of software systems specified with UML. ACM Comput. Surv. **45**(1), 2 (2012)
17. Brambilla, M., Cabot, J., Wimmer, M.: Model-Driven Software Engineering in Practice. Synthesis Lectures on Software Engineering. Morgan and Claypool, USA (2012)
18. Sommerville, I.: Software Engineering, 9th edn. Addison-Wesley, Boston (2010)
19. Berry, D.M., Kamsties, E., Krieger, M.M.: From Contract Drafting to Software Specification: Linguistic Sources of Ambiguity - A Handbook (2003). https://cs.uwaterloo.ca/~dberry/handbook/ambiguityHandbook.pdf
20. Reisner, P., Boyce, R.F., Chamberlin, D.D.: Human factors evaluation of two data base query languages: square and sequel. In: Proceedings of the AFIPS '75, 19-22 May 1975

21. Arora, C., Sabetzadeh, M., Briand, L., Zimmer, F., Gnaga, R.: Automatic checking of conformance to requirement boilerplates via text chunking: an industrial case study. In: ESEM'13 (2013)
22. Umber, A., Bajwa, I.S.: Minimizing ambiguity in natural language software requirements specification. In: Sixth International Conference on Digital Information Management (ICDIM) (2011)
23. Osborne, M., MacNish, C.K.: Processing natural language software requirement specifications. In: Proceedings of the Second International Conference on Requirements Engineering (1996)

Software Design and New Media Design

Formal and Visual Tools to Design Mobile and Sensory Interfaces and Interactive Environments

Geert de Haan[(⊠)]

Communication, Media and Information Technology, Section Media
Technology/Human Centered ICT, Rotterdam University of Applied Sciences,
P.O. Box 25035, 3001 HA Rotterdam, The Netherlands
geert.de.haan@upcmail.nl

Abstract. This paper discusses ETAG, a formal model for design representation, and ETAG-based design as a method for user interface design. The paper starts with an introduction of ETAG as a design representation. This is followed by a description of ETAG-based design and using the notation to represent relevant aspects of the work context. Next, we discuss the differences between computer software design and media product design, concluding that media design is a much more flexible, iterative process and prototyping-based process in which adaptation of the design of mobile applications extends into the maintenance phase. To cover further developments towards focusing on user needs and wishes by means of co-design practices, and to cover for ubiquitous computing and interaction with sensors and interactive environments, we propose to use sensory labs and to create living labs to move the usability lab into the real world.

Keywords: Formal modelling · ETAG · Software design · Media design · Design tools · Design methods

1 Introduction

In this paper we compare a formal design method for user interface design specification (ETAG; Extended Task-Action Grammar; [6, 15]) with examples of the collection of tools that are actually taught at a Human-Computer Interaction (HCI) educational curriculum in Media Technology at the bachelor level. The aim is to investigate the need for formal specification methods for user interface design; in particular to investigate the usefulness of formal modelling tools for modern cf. mobile and ubiquitous applications. Formal methods for user interface design, such as ETAG, were developed in the late eighties when the focus was on structured design methods and design for usability. Presently, as reflected in the Media Technology curriculum, the focus in teaching engineers is on designing creative applications of mobile and ubiquitous technology and services [7].

In this paper, Sect. 2 discusses Extended Task-Action Grammar (ETAG) as an example of a formal modelling approach to user interface design. As a formal

A. Ebert et al. (Eds.): HCIV Workshops 2011, LNCS 8345, pp. 175–187, 2014.
DOI: 10.1007/978-3-642-54894-9_13, © IFIP International Federation for Information Processing 2014

modelling tool, ETAG is a fairly advanced and refined method, based on specifying what a perfectly knowing user would know about a user interface to perform tasks with it.

Section 3 discussed ETAG-based design as a design approach which uses ETAG as its main vehicle for specifying a user interface. A main element in ETAG-based design is the formal specification of task- and user interface objects, elements and commands and command-actions with a fairly restricted application of prototyping and testing.

In Sect. 4, the paper discusses the general approach to design as taught in a contemporary Human-Computer Interaction curriculum. Among the main characteristics of the Media Technology curriculum are the focus on creativity, user-centredness and the user-experience, and in the application of a loose collection of tools which each support a particular part of the design process.

Section 5 concludes the paper with a number of conclusions about the applicability of the two general approaches to user interface design. In this section, we also discuss some of the latest developments in application development, and in particular the employment of experimentation facilities such as sensor labs and living labs for concept development, design fine tuning and design evaluation. All of these developments seem to suggest that instead of relying on specifying beforehand, user interface design moves towards increasingly agile or experimentation-based approaches.

2   Extended Task-Action Grammar

ETAG (Extended Task-Action Grammar; [6, 15]) is a formal language to represent user interfaces in terms of the knowledge that a perfectly knowing user would have (in a mental model) about performing tasks. To create a psychologically valid description of user interface for design purposes, ETAG stratifies user interface knowledge into a number of levels using existential logic and written down in a formal grammar. Sowa's Existential logic [14] is used to anchor user interface knowledge in general world-knowledge. The formal grammatical notation, adopted from ETAG's predecessor, Task-Action Grammar (TAG; [12]) ensures that the description is sufficiently precise for design and implementation purposes without sacrificing psychological validity. User interface representations are stratified into levels to meet the existence of levels in human knowledge and to reflect the major decisions that occur during the design process. ETAG representations consist of a canonical basis, a user virtual machine, a dictionary of basic tasks, and a section with production rules.

The canonical basis (an ontology) lists the universally known concepts such as object, attributes and events which are used to define the specific objects, attributes, etc. of the user interface in the type specification and the type hierarchy of the user virtual machine (Fig. 1).

The user virtual machine (UVM) describes the elements and the workings of the user interface without referring to a specific implementation. Ideally, a single UVM could be used for a mobile interface, a pc-like interface, etc. In the type specification each of the concepts in the type hierarchy is defined, and additional concepts and attributes are defined to describe how the system works, as experienced by the user (Fig. 2).

```
CONCEPT ::= [OBJECT]  |  [PLACE]  |  [EVENT]
[PLACE] ::= [place.IN ([OBJECT])]  |  [place.ON ([OBJECT])]
[EVENT] ::= [event.KILL-ON ([OBJECT], [PLACE])]   |
    [event.MOVE-TO ([OBJECT], [PLACE])]
```

Fig. 1. A fragment of a canonical basis in ETAG for an application environment in which the user has to know that there are objects, places and events. The objects may reside on or in places, and there are events to kill or delete objects on a place and to move objects between places. This type specification fragment might apply to, for instance, a filing system, a game or a messaging system.

```
type [OBJECT > MESSAGE]
  supertype:[TEXT] ;
  themes: [HEADER], [BODY] ;
  relations:[place.ON-POS(1)([MESSAGE])] for [HEADER],
    [place.ON-POS(1)([MESSAGE])] for [BODY],
    [place.POSS-AT([MESSAGE])] for [HEADER], [BODY];
  attributes: <SENDER>, <SEND_DATE>, <STATUS>
END [message]
```

Fig. 2. A specification of a message type in ETAG which describes a message a text, consisting from one header and one message body. Each message is further characterised by a sender, a timestamp and a status attribute.

The event specification is the part of the UVM describing the workings of the system as it virtually appears to work from the point of view of the users, which may be different from how it is actually built to work. It describes what the system does when it processes the tasks that are successfully invoked by the user, using a pseudo computer program notation which describes the change in the user's task world that is described in the object specification, such as changing an attribute value or creating a new object (Fig. 3).

```
type [EVENT > COPY_MESSAGES]
  description:  for { [MESSAGE: *x] }
      [event.copy-to ([MESSAGE: *x],
      [place.ON-TAIL ([MESSAGE_FILE: *y]): *p2])] ;
  precondition: [state.IS-AT ([MESSAGE: *x],
      [place.ON-POS.(i) ([MESSAGE_FILE: *z]): *p1])] ;
  comments: "copy messages from file z onto the end of
file y"
END [COPY_MESSAGES]
```

Fig. 3. A ETAG specification of an event to copy or append messages, if there are any, from one file to the end of another file.

The dictionary of basic tasks lists the tasks which are available to the user and it links the workings of the user interface to the command specification of the tasks (Fig. 4).

```
ENTRY 6:
[TASK > COPY_MESSAGES],
[EVENT > COPY_MESSAGES]
[MESSAGE_FILE: *z]
T6 [EVENT > COPY_MESSAGES]
   [OBJECT > MESSAGE: (*x)][OBJECT > MESSAGE_FILE: *y]
comments: "copy messages from the current message file
into another file"
```

Fig. 4. An ETAG basic task or a user-level task description to copy messages to a file as the invocation of the copy-messages event along with the messages and the file as arguments.

Finally, the production rules describe, for each basic task, the command procedure in terms of the command syntax, the way of referring to command elements, the naming and labelling of command elements, and the physical actions to specify each element.

The dictionary of basic tasks and the production rules is the part of ETAG which addresses the differences between interaction styles and devices like windows systems, multitouch interaction, and interactive voice-response interfaces. To complete an ETAG specification of a system, the perceptual interface should be specified next. However, ETAG has never been extended to specify the visual aspects of the user interface, mainly because it is much easier to do graphical design by means of other tools such as paper-and-pencil or interactive user interface builders.

3   ETAG-Based User Interface Design

ETAG-based design [6] is originally developed as a design method on the basis of the ETAG notation to supplement or indeed replace software engineering design methods with one that is designed as inherently user centred. ETAG-based design is a user centred design method which guarantees or, at least, stimulates the designer to consider the user. In ETAG-Based Design user interface design is regarded as the incremental specification of the mental model of a perfectly knowing user. The design process is structured into a number of discrete steps, each covering a specific set of design decisions: task and context analysis, task design or task synthesis, conceptual user interface design, and perceptual user interface design, which consists of the design of the presentation interface and the design of the interaction language between the user and the system.

In ETAG-Based Design the ETAG notation is used to represent the analysis and design results. To this purpose, it is necessary that the notation is flexibly adapted to meet the specific purposes of the design stage. Originally, ETAG was intended only for user interface specification and not for representing the results of task analysis and task design. However, by altering the level of abstraction of the specification, the amount of detail, and the inclusion of special modelling concepts, the ETAG notation becomes useful for different purposes. For example, in modelling business procedures during task analysis, the representation is specified at a high level of abstraction without much detail, and special concepts are used to represent the decomposition of tasks and procedures and to represent agency and ownership.

ETAG-based design consists of a number of discrete phases, each with its own formal modelling specification to model task analysis results, to specify task design, concept design and user interface design, and each phase includes a particular evaluation of the specification. The phases are designed in such a way as to stimulate design iteration within each phase and to minimize the need for iterate and experiment with design options between different phases; thus enabling an easy-to-manage design process (Fig. 5).

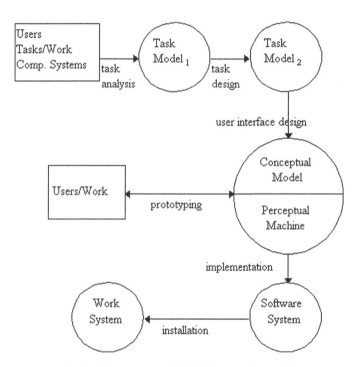

Fig. 5. The structure of ETAG-based design [6].

An advantage of using a single notation throughout design is facilitating the transitions from one design stage to the next one. Another advantage, at least in principle, is that it is easier to create tool support. This is particularly relevant for presenting ETAG as a formal model in a way which suits the background and the way of working of other stakeholders. Instead of having to translate between many different notations, in ETAG-based design, tools only need to deal with a single notation which allows for easy to automatic translation into visual specifications or programming code. This idea is similar to proposals to use a single e.g. object-oriented or XML-based representation as the underlying notation for the software engineering of user interface design specification, as proposed by Foley and Sukaviriya [5].

A final advantage of using a single notation is that designers themselves are not required to learn and use a variety of different notations. In the approaches of Paternò [11] and Constantine and Lockwood [4], for example, designers must be able to deal with a handful of different design representations, in contrast to only one notation in ETAG-based design.

ETAG was originally proposed as a competence model of the knowledge that users need to perform their tasks, much like Moran's Command Language Grammar [9] or Payne and Green's Tag Action Grammar [12] with the special addition of an ontology so that not only the translation of tasks into actions can be described but also the objects and attributes and the transitions that take place when tasks are executed. In other words, whereas TAG is able to describe what users need to know about how to delete a file, ETAG is able to describe what a file is and what happens when it is deleted.

ETAG as a formal notation is considerably harder to create than a non-formal description but it seemed worthwhile since formalisms may also be used for other purposes than mere design specification, including automatic generation of online help, generation of user interface programming specifications and code, easy calculation of usability characteristics like consistency, complexity and learnability, and the aforementioned use of a single notation throughout the whole design process (see: [6]). Not bad for a notation that is also psychologically valid, even though, at the time, the question was raised if such advantages could really counter the difficulties associated with formal representations: this might be the case for large, dependable or safety critical systems but what about the average windows utility or tablet app?

4   Designing New Media

New Media of digital media refers to all forms of purposive information transfer, carried out by digital means. Compared to analogue information carriers such as gramophone records, newspapers and paintings, digital media like web-pages and digital video, in combination with declining hardware costs and more effective tools, allow for (almost) effortless copying and editing. As a consequence of such lack of resistance to change, the design process for media products does not have to meet the same rigour of the design process for (business) software. Media products allow for a much more flexible approach to design with room for testing, experimentation, and fine-tuning of the design target with highly detailed specifications before anything can be build. In a more general way, a similar transition may be identified with every new generation of computer hardware, from the mainframe to the mini-computer, to the personal and game computer, and finally, to the smart phone and ubiquitous computing because of the technical facilities for a flexible design process in combination with increasing demand to meet market and user requirements [7].

In comparison to the design of software systems for business processes or pay rolling, the design process of new media products like interactive websites and mobile apps is lightweight, where flexibility with respect to adapting to changes in the market or the customers' wishes is a key requirement to the design and the design process. Consequently, particularly in the media area, agile design methods like Scrum [13] and Extreme Programming [2] should, at least theoretically, be most useful. In order to find out how our educational curriculum should best be adapted to the needs and wished of the companies who employ our alumni, we did a small preliminary study into design methods utilised by these companies. We asked our Media Technology students who served as their interns to name the types of product that these companies created and the main design methods used. The results indicate that virtually all of these companies either utilise scrum or comparable methods, or that they are in the process of moving from waterfall-like methods to agile design.

Because of the flexibility requirements and the lower repair costs in designing media products, the design process of media products is not only lightweight but also tends to consist of a variety of tools to suit the job without much reliance on a particular design notation. The following list contains about all user interface design representations employed in a modern Media Technology curriculum:

1   personas and mood boards
2   a design concept and view (generally, in text)
3   task lists, task descriptions and task analysis models
4   usage scenarios and storyboards
5   use cases, activity diagrams, entity relationship diagrams
6   interface sketches or paper prototypes, wireframes and screen designs
7   prototypes, demonstrators and the actual working system

Several of these design representations are exemplified in Figs. 6, 7, 8, 9, 10, 11 and 12, some in abbreviated form, taken from the Media Technology curriculum, in particular from student work and some from research.

Matthew Johnson is a 53 year old college educated male, married for over 20 years with Mary, his childhood girlfriend. They has 2 kids, Bill and Evelyn, ages 15 and 17. Matthew and Mary each have a drivers license but, as highly principled members of the green party, they don't own a car. Matthew rides the metro almost daily one the same journey between home in Leyden, where they live in an monumental house at the canal and work at the city council of Delft. He uses his commuting time to read a newspaper and if wifi is available to check for high-priority email.

Fig. 6. A example description of a persona, a typical and fictive user to represent an important class of user or customers for designers to empathise with.

You don't need a key for the building that you might want to enter: You could use a virtual key to open the door. This virtual key exists in your mobile app. You open the app, click on the door that you want to open. Of course, first the administrator will have to provide you with the proper rights. When you have the proper access rights, the door will open; otherwise it remains closed.

The system is intended to make building-access self-sufficient without a need for a doorkeeper or a reception desk. Furthermore, the administrator always knows who is inside the building.

Fig. 7. A design concept. This design concept exemplifies using an RFID/NFC wireless identification card as a key to a door-lock.

Name	Login as a Student
Summary	the student logs in on the network
Actors	Student
Assumptions	Actor is not yet logged in
Description	Actor enters username and password in the entry-fields and hits "enter" or clicks the button "login"
Exceptions	Wrong username or password
Result	Actor is logged in

Fig. 8. A description of a user task as a use case, a user task description from the point of view of the computer system interacting with the outside world.

Ms. Brown is a vital 72 year old. Two years ago she was diagnosed with type II diabetes for which a diet and medication were prescribed.

On three consecutive days, Ms. Brown's blood glucose level has been slightly higher than normal and today it is rather high. A little alarmed, Ms. Brown presses the help-button on the diabetes assistant and a friendly voice assures her that there is nothing to worry about.

The assistant suggests her to redo the measurement using the little finger of her other hand. Ms. Brown now learns that her blood glucose level is only slightly higher than normal and her assistant asks her to take her pills, including an extra TZD "you know, the big blue one" just to be on the safe side.

Fig. 9. An example user scenario presenting how a user may interact with a webpage or an application to analyse, explain or specify the design product.

The design process of media products is based on prototypes, from low-fidelity prototypes including paper prototypes, mock-ups and sketches to increasingly higher fidelity prototypes including clickable prototypes and the design product itself. Secondly, the media design process is a features-driven process, where each design cycle

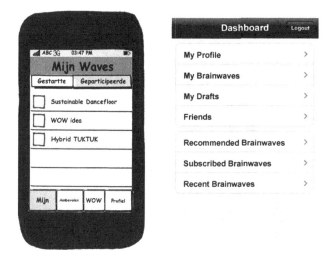

Fig. 10. A paper prototype or a user interface sketch (left) to present test-users or other designers what a design will look like. On the right a clickable prototype to present the interaction design or user-system dialogue of a smartphone application.

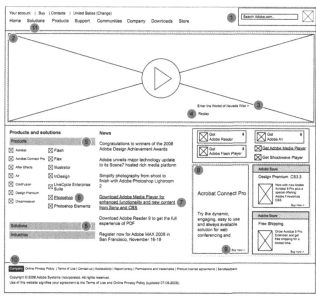

Fig. 11. A wireframe of a web page presenting the layout of a set of standard web-pages without displaying the actual content.

Fig. 12. A demonstrator (or the actual design) as a design prototype which demonstrates actual usage of a product by behaving (almost) as if it is the finished product.

or Scrum sprint focuses on the next most important features to implement. Finally, the media design process is an incremental design process with iteration both during the design process as such, as well as iteration after the design process as such, since maintenance is regarded as including further adaptation to evolving user wishes and tastes.

Media products tend to allow for much flexibility because of the distinction between the 'front-end', the website or user interface of the system and the 'back-end', the database(s) and the Content Management Systems (CMS) which act as the user interface of the application programmer.

The strict separation of the user interface and the data processing part of the application allows for easy adaptation of the front-end whilst keeping the backend stable. While a website is up and running, it is possible to present different groups of users with a different front-end, depending for example, on the basis of the local webserver they use. Next, data collected online about user preferences, conversion rate or sales figures may be used to choose the most successful front-end design. Naturally, such a process of online optimization is not restricted to a single usability evaluation trial but may take the form of a continuous process of adapting the looks and behaviour of a website or mobile app to the behaviour of its users.

Broos et al. [3] noted that a particular user interface characteristic, such as consistency, is seen as a positive characteristic of user interfaces according to HCI theory but that in designing mobile applications other requirements may become much more important. For instance, in designing a mobile social app for the skating community (board skaters, inline skaters and bmx bicyclists) it is natural to make a distinction between the tasks that users execute while they are actually mobile (hence: actively skating) and those tasks executed when the user is able to pick a steady seat to interact with the application. In the former (mobile) case, interaction should be above all automatic and minimal, utilizing sensor information like GPS location recognition instead of the demanding the user to indicate his or her choices on a keyboard or touch screen [3].

Comparable circumstances evolve in ubiquitous computing and interactive environments, and in intelligent and adaptive interfaces. According to Neerincx et al. [10] task performance should be supported by agents to the extent that human operators have sufficient cognitive capacity to focus on the task at hand; in emergency situations like in marine combat situations, agents should take over all but the most essential tasks in order to optimize total task output.

5 Comparing Design Approaches

When comparing the two design approaches listed, one heavyweight and resting on a design notation as the core of the design process, and one lightweight and utilizing whatever tools seem most appropriate to the design cycle at hand, it will be clear that the media design approach is much more flexible and less regulated and thereby better able to rapidly service any changes in customer wishes and needs, exactly as Schwaber and Beedle [13] tried to address with Scrum.

In designing web applications the media design approach works fine. However, with the ongoing transition towards mobile computing, sentient interfaces and ubiquitous computing, it is our opinion that the iterative features-driven design process has to be further adapted to the new design ecology.

First, increasing focus on user requirements and wishes has increased the employment of co-design and co-creation practices. As a consequence, large parts of application design still take place behind the software engineer's work station and perhaps in the usability lab but increasingly often design 'happens' within the actual context of use.

Secondly, computer applications increasingly make use of sensors in the computer device, in the environment or in both. Consider, for instance, using a GPS service or an application which employs the user's movement patterns, or the simple idea to shut down your phone by putting it on its belly. Of course, the experience that the research field has gathered about such interactive environments is rather limited and, as such, it underlines the need to integrate design with investigating usage and usability aspects in the real world. This provides another argument to remove the distance between the design and the application contexts.

On the basis of the utility of complex formal tools like ETAG in our work on media design, we do not opt for the introduction of new and complex tools to visualise or automate aspects of our design activities; rather, we opt to move design more into the direction of the actual context of use and away from the workstation [8]. Design is about products that enable people to act and interact in the real world, and our design specifications, models and software are just there to make designing such products possible but they are not the essence of what design is all about. To 'situate' design in the context of us, we propose two developments to support this transition.

First, we have recently introduced a sensor lab as a middle-ground between the usability lab and the real world. The sensor lab provides all the facilities for the first crude design iterations, including a range of pre-installed networked sensors and interactive display screens, observation cameras and microphones. In this manner we are able to experiment with and investigate the use of sensors in an environment which also provides usability lab facilities. Next to the 'sensorlab', we introduced a 'fablab' to extend the design facilities towards interactive objects in general rather then smart phones and other pre-designed interactive objects, and a 'citylab' was set up as a place to collect and utilise all kinds of data from the public environment; open data. All these lab facilities enable designers to experiment and do 'rapid prototyping' in each design stage, be it conceptualising, functional design, interaction design or tangible design.

Secondly, we investigate the use of self-configuring sensor networks like Almende's 'sense-os' [1]. Networks like these make it possible to hook up one's mobile phone to a network and to collect on-line sensor and usage data from the phone or other networked sensor devices thus enabling a so-called living lab which acts as a usability lab within the everyday real world environment. Actually, self-configurating networks is just another example of the transition to move our design tools to a next higher level of abstraction: what began with programming by wire and evolved alongside assembly languages and user interface toolkits will certainly move towards self-configuring sensor systems, data resources and user adaptation in the internet of things.

References

1. Almende. Observation Systems. http://www.sense-os.nl/ (2011)
2. Beck, K.: Extreme Programming Explained: Embrace Change. Addison-Wesley, Reading (1999)
3. Broos, M., van Gammeren, P., van Steenoven, T., de Haan, G.: Creating a context-aware mobile application to enlarge social cohesion: skating together. Accepted for ECCE 2011 - Designing Collaborative Activities, Rostock, Germany, 24–26 August 2011 (2011)
4. Constantine, L.L., Lockwood, L.A.D.: Software for use: a practical guide to the models and methods of usage-centered design. ACM Press, New York (1999)
5. Foley, J.D., Sukaviriya, P.: History, results, and bibliography of the User Inter-face Design Environment (UIDE), an early model-based system for user interface design and implementation. In: Paternó, F. (ed.) Interactive Systems: Design, Specification, and Verification '94, pp. 3–13. Springer, Heidelberg (1995)
6. de Haan, G.: ETAG-based design: user interface design as mental model specification. In: Palanque, P., Benyon, D. (eds.) Critical Issues in User Interface Systems Engineering, pp. 81–92. Springer, London (1996)
7. de Haan, G.: DevThis: HCI education beyond usability evaluation. In: Lenior, D., Sturm, J., Mulder, I. (eds.) Proceedings Chi Sparks, Arnhem, The Netherlands, 23 June 2011 (2011)
8. de Haan, G., Choenni, S., Mulder, I., Kalidien, S., van Waart, P.: Bringing the research lab into everyday life: exploiting sensitive environments to acquire data for social research. In: Hesse-Biber, S.N. (ed.) The Handbook of Emergent Technologies in Social Research (Chapter 23), pp. 522–541. Oxford University Press, New York (2011)
9. Moran, T.P.: The command language grammar: a representation for the user-interface of interactive systems. Int. J. Man Mach. Stud. 15(1), 3–50 (1981)
10. Neerincx, M.A., Lindenberg, J., Grootjen, M.: Accessibility on the job: cognitive capacity driven personalization. In: Proceedings of HCI International 2005, Las Vegas, USA, 22–27 July 2005 (2005)

11. Paternò, F.: Model-Based Design and Evaluation of Interactive Application. Springer, Heidelberg (1999)
12. Payne, S.J., Green, T.R.G.: Task-action grammars: a model of the mental representation of task languages. Hum Comput. Interact. **2**(2), 93–133 (1986)
13. Schwaber, K., Beedle, M.: Agile Software Development with Scrum. Prentice Hall, Upper Saddle River (2002)
14. Sowa, J.F.: Conceptual Structures: Information Processing in Mind and Machine. Addison-Wesley, Reading (1984)
15. Tauber, M.J.: ETAG: Extended Task Action Grammar: a language for the description of the user's task language. In: Proceedings Interact' 90, pp. 163–168. North-Holland (1990)

A Documentation-Centred Approach to Software Design, Development and Deployment

Brigit van Loggem[(✉)] and Gerrit C. van der Veer

Open University Netherland, Heerlen, The Netherlands
brigit.vanloggem@ou.nl, gerrit@acm.org

Abstract. In this paper, we argue how a documentation-centred approach to systems design and development could provide the different roles involved in this activity with a common ground. A large heterogeneous development team can be seen as a Community of Interest, consisting of individuals brought together from different Communities of Practice. Each group brings to the CoI not only their own skills and experience but also their own values, mental models, working practices, and communication styles. Re-shaping documentation into a boundary object offers a solution to the dual problems of (1) heterogeneous mental models within a software development team and (2) the user support role being peripheral to the team. Documentation that evolves dynamically, changing shape as the development process proceeds, can support communication both internally (between members of a software development team) and externally (between developers and end users).

Keywords: Documentation · Systems development · Communities of practice · Communities of interest · Boundary objects · Shared mental models

1 Introduction

In software design, documentation is an object of neglect. While recognized as one of the deliverables of a software engineering project, very little of it is created with any degree of enthusiasm. User documentation is routinely shrugged off as "there mainly to make up for bad interaction design" and "never read, anyhow" [1, 2]; and systems documentation is seen as a necessary evil that developers prefer to avoid.

Yet forms of communication other than documentation are engaged in without complaint. In this paper, we highlight the core characteristic of documentation as a form of communication. We propose a documentation-centred approach to organizing the work in software development teams. This approach allows for documentation to do what it is best at, which is supporting communication: internally (between members of a software development team) as well as externally (between developers and end users).

First, we discuss a number of issues related to large heterogeneous development teams, noting how these consist of individuals brought together from different backgrounds. In order to work together towards a common goal, they must reconcile

A. Ebert et al. (Eds.): HCIV Workshops 2011, LNCS 8345, pp. 188–200, 2014.
DOI: 10.1007/978-3-642-54894-9_14, © IFIP International Federation for Information Processing 2014

their different views on the system that they are building: a process that is not without difficulty. We then look at how the creation of user documentation such as manuals and online Help fits in with the overall development efforts, noting that this process is not without difficulty either. In the second section of this paper, we investigate how the notion of "boundary objects" may be applied to begin solving both areas of difficulty at the same time, and conclude by mentioning some of the challenges involved in implementing such an approach.

2   Co-operation and Information Exchange in Large Software Development Teams

Many different disciplines are involved in the design and development of any but the most trivial of information systems. In the early stages of computing the hardware formed the limiting factor. Software development was carried out by one programmer, often himself the intended user of the software. Very rapidly, however, the cost of hardware decreased; and the new possibilities offered by faster processors and disk drives and larger memories equally rapidly led to larger and more complex programs being written—"any program will expand to fill available memory", as a jocular maxim of computer science known as the Fifth Law of Computer Programming will have it. Soon, software systems became too complex for one individual to write. Nowadays, almost no commercial software is written by one single programmer. Much software even takes many dozens of man-years to develop, in a process known as "software engineering". The development of computer software has become a collaborative activity for which new languages have been developed, new working methods, and new professional specializations [3].

A quick and by no means exhaustive inventory of a number of IT-related job sites on the Internet conducted on 19 July 2012 revealed that it is no longer sufficient to open a can of programmers to have a software system built. Software engineering calls for project teams to be formed which may include not only programmers but analysts, application administrators, application programmers, application specialists, business analysts, business architects, documentation analysts, enterprise-wide information specialists, HCI designers, information architects, internet engineers, IT consultants, multimedia architects, network designers, network engineers, operations analysts, product specialists, requirements analysts, software analysts, software architects, software engineers, software test specialists, solutions specialists, support analysts, system administrators, systems developers, systems analysts, systems engineers, technical authors, technical consultants, technical designers, technical support engineers, test engineers, testers, trainers, usability designers, usability engineers, web designers, web developers, web producers and many, many more. All these bring to the work their own skill set, which may be any combination of some 75–100 skills directly related to software development[1].

---

[1] See: the Skills Framework for the Information Age (www.sfia.org).

This list does inevitably contain synonyms; especially as there exists no generally-accepted taxonomy of IT-related professions. In an attempt to steer clear of the bewildering array of job titles, we have opted to highlight the widely divergent backgrounds, interests, and skills represented in software development teams by distinguishing the following roles, each responsible for a different aspect of the to-be-built system:

- Functional analysts (FA). These are responsible for eliciting requirements and defining a functional specification of the system.
- System architects (SA). Based on the functional specification delivered by the analysts, the architects are responsible for defining a technical specification of the system.
- Interaction designers (ID). These are responsible for the usability of the system.
- Software programmers (SP). Based on the technical specification delivered by the architects, the programmers are responsible for writing the code.
- User support (US). These are responsible for supporting the end users of the system after it has been built, through user manuals and Help systems.

This simple description of a software development team is, of course, a gross over-simplification. It does, however, have the virtue of allowing us to acknowledge and discuss fundamental differences within such teams, without losing ourselves in subtle detail that is not pertinent to the line of our argument.

2.1   Communities of Practice and Communities of Interest

The different roles within a software development team are set off from one another not just by having different responsibilities and different skill sets, but also by belonging to different "Communities of Practice". A Community of Practice or CoP is made up of "practitioners who work as a community in a certain domain doing similar work" [4]. Any particular CoP has its own standards, values, and ways of doing things. Members of a particular CoP join that CoP's professional organization; read that CoP's professional literature; and learn "on the job" what is "relevant" and what is not. FA sees the to-be-built system in terms of its alignment to business require-ments. SA sees it as an intricate construction of interrelated components. ID is involved with the user interface of the system, while SP's interest is with the way the system consists of blocks of code. US, finally, is set apart even further by focusing on a mental construct, known as the "User Virtual Machine" or UVM; which is defined as "not only everything that a user can perceive or experience (as far as it has a meaning), but also aspects of internal structure and processes as far as the user should be aware of them" [5]. The visible part of the UVM is what these authors refer to as the "perceptual interface" and what is more commonly referred to as the user interface (created by ID); but the UVM as a whole is a much larger conceptual machine that presents itself to the end user.

These different views on the to-be-built system become entrenched over time. Within each CoP, sustained engagement and collaboration leads to boundaries, based on a shared history of learning which is set off against that of other CoPs [6]. Knowledge remains localized, embedded, and invested in practice, so that it is difficult to share with outsiders [7].

When members of multiple CoPs are joined together in a team, with a view to jointly realize a particular well-defined result, they are said to form a Community of Interest or CoI. This is defined as a group of people "from different backgrounds coming together to solve a particular (design) problem of common concern" [4]. A software development team is such a CoI. The members of the CoI that is a development team bring to the efforts their own ideas as to what the system is about and how it works. They have different mental models of the system.

2.2 Mental Models

Although "mental model" is a term traditionally reserved for the understanding that a user constructs of a software artefact during the process of applying it to real-world tasks over a period of time, lately it has been extended [e.g. 8, 9]. By removing the condition of application to a real-world task from the definition, a user becomes any human actor who interacts with a software system over a period of time. Interaction then includes the interaction involved in the construction of the system.

It is not our intention to provide a complete review of the mental models literature. For a wide-ranging and multi-disciplinary overview of mental model theories and their various applications, see [10]. An older seminal work is [11]. Finally, [12] provides a thorough overview of mental models theories. There is little consensus on what the term "mental models" means exactly [see also 13, p. 73, and 14, pp. 109–111]. We can, however, distil a common narrative leaning most heavily on [15] and [16].

According to theory a *mental model* is continuously being constructed in the mind during interaction with a complex system, during all stages of learning from the very beginning all the way to the highest proficiency. Like any model, it is a simplified abstraction that is used to predict behaviours of the referent (the *target system*). In order to predict what the target system will do under certain conditions, the user will mentally apply those conditions to the model, "run" it, and (still mentally) observe the outcome. The model is seen as viable if running it results in reliable predictions about the behaviour of the target system. In situations where the target system is man-made, we can identify on the one hand the *user mental models* held by end users and on the other the *internal models*, held by the system's makers. Information on how the communication between end user and system unfolds may contain a *conceptual model*, which is any model that is explicitly worked out by the User Support role to stimulate meaningful learning in those being instructed.

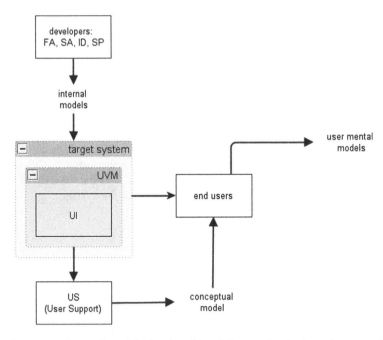

Fig. 1. Overview of mental models developed by different roles in the software engineering process.

As we have seen, the different roles within a software development team interact with different aspects of the system. Therefore, there is not just one internal model but rather a multitude. Rather than converging, team members' understanding of the system, the work, and other team members' expertise has been found to diverge over time. As time goes by, their mental models become increasingly dissimilar [9]. This is related to a decrease in interaction: the further into the project, the less team members engage in meetings and other such forms of communication.

2.3   Communication and Co-operation

Where many people work together towards a common goal, they need to communicate: if they don't, then achieving the goal will be very difficult if not impossible [3, 17] and the CoI will be unsuccessful. It is a sad fact of life that this does indeed happen. Complex software projects regularly fail to meet expectations.

Face-to-face communication is natural and often found to be the preferred channel for information exchange within a software development team. LaToza et al. found that programmers prefer face-to-face communication over every other method for obtaining an understanding of code written by somebody else [8]. However, face-to-face communication goes unrecorded and has spatial and temporal restrictions. Geographically distributed development teams are increasingly common and the system, once built, must be maintained and supported by others than those involved in the original development efforts [18]. For these reasons, most software engineering approaches call for extensive documentation of the development process. A potentially very large number of documents is created in the course of developing a software system [19].

Unfortunately, all this paperwork does not necessarily serve the desired communication. Programmers have been shown to conform to stereotype and go to great lengths to develop an understanding of the code; but they turn to its documentation only when everything else fails. Internal design documents are mostly read by newcomers to a team [8]. Furthermore, programmers have a strong sense of personal ownership of the code and hold enormous amounts of knowledge on the system in their heads. Their concept of "team" is limited to a very small number of direct colleagues, working on the same part of the code; and it is within these small teams only that achievements are documented. LaToza and his co-authors further found that for programmers the documentation serves not so much for information exchange as for information protection; for digging, as the authors call it, a "moat" around the work that has been done. Rather than describe the internal workings of a particular piece of coding, the documentation delineates the code by providing detail on its interface with other code.

To know which document to turn to in order to satisfy a need for information, an understanding is required of all that is available. The closer people are to each other in the team, the more they have the same understanding of what a particular document is good for; to such a degree that it has proven possible "to reconstruct an approximation of the development process based on statements solely about the documentation" [19]. As design documentation documents are read as well as written within the team, it follows that most of the internal documentation is well understood only by those whose work is closely related to that of the author. Communication within the CoI is severely hindered by the different representations that the different CoPs use for external cognition [4], and for actors to reconcile the different meanings is labour-intensive [20].

2.4   User Documentation

Thus far, we have discussed the documentation produced by the User Support (US) role only tangentially; and paid attention mostly to the documentation produced and used by the other roles in the development team. Where the latter's function is one of internal communication within the CoI, be it distributed or co-located and concurrent or over time, the former embodies communication with stakeholders outside the team: the end users of the system. For US documentation is an end rather than a means. This sets US off from the other roles in the CoI even more than the other roles are set off from one another (see Fig. 1). US's primary responsibility is to produce user manuals and Help systems. They describe the system after it has been completely built rather than during its construction; and indeed, frequently they are not even part of the development team but called in at a later stage, when the CoI is about to be or even has already been disbanded. US do not create that aspect of the system that they describe (the UVM) but identify the UVM as it emerges from the other roles' efforts. A software system is a self-contained "world" with its own objects (think of the Clipboard in many operating systems; of templates, style sheets and fields in a word processing environment; or of layers in an image editor). These software-specific objects, with their mutual dependencies and the rules governing their behaviour, are as much part of the UVM as is the interaction layer through which they are accessed. A user needs a thorough understanding of the UVM to gain complete mastery of a particular software tool, and apply it successfully to every task it can possibly be applied to. Such understanding is fostered through meta-communication in the shape of documentation or training [16]. As a "correct" user mental model is crucial to the end user's gainfully applying the system to real-world work, US strives to guide the formation of such a correct model; by explicitizing established misconceptions and subsequently eradicating them [21], or by presenting a conceptual model as depicted in Fig. 1 [22, 23].

In order to create a conceptual model for end users to learn from, US first need to develop their own correct mental model of the UVM. They do so by studying the internal documentation left behind by the development team and by holding formal or informal interviews with those of the development team who are still available. Then, they apply their knowledge of documentation and instruction to the scattered knowledge gleaned. This is a rather haphazard process, the result of which is often unsatisfactory. There is a strong need for US to be truly part of the CoI that creates the system. Only then will they be able to create user support materials that are genuinely helpful to end users.

3   Documentation as a Boundary Object

All design efforts, including the design of complex software systems, require the sharing of work artefacts [3]. Incremental creation of external representations is a strong mechanism for negotiating a shared understanding of the task at hand [4, 24]. In a seminal article [20], Susan Leigh Star presented the concept of boundary objects binding together heterogeneous groups of actors. Star's own words cannot be surpassed in describing the concept, as follows: "objects which inhabit several intersecting social worlds [...] *and* satisfy the informational requirements of each of them. Boundary objects are plastic enough to adapt to local needs and the constraints of the several parties employing them, yet robust enough to maintain a common identity across sites. They are weakly structured in common use, and become strongly structured in individual-site use. These objects may be abstract or concrete. They have different meanings in different social worlds but their structure is common to more than one world to make them recognizable, a means of translation. The creation and management of boundary objects is a key process in developing and maintaining coherence across intersecting social worlds" [20, p. 393].

The current approach to documentation, in which every CoP within the CoI develops their own documentation separate from the others, is unsatisfactory; for a number of reasons:

- It further reinforces existing barriers (or "digs moats") between the different groups [8], as always one CoP is forced to discuss a document written in another CoP's language.
- It leads to information being lost, as translations have to be made between the different perspectives on the system.
- It is resource-intensive, as the different documents are all created from scratch.
- It is wasteful, as the separate documents have a limited life-span that is restricted to a particular development stage.
- It offers no guarantees for providing an exact description of what has been actually built at any given moment in time, as documenting and designing/developing are separate activities.
- It backfires, as people lose track of what has been documented; in which document a particular information item can be found; and where the different documents are stored [19].

In this paper, we propose a solution to the dual problems of (1) heterogeneous mental models within a software development team and (2) the user support role being peripheral to the team. The solution we propose is based on re-shaping documentation into a boundary object.

3.1   A Revised Role for Documentation

When carefully thought-out, one and the same set of documents could fulfil the roles of internal design documentation and user documentation. A semi-formal structure can be envisaged in which user requirements are laid down, after which the resulting documents are at every step further refined so that they become first the design specification and finally the user documentation.

A semi-formal description is one that combines the rigidity of a formalism with the flexibility of narrative. Within a pre-described framework, where building blocks are identified by (for example) fixed headings, a document's required content can be assembled at any given stage. Such a document is accessible to and can be a base for discussion between FA, SA, ID, SP, US and end users, who can then co-operate throughout the development cycle without loss and without spending any time or other resources in duplication; developing an ever-more detailed shared mental model over time.

Figure 2 gives a schematic overview of what such a revised approach could look like. Requirements are collected by the prospective end users together with FA; through whichever method is deemed appropriate. The resulting requirements are then recorded in a semi-formal document. This is agreed on by all those involved, and handed over to SA and ID for transformation into a functional description of the User Virtual Machine or UVM. Before SP starts working on its implementation, the UVM may be evaluated together with the users by means of any prototype-based method. Whichever form the prototype takes, however, the final, agreed-on version will become part of the documentation. SP then designs the implementation details and builds the tangible product. Finally, the documentation is worked up into an As Built description. Parts of this will now function as user documentation, while other parts will serve as systems documentation to be referred to for maintenance and updates. The documentation will now always exactly mirror the current state of the system. As a result, significantly higher quality should be achievable at significantly lower cost.

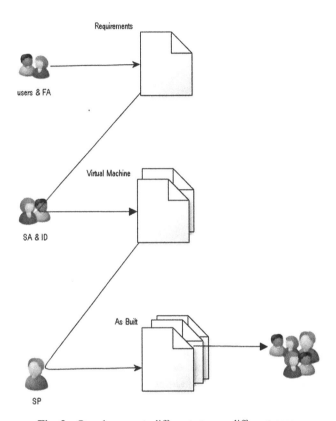

Fig. 2. One document, different stages, different uses.

In this approach, the documentation is at all times a boundary object in the meaning of the term defined by Star, inhabiting the worlds of all CoPs involved in the CoI. Being developed incrementally by all, it will satisfy the informational requirements of all parties, maintaining a common identity yet allowing for local detail. Bridging boundaries rather than digging moats, the ever-elusive quest for consensus is made redundant. "When participants in the intersecting worlds create representations together, their different commitments are resolved into representations – in the sense that a fuzzy image is resolved by a microscope. This resolution does not mean consensus." It is important to maximize not just the communication between worlds, but equally well their autonomy [20].

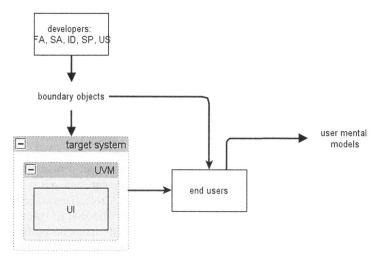

Fig. 3. Documentation as a boundary object.

3.2 A Revised Role for User Support

In the revised workflow described in the previous paragraph, mental models development is concentrated in the co-creation of documentation. Internal mental models as depicted in Fig. 1 are aligned as they develop. Moreover, the desired mental models of the intended end users are taken into account from the beginning. It follows then that there is no longer a need for User Support to separately develop their own mental models and then translate these into conceptual models to instruct end users (see Fig. 3). However, this does not mean that User Support has become superfluous. On the contrary, the particular expertise held by this role is indispensable now: not at the end of the development process, but rather throughout.

For boundary objects to function as such, standardization of methods is required [20]. As the process now hinges on one set of documents, any flaws in these will have repercussions at every subsequent stage. The semi-formal structure underlying the documentation must therefore be very carefully designed in its own right, to be tightly incorporated in the methodology that is applied. If this approach is to yield the desired benefits, a number of requirements must be met:

- The FA, SA, ID and SP roles must be supported in their endeavours to write in such a manner that the result is of value not only to themselves but to all other roles as well. This can be expected to require a major effort. Software developers are not known for either their willingness or their capacity to write and they will need to be motivated to do so. Then, they will need to be provided with instruction, guidelines and templates and most of all, they will need continuous monitoring and coaching.
- It must be clear who "owns" the documentation at any given stage. Transfer of ownership of the document marks the transition from one stage to the next.

- At every stage, the documentation must be able to incorporate additional new content such as requirements and features, systems logic and user interaction, and the nitty-gritty of coding solutions.
- Not only must the documentation provide room for all the content, it must also clearly prescribe the nature and scope of the content that is needed at every stage. A document set that is owned by different groups of people at different moments in time must be self-explanatory and self-directing: its contents cannot be left to chance or the personal preference of whoever happens to be working on a particular section.

Whereas initially the documentation consists of little more than a structure allowing for requirements and features to be recorded, the requirements analysis is concluded by creating "slots" for the design of the UVM by the SA role. This stage in turn is completed with not just production of the prototype, but also that of "slots" for the implementation design details that will be added by the SP role. Consolidation of all the information into an As Built deliverable that truthfully reflects that which has been delivered, finally, must be executed with a view to the final task of the documentation: that of supporting users on the one hand and providing a starting point for maintenance and further development on the other.

All these requirements mean that existing methodologies are no longer applicable and must be re-invented. Making software engineering documentation-centred can succeed only if the software development team includes a documentation specialist from the very beginning. User Support, with its core competence of documentation, is perfectly placed to truly make documentation into a boundary object.

4   Conclusion

Documentation has long been regarded as a necessary evil and treated accordingly. Internal design documents are discarded when the next stage of development begins. Development is often not documented beyond comments in the code, which tend to be few and far between. End user documentation is produced, if at all, at the very last moment by someone not involved in the design or development of the system. A recently proposed methodology for software engineering known as agile development calls for as little documentation as possible, and suggests internal communication is best carried out face-to-face. (Yet although agile developers on the shop floor may not be keen to produce documentation, they do feel that there should be more of it than there is [18].)

Documentation is recorded communication; and communication is what allows people to work together, creating something that one single person could not possibly achieve. Without communication, we cannot expect to build an interactive system that genuinely meets people's needs. The multitude of written documents produced between an interactive system's inception and the day on which it is last used, represent a missed opportunity for effective communication. All are written in their own language: some formal, some informal. Rather than facilitating the exchange of ideas and insights between different roles and across different stages of the system's life cycle, they scatter knowledge to such a degree as to make it effectively inaccessible.

The proof of the pudding is, of course, as always in the eating. Applying the approach described in this paper, in which one semi-formal, continuously evolving set of documents forms the focal point for everybody's contribution, will not be trivial. To test the approach in a real-life environment where a complex piece of software is developed to a real-life end, a large number of people need to believe in the concept and have enough faith in it to actually see it through. We believe that this will be an extremely rewarding and constructive exercise.

References

1. Mehlenbacher, B.: Documentation: not yet implemented, but coming soon. In: Jacko, J.A., Sears, A. (eds.) The HCI Handbook: Fundamentals, Evolving Technologies, and Emerging Applications, pp. 527–543. Lawrence Erlbaum, Mahwah, NJ (2003)
2. van Loggem, B.E.: User documentation: the Cinderella of information systems. In: Rocha, Á., Correia, A.M., Wilson, T., Stroetmann, K.A. (eds.) Advances in Information Systems and Technologies, vol. 206, pp. 167–177. Springer, Berlin (2013)
3. Barthelmess, P., Anderson, K.M.: A view of software development environments based on activity theory. Comput. Supp. Cooper. Work **11**, 13–37 (2002)
4. Arias, E.G., Fischer, G.: Boundary objects: their role in articulating the task at hand and making information relevant to it. In: International ICSC Symposium on Interactive and Collaborative Computing (ICC'2000) (2000)
5. van der Veer, G.C., van Vliet, H.: The human-computer interface is the system: a plea for a poor man's HCI component in software engineering curricula. In: Ramsey, D., Bourque, P., Dupuis, R. (eds.) 14th Conference on Software Engineering Education and Training, pp. 276–286. IEEE Computer Society (2001)
6. Wenger, E.: Communities of Practice: Learning, Meaning, and Identity. Cambridge University Press, Cambridge, England (1998)
7. Carlile, P.R.: A pragmatic view of knowledge and boundaries: boundary objects in new product development. Org. Sci. **13**, 442–455 (2002)
8. LaToza, T.D., Venolia, G., DeLine, R.: Maintaining mental models: a study of developer work habits. In: 28th International Conference on Software Engineering, pp. 492–501. ACM, Shanghai, China (2006)
9. Levesque, L.L., Wilson, J.M., Wholey, D.R.: Cognitive divergence and shared mental models in software development project teams. J. Org. Behav. **22**, 135–144 (2001)
10. Rogers, Y., Rutherford, A., Bibby, P.A. (eds.): Models in the Mind: Theory, Perspective and Application. Academic Press, London (1992)
11. Gentner, D., Stevens, A. (eds.): Mental Models. Erlbaum, Hillsdale, NJ (1983)
12. Schwamb, K.B.: Mental Models: A Survey (1990)
13. O'Malley, C., Draper, S.: Representation and interaction: Are mental models all in the mind? In: Rogers, Y., Rutherford, A., Bibby, P.A. (eds.) Models in the Mind: Theory, Perspective and Application, pp. 73–92. Academic Press, London (1992)
14. Payne, S.J.: On mental models and cognitive artefacts. In: Rogers, Y., Rutherford, A., Bibby, P.A. (eds.) Models in the Mind: Theory, Perspective and Application. Academic Press, London (1992)

15. Norman, D.A.: Some observations on mental models. In: Gentner, D., Stevens, A. (eds.) Mental Models, pp. 131–153. Erlbaum Press, Hillsdale, NJ (1983)

16. van der Veer, G.C., Tauber, M.J., Waern, Y., van Muylwijk, B.: On the interaction between system and user characteristics. Behav. Inf. Technol. **4**, 289–308 (1985)

17. Curtis, B., Krasner, H., Iscoe, N.: A field study of the software design process for large systems. Commun. ACM **31**, 1268–1287 (1988)

18. Stettina, C.J., Heijstek, W.: Necessary and neglected? An empirical study of internal documentation in agile software development teams. In: SIGDOC '11, pp. 159–166. ACM (2011)

19. de Boer, R.C., van Vliet, H.: Writing and reading software documentation: how the development process may affect understanding. In: 2009 ICSE Workshop on Cooperative and Human Aspects on Software Engineering, pp. 40–47. IEEE Computer Society, Vancouver, Canada (2009)

20. Star, S.L., Griesemer, J.R.: Institutional ecology, translations and boundary objects: amateurs and professionals in Berkeley's museum of vertebrate zoology, 1907-39. Soc. Stud. Sci. **19**, 387–420 (1989)

21. Uzuntiryaki, E., Geban, Ö.: Effect of conceptual change approach accompanied with concept mapping on understanding of solution concepts. Instr. Sci. **33**, 311–339 (2005)

22. Mayer, R.E., Gallini, J.K.: When is an illustration worth ten thousand words? J. Educ. Psychol. **82**, 715–726 (1990)

23. Allbritton, D.W., McKoon, G., Gerrig, R.J.: Metaphor-based schemas and text representation: making connections through conceptual metaphors. J. Exp. Psychol. Learn. Mem. Cogn. **21**, 612–625 (1995)

24. Stettina, C.J., Heijstek, W., Fægri, T.E.: Documentation work in agile teams: the role of documentation formalism in achieving a sustainable practice. AGILE Conference (AGILE 2012), Dallas, TX (2012)

eCITY: Evolutionary Software Architecture Visualization – An Evaluation

Taimur Khan[1(✉)], Henning Barthel[2], Liliana Guzman[2],
Achim Ebert[1], and Peter Liggesmeyer[1]

[1] Computer Graphics and HCI Group, University of Kaiserslautern,
Gottlieb-Daimler-Str., 67663 Kaiserslautern, Germany
{tkhan,ebert,liggesmeyer}@cs.uni-kl.de
[2] Fraunhofer IESE, Fraunhofer-Platz 1, 67663 Kaiserslautern, Germany
{Henning.Barthel,Liliana.Guzman}@iese.fraunhofer.de

Abstract. An essential component in the evolution and maintenance of large-scale software systems is to track the structure of a software system to explain how a system has evolved to its present state and to predict its future development. Current mainstream tools facilitating the structural evolution of software architecture by visualization are confined with easy to integrate visualization techniques such as node-link diagrams, while more applicable solutions have been proposed in academic research. To bridge this gap, we have incorporated additional views to a conventional tool that integrates an interactive evolving city layout and a combination of charts. However, due to a limited access to the stakeholders it was not possible to solicit them for a formal modeling process. Instead, an early prototype was developed and a controlled experiment was conducted to illustrate the vital role of such in-situ visualization techniques when aiming to understanding the evolution of software architecture.

Keywords: Software architecture visualization · Software comprehension · Software evolution · Experiment

1 Introduction

Mainstream software systems undergo continuous changes in order to adapt to new technologies, to meet new requirements, and to repair errors [1]. Inevitably, the software in question expands in both size and complexity, often leading to a situation where the original design gradually decays unless proper maintenance is performed [2]. However, due to the "complex, abstract, and difficult to observe" nature of software systems performing visually supported maintenance can be quite complicated [3]. The field of software visualization aims to ease this task by providing visual representations and techniques that make the software more comprehensible. A key ingredient of these visualizations is a visual representation of the software structure that assists in creating a mental map of the system. Such a mental map provides a means to examine product properties such as size and quality indicators and process events such as errors found or changes made [4].

A. Ebert et al. (Eds.): HCIV Workshops 2011, LNCS 8345, pp. 201–224, 2014.
DOI: 10.1007/978-3-642-54894-9_15, © IFIP International Federation for Information Processing 2014

With respect to the analysis of the evolution of software, it is essential to track the structure of the software system to explain and document how a system has evolved to its present state and to predict its future development [5]. There are a number of free and commercial tools that can be found in both academic and industrial research with the sole purpose of improving software architecture evolution comprehension through the use of visualization. On the one hand, industrial applications are confined to easy to integrate visualization methods and metaphors that lack the sophistication to handle informative large-scale software architecture evolution visualization. While on the other, academic researchers have developed numerous solutions that have not made it to the mainstream [6–8]. The work of Telea et al. [7] indicates two inter-related reasons for this phenomenon and we agree with their findings; (1) stakeholders do not have the time to try new tools to see if it fits in their context, and (2) tool developers cannot create an product that satisfies all possible needs. Our aim is to bridge this gap by addressing the following two factors: (1) propose visualization methods and metaphors that do not significantly deviate from current solutions - analysts should be comfortable with the software architecture representations visually, and (2) the ability to monitor, visualize, and interact with large-scale software systems in real-time - be able to deal with the scale and complexity of real-world software applications.

The goal of this project is to utilize research ideas in the area of software architecture evolution visualization and to apply these modern techniques in the context of mainstream software architecture maintenance and evolution tools. To achieve this goal we have been working together with the Fraunhofer IESE, to enhance their conventional SAVE (Software Architecture Visualization and Evaluation) tool that evaluates software architectures while they are constructed as well as after their construction [9]. However, due to a limited access to the stakeholders it was not possible to solicit them for a formal modeling process. Instead, a prototype was developed to augment SAVE through the use of different views to further the daunting task of large-scale software architecture evolution analysis. While the experimental results show that some details were missed through this non-formal approach, they also show that an improved configuration of the visualization influences the efficiency and effectiveness of basic software architecture evolution tasks significantly. More specifically, a gain of efficiency by 170 % and a gain of effectiveness by 15 % in these basic tasks were realized simply by selecting a different set of views. Based on these results we claim that considerable benefits can be attained by incorporating such in-situ visualization methods and metaphors to a conventional software architecture maintenance and evolution tool.

The organization of this paper is as follows: related work is examined in Sect. 2, the eCITY tool is described in Sect. 3, and the experiment setup and results are reported in Sect. 4. Finally, we conclude this paper and look at possible future work in Sect. 5.

2 Related Work

As software maintenance is mainly performed at code level, majority of the visualizations employ a 2D line-based approach to represent software evolution [10–12]. In such scenarios, the adopted procedure is to visually map a code line to a pixel line and to utilize color to depict the age of a code fragment [10]. Additional focus has been to enhance interaction techniques to improve navigation and exploration of the underlying data [11,12]. While these techniques thrive in tracking the line-based structure of software systems and reveal change dependencies at given moments in time, they lack the sophistication to offer insight into attribute and structural changes made throughout the development process.

In contrast, there are only a small number of visualizations that represent structural changes of a system architecture over time [8]. Holten and van Wijk present a technique that compares the software hierarchies of two software versions [13]. The algorithm positions matching nodes opposite to each other to better compare the two versions. They utilize shading to highlight nodes that are present in one version but not the other. Further, Holten employs his well-known edge bundling technique to highlight and track the selected hierarchy.

Collberg et al. illustrate the use of a graph drawing technique, that has a temporal component for the visualization of large graphs, to visualize the evolution of a software system [14]. They employ force-directed layouts to plot call graphs, control-flow graphs, and inheritance graphs of Java programs. Changes that the graphs have gone through since inception are highlighted through the use of color. Nodes and edges are initially given the color assigned to its author (red, yellow, or green) and progressively age to blue.

A recent research focus is to utilize and extend intuitive metaphors to aid in the visualization of software systems. Our work is in fact inspired by the original contribution of Steinbrückner et al., where they propose the idea of stable city layouts for evolving software systems [4]. They describe a three-staged visualization approach, where the first stage constitutes of a primary model responsible for capturing the software system structure and its evolution details. The second stage refers to a secondary model that initially adds geometric information to the primary model. This model is then further enhanced through the use of elevation levels to directly depict a software systems development history in the layout. Finally the third stage is comprised of tertiary models that are derived from secondary models by applying projections, coloring, or the imposition of symbols or diagrams. While we employ the above-mentioned basic secondary model, we utilize a combination of animated transitions to grow or shrink the city instead of using different elevation levels and color interpolations to highlight the evolution of components.

3 eCITY: An Evolving City

The eCITY tool follows the methodology of Eick et al. [15] to employ the well-known idea of multiple architectural views of large and complex software systems with a focus on evolution tasks. This approach was adopted to enhance the architects' current workflow that relies solely on the SAVE Diagram View (Sect. 3.1) - a view that provides extensive evaluation possibilities but one that does not have the best design to handle the complexities of exploring the systems evolution. To address this shortcoming, we have implemented a combination of views; a Timeline View (see Sect. 3.2) and an evolving city layout (see Sect. 3.3).

eCITY exploits the core functionality provided by the Fraunhofer SAVE tool. One of these features is responsible for extracting the underlying architectural model from the software systems source code. This model is generated through a combination of an initial fact extraction and a number of delta fact extractions, to produce a data model that contains architectural data about a software system over a period of time. In this section, we describe the three main views of the eCITY tool that utilize this data model to perform evolutionary software architecture tasks; namely the *SAVE Diagram View*, the *Timeline View*, and the *City View*. Here, it is important to note that although the SAVE Diagram View is part of the original SAVE tool, it has been incorporated in the eCITY tool so that the users have access to their original workflows. Both the Timeline and City Views have been designed to help the architects in accessing the structural changes of the software system in a more effective and efficient manner than using the SAVE Diagram View alone. We support this claim through the results of our experiment that are presented in Sect. 4.

3.1   SAVE Diagram View

The SAVE Diagram View (Fig. 1a) is the main view used by the software architects at the Fraunhofer IESE to explore and assess a software systems architecture. The main features of this view are: its configurability (enabling and/or disabling certain graphical elements), the expressiveness of its graphical elements, and its rich-features that allow for extensive evaluations. Projects, packages, and classes are all represented as components in the SAVE Diagram View, while edges between components depict their relationships to one another. In general, SAVE has a nested approach in which high-level components have rectangular representations that may be either expanded one-level deeper into the hierarchy or expanded completely to show the entire underlying hierarchy. Conversely, components may be collapsed in a similar manner. The work of Knodel et al. [9] discusses these elements and their features in further detail.

The complexity of a structural diagram is typically reduced by either creating new diagrams of selected components or through the use of various filters. For the purpose of analyzing the underlying software structure over time, the analysts rely on two distinct filters: the *Relation Type* filter and the *Point-In-Time* diagram filter. The user may reduce visual clutter, while solely examining the software structure, by applying a *Relation Type* filter to hide some or all of the displayed dependencies. Additionally, the user may apply a *Point-In-Time* diagram filter to explore the system at a particular point in time. As shown in Fig. 1b applying a *Point-In-Time* diagram filter updates the SAVE Diagram View with icons to depict the modification status at a certain point in time

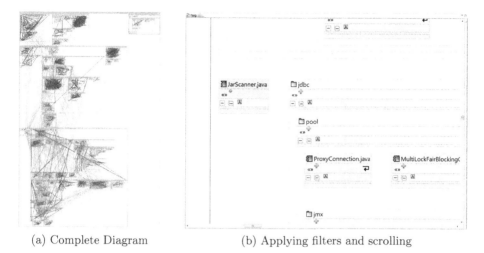

(a) Complete Diagram   (b) Applying filters and scrolling

Fig. 1. SAVE diagram view

according to the chosen parameters: a triangle depicts modifications, addition symbol depicts insertions, minus symbol depicts removals, and a circle depicts no change.

It was a conscious decision to incorporate the same view into eCITY, thereby not completely replacing the architects' normal workflow. Instead, we provide them with the views described in Sects. 3.2 and 3.3 to have additional perspectives of their evolution data.

3.2   Timeline View

In the original SAVE workflow, architects apply a *Point-In-Time* filter to update the SAVE Diagram and manually track the number and type of changes made - a process which is deemed not only tedious but also error prone. The first step of this workflow requires the user to load the underlying data model that represents the software system being analyzed. It is during this process that data regarding the modification status of both the individual components as well as the overall hierarchy is stored; i.e. the distribution of these changes over time are stored in a convenient and easy to access manner.

As such, the main purpose of the Timeline View is to provide the user with an overview of changes made to the system over time. A combination of interactive bar charts that represent the number of modifications, insertions, and removals made to packages and classes are employed to achieve this task. A typical color scheme was employed to depict these changes; modifications, insertions, and removals are represented using yellow, green, and red colors respectively.

The initial view consists of a combined plot (Fig. 2a left); one of which is an overview where the user can select and manipulate a rectangular region, the other provides details on the selection (Fig. 2a right). Further, the user may

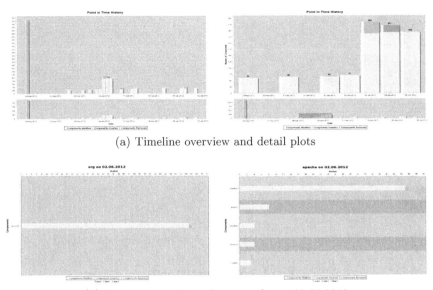

(a) Timeline overview and detail plots

(b) Top components and org.apache on 02.06.2012

Fig. 2. Timeline view

interactively select a point in time and update all three views simultaneously. Such a selection, changes the plot and provides details of the top level component at the chosen time stamp (Fig. 2b left). Further, the user may recursively explore the distribution of changes over the hierarchy (Fig. 2b right). The user may also navigate back to the previous chart or directly to the overview chart of Fig. 2a. There are additional interaction possibilities with the charts; hovering over a chart component highlights the relevant subtree in the City View and selecting the chart component zooms onto the graphical representation of that particular component in the City View.

3.3 City View

An additional mode of analysis while monitoring the structural changes made to a software system is to track where these changes are made, i.e. where are packages and classes added, modified, or removed over time. In order to achieve this goal in the original SAVE workflow, architects apply multiple *Point-In-Time* filters and have to keep a mental map of these changes - this process is also deemed tedious, error prone, and depending on the size of the system hierarchy quite difficult. The City View (Fig. 3) addresses these concerns by providing an overview of the entire system architecture at a particular point in its evolution process and provides the user a means to interactively explore these changes over the system hierarchy.

It was mentioned in related works that our approach is inspired by the work of Steinbrückner et al. [4] and in particular the secondary model they present.

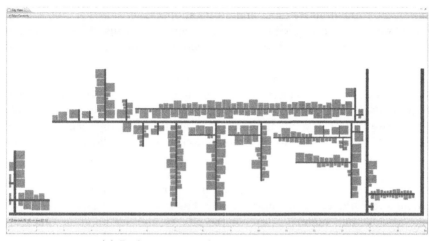

(a) Package org.apache.tomcat on 26.06.2012

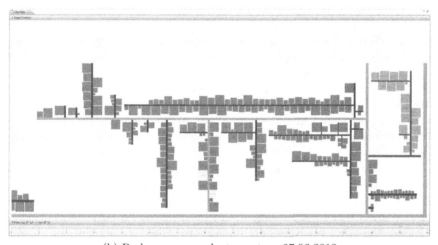

(b) Package org.apache.tomcat on 27.06.2012

Fig. 3. Exploring org.apache.tomcat with eCITY (see Appendix C for details) (Color figure online)

While they focus on geometrically mapping different details of the development history onto this model, we choose to manipulate this layout to highlight structural changes over time. Figure 3a depicts our implementation of their secondary model, where packages are represented by streets and classes are symbolized by plots. The vertical or horizontal orientation of a street alters depending on its parent street/package orientation. Plots are positioned along the street representing the package they belong to; to reduce space requirements, they are positioned on both sides of the street. The layout algorithm adjusts the length of the street to hold all its plots and all its subpackages. Further, the size of a plot may vary according to a given scaling parameter; because connectivity is an important measure for an architect, we scaled plots according to its connectivity to other artifacts.

While the user loads the SAVE data model, we calculate the initial layout as described above and sequentially go through the *Point-In-Times* to update the layout by adding and removing both classes and packages. Such details of the city layout as well as the modification status of its components are stored in key frames to allow for real-time interaction. Utilizing a slider and key frame animation techniques colors are interpolated and the city suburbs grow and shrink to represent changes made between two points in time.

The city may be explored using the mouse to pan and zoom to examine its suburbs or different parts more closely. Further, the user may interactively invoke a slider and manually update the city to another point in time. This interaction mechanism animates the city through the use of colors that depict the modification status and the growing and shrinking of suburbs to represent the addition and/or removal of classes and package. This functionality may be observed by comparing Fig. 3a with Fig. 3b, where certain classes are modified (color changes to yellow) and a package is inserted in the top right corner (colored green). The color scheme employed is quite similar to that of the Timeline View charts, where yellow, green, red, and grey are used to depict the modification, insertion, removal, and unchanged modification status of each component.

Besides panning and zooming capabilities, two distinct modes of operation have been incorporated into this view; one of these modes is triggered when the user selects a point in time in the combined plot of Fig. 2a, while the other mode requires the user to interact with a time slider. In the former mode the city may either animate or instantaneously update itself to the chosen point in time depending on whether the *Time Animation* is enabled or disabled. On the other hand, interacting with the time slider interactively updates the city to an older or a newer version depending on the direction chosen. As soon as the slider is released, the other two views are updated to reflect the active point in time. The user also has the possibility to reset the views or toggle certain animations using the popup menu. Finally, with mouse-over he is able to see the name of the underlying component, which comes in handy when he is zoomed out of the city.

4   Experiment

We proposed eCITY for improving the analysis of software architecture evolution over time. In particular, we assume that through the use of the Timeline and City views, software architects would be more efficient and effective in analyzing architectural changes. We also expect that eCITY will be better accepted and perceived as more useful than SAVE. For testing these assumptions, we designed and performed a controlled experiment.

4.1   Research Purpose and Hypotheses

The first goal was to compare the SAVE and eCITY configurations with respect to the efficiency and effectiveness achieved by analysts when they analyze architectural changes. Thus, we defined the following research hypotheses:

- H_1: Analysts using the eCITY configuration are more efficient than analysts using the SAVE configuration when they analyze the evolution of software architectures.
- H_2: Analysts using the eCITY configuration are more effective than analysts using the SAVE configuration when they analyze the evolution of software architectures.

The second goal was to compare SAVE and eCITY with respect to their acceptance and usability. Therefore, we define the two additional research hypotheses:

- H_3: Analysts accept the eCITY configuration more than the SAVE configuration when they analyze the evolution of software architectures.
- H_4: Analysts consider the eCITY configuration more useful than the SAVE configuration when they analyze the evolution of software architectures.

4.2   Operationalization

In order to test the above hypotheses, we operationalized the four variables of interest, selected a software system to be analyzed, and designated the tasks to be performed. First, the variables of interest were operationalized as follows:

i.   Efficiency is the time required for accomplishing a set of given tasks.
ii. Effectiveness is the difference between the true and actual score related to a task.
iii. Acceptability is measured using the Technology Acceptance Model (TAM), which is a valid and reliable questionnaire for assessing technology acceptance and use [16]. Out of 31 questions in the original TAM, we selected 7 questions focused on performance and effort expectancy (Appendix A). All questions were rated using a five-point Likert scale (1: I strongly disagree, 5: I strongly agree).
iv. Usability is measured using the questionnaire proposed by Nestler et al. [17]. Considering the purposes of the eCITY configuration, we selected 4 out of 5 defined dimensions and 15 out of 269 questions. The selection was discussed with evaluation experts. The dimensions and related questions are listed in Appendix B. Each question is rated using a five-point Likert scale (1: I strongly disagree, 5: I strongly agree).

Second, we selected the Apache Tomcat system as the system to investigate because it is a real software system and its architectural models were available in SAVE. Finally, three types of architectural evolution tasks were identified with the support of experts. These are:

i. *Counting:* Identifying changes made to the system on a specific date or changes made to a subcomponent in a time period.
ii. *Find Date:* Identifying the time period with the most number of changes or when a component has been changed the most.
iii. *Find Package/s:* Identifying the subcomponents of a chosen component that have been changed in a time period, find modules/subcomponents that are present since the earliest version and have not been changed since, or find modules/subcomponents that have changed a lot in a particular time period.

4.3   Pilot Study

A pilot study was conducted with two experts in the field of software architecture. Our purpose was to get an early feedback regarding the experimental design, the selected tasks, and the time required for solving them.

The first expert completed the tasks using the SAVE configuration in an hour and fifteen minutes. He considered the tasks to be realistic. However, he suggested that while asking the user if certain components are changed often or not at all, we should focus on a smaller sub-package rather than the entire system. Hence reducing the time required to perform the tasks related to finding packages.

The second expert solved the tasks using the eCITY configuration in forty five minutes. He also considered the set of selected tasks to be realistic. Additionally, he made recommendations regarding the visualization. These included: (1) keeping the date format and color coding uniform, (2) adding the option to enable and disable animations, and (3) adding feedback regarding the enabled/disabled features in the City popup menu. These issues were discussed and solved.

Consequently, the original set of tasks were tweaked to address the experts' feedback.

4.4   Controlled Experiment

Subjects. The controlled experiment was conducted with 38 participants. Out of the 38 participants, 3 were software engineering experts of the Fraunhofer Institute for Experimental Software Engineering (IESE) and 35 were graduated students in computer science from the Technical University of Kaiserslautern. The three experts involved have a deep knowledge in the field of software architecture and prior experience in SAVE, while all the students have theoretical knowledge about software architectures.

Due to the lack of experts available and their previous experience in SAVE, experts were asked to work with SAVE and then with eCITY. Students were randomly distributed in two groups working either with SAVE or eCITY. This was intended for avoiding learning effects.

Experimental Setup. The same software architecture was explored using either SAVE or eCITY. Thus, two computers were prepared for the experiment:

one with Eclipse and the SAVE Configuration and the other with Eclipse and the eCITY configuration. The Eclipse workspace was prepared for both installations to contain the required data: a SAVE data model containing 16 fact extractions of the Apache Tomcat system between the time period 14.05.2012 and 02.07.2012. Each instance of the Apache Tomcat system was extracted from its public repository. Four of these instances were complemented with the insertion, modification, and removal of some fictitious packages and classes to create some interesting artifacts.

Each workspace was completely restored at the beginning of each experiment session. A different visualization introduction handout was provided to each participant depending on the installation used. Additionally, the participants were afforded with a walkthrough of the functionalities and features that would assist them in the experiment process. The participants were then asked to perform the tasks and questionnaires described in Sect. 4.2.

Each participant was allowed unlimited time to finish the tasks and to fill the questionnaires regarding Acceptability and Usability. The resulting materials were then collected and analyzed.

Data Collection. The time and the answer to each task was collected using an exercise sheet. Additionally, a printed questionnaire was used for eliciting the perception of the participants regarding the acceptance and the usability of the corresponding configurations, i.e. SAVE or eCITY.

Data Analysis. A transcript of the collected efficiency, effectiveness, acceptability, and usability data was compiled in excel. The subject data is kept anonymous and confidential. Regarding effectiveness, tasks were weighted according to their difficulty: Counting and Find Date tasks were awarded 3 points each and Find Package/s tasks were awarded 4 point each. The latter sets of tasks were weighted higher as they were deemed to be more complex.

We applied descriptive statistics methods such as the sample mean, standard deviation, median, and range to the experimental data. Further, we used the *MegaStat* excel plug-in to statistically test our hypotheses using the Mann-Whitney-U-Test. It is appropriate for our scenario due to the size of the data and its ability to handle both normal and non-normal distributions. We performed the tests with a confidence level for rejecting the null hypotheses at 99 %.

4.5   Results

The statistical evaluation of the experiment is presented in this section. As such, the time required for tasks, the results of the tasks, the acceptability of the configuration, and the usability of each configuration is presented. Further, we argue for the earlier stated hypotheses by performing hypotheses testing on the collected data. We conclude this section by examining the threats to validity

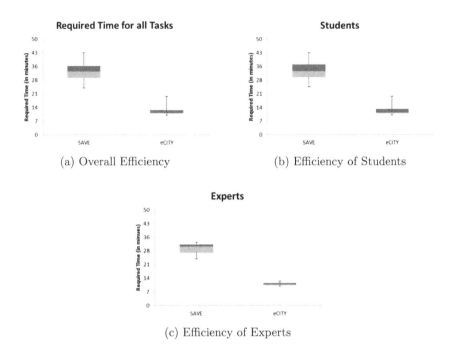

(a) Overall Efficiency   (b) Efficiency of Students

(c) Efficiency of Experts

Fig. 4. Efficiency box-plots (x-axis: left SAVE, right eCITY, y-axis: required time in minutes)

Efficiency Results. The time required for each participant to complete a task was measured to compare the efficiency with which the participants performed using each one of the two configurations. The results are presented in the box-plots of Fig. 4; Fig. 4a depicts the efficiency of the participants with respect to the SAVE and eCITY configurations, while Fig. 4b and c examine the efficiency of students and experts respectively. Based on these results, the following observations can be made:

– Independent from being experts or students, members of the eCITY group were on average more efficient.
– There is a larger variance from the average required time in the SAVE group than the eCITY group.
– Independent from the configuration used, students were on average as efficient as experts.
– The variance of the results is larger for students than experts

The mean, median, and standard deviation values of the efficiency with which the participants performed are presented in Table 1. The results presented have been broken down to the type of tasks, to inspect the level of efficiency reached for each type. It is not surprising to see such a significant improvement in the efficiency of counting tasks as the SAVE configuration required the participant

Table 1. Participants efficiency (time required in mm:ss)

		Mean	Median	Std. deviation
Counting	SAVE	11:20	11:15	2:11
	eCITY	1:59	1:58	0:32
Find Date	SAVE	8:09	7:29	2:46
	eCITY	2:12	2:07	0:42
Find Package/s	SAVE	13:50	13:19	2:11
	eCITY	8:10	7:50	1:39

to pan and zoom on an extremely large viewing area and physically count the changes while the eCITY configuration required them to look up charts and interact with sliders. The participants needed to interact with the eCITY configuration in much the same manner for the Find Date tasks, however, for the SAVE configuration they had to apply filters and compare the densities of each updated diagram. The biggest challenge they faced was having to keep a mental map of these changes. Similarly, the participants were more efficient in the Find Package/s tasks using the eCITY configuration as they found it easier to interactively update the city and locate both stable and heavily constructed areas.

In Table 2, we further examine the results from the SAVE (A) and eCITY (B) configurations. Using this table we can compare the efficiency gain of the eCITY configuration to that of the SAVE configuration. The following efficiency gains were recorded: 470 % for counting tasks, 271 % for finding significant dates, and 69 % for finding packages with certain changes. This equates to an overall efficiency gain of 170 % for the eCITY configuration compared to the SAVE configuration. Knodel et al. [18] conduct a similar empirical experiment where they also evaluate the results with respect to the effect size, a representation of the difference in mean values as compared to the standard deviation. Similarly, we calculate the standard deviation in Table 2 using the formula of Hedges et al. [19] and claim an overall effect size of 5.77 standard deviations to be highly significant [20].

The corresponding efficiency hypothesis was tested using the Mann-Whitney-U-Test. These results indicate that on average the eCITY configuration is significantly more efficient than the SAVE configuration.

Table 2. Efficiency gain and effect size (mm:ss)

	Mean A	Mean B	Dev.	Gain	Effect
Counting	11:20	1:59	1:20	469.91	6.99
Find Date	8:09	2:12	1:42	270.78	3.49
Find Package/s	13:50	8:10	1:55	69.37	2.97
Overall	33:18	12:21	3:38	169.65	5.77

- $H_{0,1}$: $Time_{SAVE} <= Time_{eCITY}$
  Test input: the time required to complete tasks
  Test: Mann-Whitney U test (one-tailed)
  Result: $Z = 5.46$, $p < 0.001$; thus, the null hypothesis is rejected

Effectiveness Results. The accuracy with which each participant completed a task was measured to compare the effectiveness with which the participants performed using either one of the two configurations. As such, the answers to the tasks were evaluated against the expected results. The maximum score was 24 points (6 points for Counting tasks, 6 points for Find Date tasks, and 12 points for Find Package/s tasks). The results are presented in the box-plots of Fig. 5. A similar pattern to the efficiency evaluation is followed: Fig. 5a depicts the effectiveness of the participants with respect to the SAVE and eCITY configurations, while Fig. 5b and c examine the effectiveness of students and experts respectively. The following observations can be made from the results presented:

- Independent from being experts or students, members of the eCITY group were on average more effective.
- There is a larger variance from the average value in the SAVE group than the eCITY group.

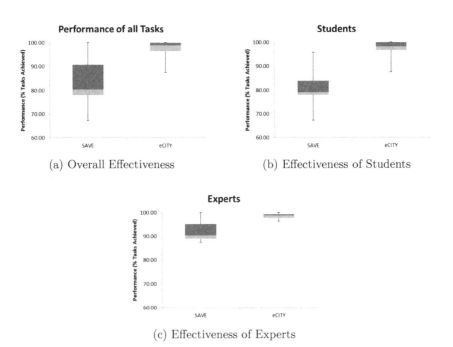

(a) Overall Effectiveness   (b) Effectiveness of Students

(c) Effectiveness of Experts

Fig. 5. Effectiveness box-plots (x-axis: left SAVE, right eCITY, y-axis: % tasks achieved)

Table 3. Participants effectiveness (% of task results achieved)

		Mean	Median	Std. deviation
Counting	SAVE	70.00	66.67	16.75
	eCITY	99.21	100.00	3.64
Find Date	SAVE	70.00	50.00	29.91
	eCITY	97.62	100.00	10.91
Find Package/s	SAVE	95.95	97.62	5.34
	eCITY	96.94	97.62	3.03

– Experts were on average more effective than students using the SAVE configuration, however, the students performed almost as well as experts with the eCITY configuration.
– The variance of the results is larger for students than experts.

The mean, median, and standard deviation values of the effectiveness with which the participants performed are presented in Table 3. Again, to examine the level of effectiveness reached for each type of tasks, the results have been broken down for each type. Our findings show that panning and zooming on a large view to count the changes leads to more errors than using the chart and slider combination of the eCITY configuration. It was difficult for the participants to keep track of which components they had already counted. The participants also made more mistakes with the SAVE configuration while looking for dates with the most changes as they found it difficult to compare the mental maps of the densities of each updated diagram. It was hard for them to distinguish between the relatively few changes between two different time stamps. For the last category of tasks, the participants performed equally well to find certain packages that were modified in a particular time frame. However, there was a larger variance from the average effectiveness using the SAVE configuration as compare to the eCITY configuration.

We further examine the effectiveness results from the SAVE (A) and eCITY (B) configurations in Table 4. The following effectiveness gains were recorded: 29 % for counting tasks, 28 % for finding significant dates, and 1 % for finding packages with certain changes. This equates to an overall effectiveness gain of 15 % for the eCITY configuration compared to the SAVE configuration. The effect size for all tasks is 2.52 standard deviations, which according to Cohen [20] is considered to be a large effect size.

The corresponding effectiveness hypothesis was tested using the Mann-Whitney-U-Test. These results indicate that on average the eCITY configuration is significantly more effective than the SAVE configuration.

– $\mathbf{H_{0,2}}$: Effectiveness$_{SAVE}$ >= Effectiveness$_{eCITY}$
  Test input: the effectivess (accuracy) of the task results
  Test: Mann-Whitney U test (one-tailed)
  Result: Z = −4.81, p < 0.001; thus, the null hypothesis is rejected

Table 4. Effectiveness gain and effect size (%)

	Mean A	Mean B	Dev.	Gain	Effect
Counting	70.00	99.21	10.04	29.44	2.91
Find Date	70.00	97.62	20.18	28.29	1.37
Find Package/s	95.95	96.94	4.16	1.02	0.24
Overall	82.98	97.68	5.83	15.05	2.52

Acceptability Results. The participants of the experiment were asked to give their personal assessment on the acceptability of the two configurations. As mentioned in Sect. 4.2, we applied certain parameters of the performance and effort expectancy dimensions of the Technology Acceptance Model. The participants responses ranged from 1 (Strongly Disagree) to 5 (Strongly Agree) for each parameter. The aggregated mean, median, and standard deviation values for the dimensions mentioned above and the average overall acceptability score are presented in Table 5. These results indicate that the average values in all of these cases are very similar for both configurations.

Using the box-plots of Fig. 6, we can make the following observations regarding the acceptability scores for each configuration by participant type:

– The average acceptability score for the experts differs more than the score of the students.
– Independent from being experts or students, the acceptability score of the eCITY group was higher on average.
– Students voted higher for the acceptability of the SAVE configuration than experts, whereas experts voted higher still for the eCITY configuration.
– The difference in expert acceptability scores for the two configurations is higher than the difference in student acceptability scores.

At first the last observation was a bit surprising, however, after careful consideration it was in fact quite a reasonable result. We claim this to be the case due to the fact that the student evaluations were blind, that each student used only one configuration, and most importantly the experts were more aware of the shortcomings in the SAVE configuration.

Table 5. Acceptability response for the comparison of configurations

		Mean	Median	Std. deviation
Performance E.	SAVE	3.72	4.33	1.20
	eCITY	4.38	4.33	0.43
Effort E.	SAVE	3.56	3.75	0.86
	eCITY	3.94	4.00	0.52
Overall	SAVE	3.63	3.93	0.94
	eCITY	4.13	4.14	0.42

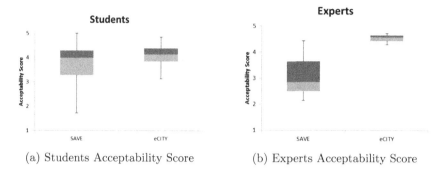

(a) Students Acceptability Score   (b) Experts Acceptability Score

Fig. 6. Acceptability response of students and experts (x-axis: left SAVE, right: eCITY, y-axis: acceptability score)

The corresponding acceptability hypothesis was tested using the Mann-Whitney-U-Test. These results indicate that on average the eCITY configuration achieves the same acceptability as SAVE configuration.

- $H_{0,3}$: Acceptability$_{SAVE}$ >= Acceptability$_{eCITY}$
  Test input: results of the acceptability questionnaire
  Test: Mann-Whitney U test (one-tailed)
  Result: $Z = -1.55$, p $= 0.0608$; thus, the null hypothesis cannot be rejected

Usability Results. The participants of the experiment were also questioned for an assessment on the usability of the two configurations. Earlier in Sect. 4.2, we defined Usability in terms of various Utility, Intuitiveness, Learnability, and Personal Effect parameters. Usability was evaluated in the same manner as Acceptability where the participants used an ordinal scale with five values for their responses. The aggregated mean, median, and standard deviation values for the dimensions mentioned above and the average overall usability score are presented in Table 6. These results indicate that the average values in three of the four dimensions are marginally higher for the eCITY configuration, while the average value in the fourth dimension (Personal Effect) is significantly more. Overall, the average usability score of the SAVE configuration leans towards *neutral* on the scale, while the eCITY configuration tilts towards *agree* on the scale.

By examining Fig. 7 we can make the following remarks about the usability scores for each configuration by participant type:

- The average usability score for the experts differs more than the score of the students.
- Independent from being experts or students, the usability score of the eCITY group was higher on average.

Table 6. Usability response for the comparision of configurations

		Mean	Median	Std. deviation
Utility	SAVE	3.48	3.67	0.97
	eCITY	4.22	4.00	0.53
Intuitiveness	SAVE	3.29	3.75	0.84
	eCITY	3.81	4.00	0.61
Leanability	SAVE	3.30	4.00	1.22
	eCITY	4.14	4.14	0.65
Personal Effect	SAVE	3.02	2.90	0.94
	eCITY	4.03	4.20	0.43
Overall	SAVE	3.24	3.30	0.79
	eCITY	4.99	4.07	0.40

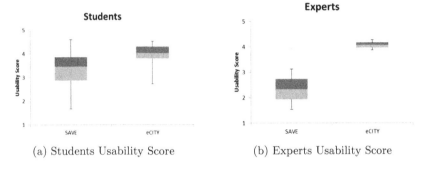

(a) Students Usability Score   (b) Experts Usability Score

Fig. 7. Usability response of students and experts (x-axis: left SAVE, right: eCITY, y-axis: usability score)

- On average, the students voted a whole ordinal scale higher for the usability of the SAVE configuration than experts.
- The difference in expert usability scores for the two configurations is higher than the difference in student usability scores.

The corresponding usability hypothesis was tested using the Mann-Whitney-U-Test. These results indicate that on average the eCITY configuration is perceived to be more useful than the SAVE configuration.

- $\mathbf{H_{0,4}}$: Usability$_{\text{SAVE}} >=$ Usability$_{\text{eCITY}}$
  Test input: results of the usability questionnaire
  Test: Mann-Whitney U test (one-tailed)
  Result: Z = −3.33, p < 0.001 thus, the null hypothesis is rejected

Threats to Validity. Threats to internal and external validity are discussed in this section. Threats to internal validity refer to conditions that constrain the confidence level of the results, while threats to external validity are conditions that limit the generalizability of the study.

Internal Validity: We tried to prevent the effects of confounding variables, between a tool (independent variable) and a dependent variable (efficiency, effectiveness, acceptability, and usability). Student participants received the same training for either the SAVE or eCITY configurations. None of the thirty five students had any prior experience with SAVE or eCITY and were randomly distributed in to one of the two study groups. We then ran the experiment with SAVE experts to make sure that the results were representative. The three experts had no experience with the eCITY configuration and were given the same training as the students. As our statistical results show, there was not a lot of difference in the dependent variable within each configuration. Further, we verified that the tasks for each configuration were performed with similar performance and time. The acceptability and usability aspects we choose are quite reliable, but certainly there are other measures. We applied the widely accepted Technology Acceptance Model and the usability study of Nestler et al. to break down the two aspects into 22 distinct measures. Lastly, we argue that the Apache Tomcat servlet container is representative of a real-world software system. It is used in a diverse range of industries and organizations to power numerous large-scale web applications.

External Validity: A real and complete system, the Apache Tomcat, was evaluated by the participants using the two configurations. Although, our results show that our solution was as acceptable as the original configuration, but more efficient, effective, and perceived as more useful, it would be interesting to repeat the experiment with other representative systems to check if the validity holds. Further, since a small number of participants were involved, the experiment should be repeated with more participants. These two measures should ensure that our approach has a practical value for other projects that look to improve analysis of software evolution.

5   Summary and Outlook

The quality of a software system's architecture is one of the most significant factors for its success, a characteristic that is even more prevalent in the development of large and complex software systems. A precursor to accessing the quality of the underlying software architecture is to comprehend the structure of its elements. Further, the structure of the architecture continuously undergoes changes to adapt to functional or quality requirements, making the comprehensibility of the existing architecture an effort intensive activity. These problems are addressed through the use of visualization tools that examine the evolution of software architectures. The experiment we conducted showed the significance of employing appropriate visualization techniques and metaphors to conduct such analyses. By means of a more appropriate configuration, participants achieved an average gain of 170 % in the efficiency and an average gain of 15 % in the effectiveness in basic software architecture evolution tasks.

For the realization of our goals, we worked with Product Line Architects at the Fraunhofer IESE to augment their workflow with additional views of their data. In this paper, we introduced an implementation of an interactive evolving city view through a non-formal modeling process that proved to be both efficient and effective. Initially, the stakeholders were reluctant with the idea of a city layout as it deviated from traditional node-link layouts. However, they revised this opinion by working with the eCITY prototype and even found the interactive city to be both natural and intuitive. Having said that, by not following a formal modeling process there are certain details that we need to address further. The most critical limitation is that we currently do not examine how the software architecture's interdependency evolves over time. While the experts can still use their traditional workflows to examine these dependencies, "it would be quite nice to add them to the city view". Other possible improvements include a better mechanism for locating packages and classes such as an integrated search engine, highlighting of suburbs undergoing change in a time interval using multiple fish-eye views, the implementation of an alternate color scheme to address colorblindness, and an interface scheme that allows users to perceive and interact with focused and contextual views through overview-and-detail or focus-and-context. We are also aware that at times the analyst needs to directly compare the architecture at two disjoint points in time and will be addressing this in the near future.

Overall, the results show that our solution was in average as acceptable as the original configuration, but was more efficient, effective, and perceived as more useful. These results are a positive indication of the quality of our solution in terms of efficiency, effectiveness, acceptance, and usability. However, further empirical studies are required for confirming these results and deriving conclusive outcomes; i.e. using a larger sample, analyzing different systems, etc.

Acknowledgment. The authors wish to thank the members of both the Computer Graphics and Human Computer Interaction Group at the University of Kaiserslautern and the Product Line Architectures at the Fraunhofer IESE for their cooperation. This work was supported by the Innovation Center Applied System Modeling through the Applied System Modeling for Embedded Software Systems project.

A   Acceptability Questions

– **Performance ExpectanQuestiocy:**
    i. *I would find the visualization useful in my job*
    ii. *Using the visualization enables me to accomplish tasks more quickly*
    iii. *Using the visualization increases my productivity*
– **Effort Expectancy:**
    i. *My interaction with the visualization would be clear and understandable*
    ii. *It would be easy for me to become skillful at using the visualization*
    iii. *I would find the visualization easy to use*
    iv. *Learning to apply the visualization is easy for me*

B   Usability Questions

– **Utility**; Productivity:
    i. *I find the visualization highly appropriate to get details on the software's architectural evolution*
    ii. *The visualization supported the handling of all the tasks I needed to perform*
    iii. *I was highly successful in accomplishing the given tasks with the visualization*
– **Intuitiveness**; Affordance, Transparency, Memorability, and Perspicuity:
    i. *The visualization clearly indicated all the possible inputs to me*
    ii. *I find the terms, abbreviations, and symbols used in the visualization easy to understand*
    iii. *I find the visualization to be highly understandable*
    iv. *I find the effects of actions to be highly transparent*
    v. *I find the visualization helped reduce my memory load in accomplishing the given tasks*
    vi. *It was easy for me to find the important commands and actions*
– **Learnability**; Feedback:
    i. *The visualization provided appropriate feedbacks to me when I interacted with it*
– **Personal Effect**; Novelty, Satisfaction, and Stress
    i. *I feel that the visualization provided a novel approach*
    ii. *I was totally comfortable with using the visualization*
    iii. *I find interaction with the visualization to be pleasant*
    iv. *I am satisfied with the information provided to me by the visualization*
    v. *I felt insecure, discouraged, irritated, or stressed while using the visualization*

C   Detailed eCITY View (rotated) –
Left: Classes modified and Right: Package inserted

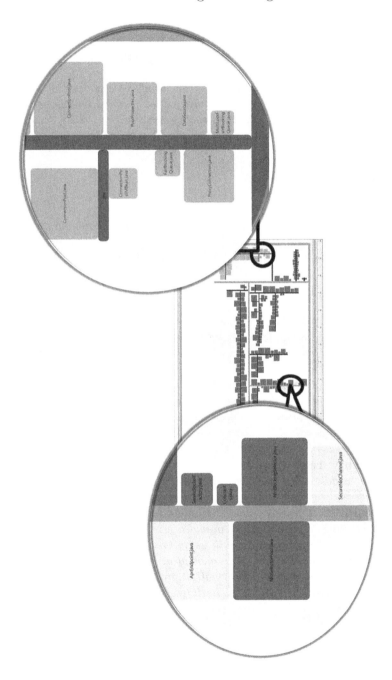

References

1. Lehman, M.M., Belady, L.A. (eds.): Program Evolution: Processes of Software Change. Academic Press Professional Inc., San Diego (1985)
2. D'Ambros, M., Lanza, M.: Visual software evolution reconstruction. J. Softw. Maint. Evol. **21**, 217–232 (2009)
3. Petre, M., Quincey, E.: A gentle overview of software visualization. PPIG News Letter, 1–10 (September 2006)
4. Steinbrückner, F., Lewerentz, C.: Representing development history in software cities. In: Proceedings of the 5th International Symposium on Software Visualization, SOFTVIS '10, pp. 193–202. ACM, New York (2010)
5. D'Ambros, M., Lanza, M.: Reverse engineering with logical coupling. In: Proceedings of the 13th Working Conference on Reverse Engineering, pp. 189–198. IEEE Computer Society, Washington, DC (2006)
6. Ghanam, Y., Carpendale, S.: A survey paper on software architecture visualization. Technical report, University of Calgary, pp. 1–10, June 2008
7. Telea, A., Voinea, L., Sassenburg, H.: Visual tools for software architecture understanding: a stakeholder perspective. IEEE Softw. **27**, 46–53 (2010)
8. Khan, T., Barthel, H., Ebert, A., Liggesmeyer, P.: Visualization and evolution of software architectures. In: Garth, C., Middel, A., Hagen, H. (eds.) Visualization of Large and Unstructured Data Sets: Applications in Geospatial Planning, Modeling and Engineering - Proceedings of IRTG 1131 Workshop 2011. OpenAccess Series in Informatics (OASIcs), vol. 27, pp. 25–42. Schloss Dagstuhl-Leibniz-Zentrum fuer Informatik, Dagstuhl (2012)
9. Knodel, J., Muthig, D., Naab, M., Lindvall, M.: Static evaluation of software architectures. In: Proceedings of the Conference on Software Maintenance and Reengineering, CSMR '06, pp. 279–294. IEEE Computer Society, Washington, DC (2006)
10. Eick, S.G., Steffen, J.L., Sumner Jr, E.E.: Seesoft - a tool for visualizing line oriented software statistics. In: Card, S.K., Mackinlay, J.D., Shneiderman, B. (eds.) Readings in Information Visualization, pp. 419–430. Morgan Kaufmann Publishers Inc., San Francisco (1999)
11. Telea, A., Auber, D.: Code flows: visualizing structural evolution of source code. Comput. Graph. Forum **27**(3), 831–838 (2008)
12. Voinea, L., Telea, A., Chaudron, M.R.V.: Version-centric visualization of code evolution. In: Brodlie, K., Duke, D.J., Joy, K.I. (eds.): EuroVis, pp. 223–230. Eurographics Association (2005)
13. Holten, D., van Wijk, J.J.: Visual comparison of hierarchically organized data. Comput. Graph. Forum **27**(3), 759–766 (2008)
14. Collberg, C., Kobourov, S., Nagra, J., Pitts, J., Wampler, K.: A system for graph-based visualization of the evolution of software. In: Proceedings of the 2003 ACM Symposium on Software Visualization, SoftVis '03, pp. 77–86. ACM, New York (2003)
15. Eick, S.G., Graves, T.L., Karr, A.F., Mockus, A., Schuster, P.: Visualizing software changes. IEEE Trans. Softw. Eng. **28**(4), 396–412 (2002)
16. Venkatesh, V., Morris, M.G., Davis, G.B., Davis, F.D.: User acceptance of information technology: toward a unified view. MIS Q. **27**(3), 425–478 (2003)
17. Nestler, S., Artinger, E., Coskun, T., Yildirim, Y., Schumann, S., Maehler, M., Wucholt, F., Strohschneider, S., Klinker, G.: Assessing qualitative usability in life-threatening, time-critical and unstable situations. GMS Med. Inform. Biom. Epidemiol., 7(1) (2011)

18. Knodel, J., Muthig, D., Naab, M.: An experiment on the role of graphical elements in architecture visualization. Empirical Softw. Eng. **13**(6), 693–726 (2008)
19. Hedges, L., Olkin, I.: Statistical Method for Meta-Analysis. Academic Press, New York (1985)
20. Cohen, J.: A power primer. Psychol. Bull. **112**, 155–159 (1992)

Author Index